CW01150299

Britain's Triumph and Decline in The Middle East

Military Campaigns 1919 to the Present Day

Also from Brassey's:

MUTINY AT SALERNO
An Injustice Exposed
DAVID

BRASSEY'S DEFENCE YEARBOOK 1996
Edited by
MICHAEL CLARKE

THE PRINCELY SAILOR
Mountbatten of Burma
MCGEOCH

Britain's Triumph and Decline in The Middle East

Military Campaigns 1919 to the Present Day

WILLIAM JACKSON

A Sequel to

The Pomp of Yesterday:
The Defence of India and the Suez Canal
1798–1918

BRASSEY'S
London • Washington

Copyright © 1996 Brassey's (UK) Ltd.

All Rights Reserved. No part of this publication may be reproduced, stored in a retrieval system or transmitted in any form or by any means: electronic, electrostatic, magnetic tape, mechanical, photocopying, recording or otherwise, without permission in writing from the publishers.

First English edition 1996

UK editorial offices: Brassey's Ltd, 33 John Street, London WC1N 2AT
UK Orders: Marston Book Services, PO Box 269, Abingdon, Oxford OX14 4SD

North American Orders: Brassey's Inc,
PO Box 960, Herndon, VA 22070, USA

William Jackson has asserted his moral right to be identified as the author of this work.

Library of Congress Cataloging in Publication Data
available

British Library Cataloguing in Publication Data
A catalogue record for this book is available from the British Library

ISBN 1 85753 123 X Hardcover

Typeset by M Rules
Printed in Great Britain by
Bookcraft (Bath) Ltd.

CONTENTS

	List of Maps	vii
PROLOGUE	WITH NINEVEH AND TYRE	1
CHAPTER 1	MANDATES, NOT EMPIRES *The Inter-War Years 1919–39*	3
CHAPTER 2	MUSSOLINI'S HOLLOW CHALLENGE *The Defence of Egypt and the British Riposte 1940–41*	34
CHAPTER 3	DEFEATING HITLER'S CHALLENGE *Rommel versus Wavell, Auchinleck and Montgomery 1941–42*	59
CHAPTER 4	THE UNEASY ANGLO-AMERICAN PARTNERSHIP *Palestine to Suez 1945–56*	109
CHAPTER 5	AMERICA TAKES OVER *The Israeli Wild Card 1957–78*	136
CHAPTER 6	PARTNERSHIP IN THE GULF *The Iranian Revolution and Desert Storm 1979–91*	159
	Bibliography	177
	References	179
	Index	181

LIST OF MAPS

1. The Turkish Peace Settlement; 1919–23 — 5
2. The Iraq Revolt of 1920 — 16
3. The Campaign in Northern Iraq — 25
4. Opposing Forces in the Middle East in June 1940 — 36
5. The Battle of Sidi Barrani: 7–11 December 1940 — 42
6. O'Connor's Seizure of Cyrenaica in 1941 — 48
7. The 1941 Campaign in East Africa — 54
8. Rommel's 1st Invasion of Cyrenaica: April 1941 — 61
9. *Battleaxe*: 15–17 June 1941 — 71
10. British and German Plans for *Crusader*: November 1941 — 78
11. The Four Phases of *Crusader* — 80
12. The Gazala Line in May 1942 — 86
13. The Four Phases of the Battle of Gazala: 26 May–21 June 1942 — 91
14. Rommel's Advance to El Alamein: July–August 1942 — 96
15. The El Alamein Line at the end of August 1942 — 100
16. The Battle of Alam Halfa: 30 August–3 September 1942 — 103
17. The First Phases of the Battle of El Alamein: 24–31 October 1942 — 105
18. The Final Phase of the Battle of El Alamein: 1–4 November 1942 — 107
19. The First *Musketeer* Plan for September 1956 — 126
20. The Anglo-French and Israeli attacks on Egypt in November 1956 — 130
21. The Aden Protectorates — 143
22. The Yom Kippur War: October 1973 — 153
23. The Persian Gulf in the 1980s — 161
24. The Land Battle: *Desert Sword*, 24–28 February 1991 — 170
25. 1st Armoured Division's Operations: 25–28 February 1991 — 173

PROLOGUE

WITH NINEVEH AND TYRE

*Lo, all our pomp of yesterday
Is one with Nineveh and Tyre!
Judge of the nations, spare us yet
Lest we forget; lest we forget.*

Kipling's Recessional, 1897

British military operations in the Middle East have been almost continuous for the last two hundred years since Nelson destroyed Napoleon's fleet at the Battle of the Nile in 1798, and thwarted the first overland threat by a European power to the British Indian Empire. The story of the first century was told in *The Pomp of Yesterday: The Defence of India and the Suez Canal; 1798–1918*, published in 1995. This book, *Britain's Triumph and Decline in The Middle East: 1919 to the Present Day*, is its sequel, covering the second century and ending with the Gulf War of 1990–91.

British strategic policy during the 19th century was centred upon blocking any threat to 'The Jewel in the Crown', be it from Revolutionary France, Tsarist Russia, the Ottoman Empire or Imperial Germany. Once the Napoleonic threat faded, the greatest danger came from ambitious Tsarist administrators, diplomats and generals intent on their own aggrandisement by advancing Russia's Asian frontiers eastwards and southeastwards, often without reference to Saint Petersburg. They were countered by the British policy of propping up the fragile Ottoman Empire to bar the routes through Caucasia and Persia during the international wrangles over the 'Eastern Question'; and by the extraordinary initiatives and bravery of British Army officers, seconded to the Indian Political Service, who played the 'Great Game' amongst the Moslem peoples of Central Asia, winning their loyalties to check Russian influence in the Khanates bordering India.

The opening of the Suez Canal and the discovery of oil in south-west Persia caused major changes in British strategic policy. The safe operation of the Canal could only be guaranteed by the British occupation of Egypt and the Sudan, which was not achieved without severe fighting, the death of Gordon and the victories of Kitchener of Khartoum. Ere long Imperial

Germany was vying for a 'Place in the Sun', and saw a chance of unseating the British in both the Middle East and India by backing the Islamic cause in co-operation with the Ottoman Porte. The resulting Turco-German *Jihad* might have succeeded had it not been for the hard and costly campaigns fought by British and Indian troops in Mesopotamia, Egypt and Palestine, and for the success of the Arab Revolt against the Turks. Both the Canal and the oil were finally secured when Allenby defeated the Turco-German forces at the decisive Battle of Megiddo in northern Palestine in September 1918.

This sequel tells a different tale; the same great military endeavour and new triumphs, but an eventual decline of British influence in the Moslem world. After re-shaping the political map of the discarded Ottoman Empire and defeating Mussolini's Italy and Hitler's Germany, the dragon's teeth of the conflicting British promises made to the Arabs and Jews during the Arab Revolt of 1917–18, started to germinate. Arab and Jewish nationalism became unbridled; the United States entered the fray; and Whitehall was forced, step by step, to surrender paramountcy to Washington due to Britain's political and economic decline set in train by the debilitating losses suffered in the two World Wars, which weakened her will and capacity to rule. Fortunately, the damage done to the uneasy and unequal post-war Anglo-American partnership by the Suez crisis of 1956 was fully restored by their close relations demonstrated during the Gulf War of 1990–91. Sadly, Kipling's *Recessional* is grimly apt: our former triumphs are indeed one *with Nineveh and Tyre*.

WGFJ
West Stowell
1995

CHAPTER 1

MANDATES, NOT EMPIRES
The Inter-War Years
1919–39

The Turkish portions of the present Ottoman Empire should be assured a secure sovereignty, but the nationalities which are now under Turkish rule should be assured an undoubted security of life and an un-molested opportunity of autonomous development, and the Dardanelles should be permanently open as a free passage to the ships of all nations under international guarantee.

President Woodrow Wilson's 'Twelfth Point'[1]

The demise of the Ottoman Empire in November 1918 brought Britain to the apogee of her power in the Middle East. Her military administrations were governing the whole of the Fertile Crescent from Egypt through Palestine and Syria to Mesopotamia, which was now given its Arabic name, *Iraq*, instead of the Greek, Mesopotamia – the land between the two rivers, the Euphrates and Tigris.

If these successes had occurred a century earlier, the whole vast area might have been annexed by the Crown and ruled like the Indian Empire for the good of the indigenous people – Kipling's 'lesser breeds without the law' – and for British trading and strategic advantage. But times had changed: imperialism was on the wane with the United States leading anti-colonialist sentiment in international politics. And there were other claimants – France, Italy, Greece, the Jews and, not least, the Arabs – to a share of the spoils of the Ottoman collapse. Sadly, Britain had been psychologically and materially drained by the titanic struggle on the Western Front, which had cost her a generation of young men who might have been her pro-consuls in an expanding empire. The most pressing item on her post-war political agenda was not the extension of her rule, but the return of men and women to peacetime industrial production to stave off bankruptcy.

The immediate problem faced by the peace-makers in Paris, as far as the Middle East was concerned, was how the non-Turkish Ottoman provinces should be governed and by whom. If the colonial powers had had their way, the Middle East would have been carved up between them and governed as protectorates and spheres of influence. Each would have imported its own style of colonial government: the British copying their Egyptian Protectorate or Indian Empire; the French creating new French provinces in image of and closely tied to metropolitan France like Algeria; the Italians using Roman colonisation; the Greeks reinforcing their residual minorities in Asia Minor and trying to re-establish Byzantine Greece; and the Jews expanding their communities in Palestine by migration from Europe. The Arabs would have been left with the deserts of Arabia as their heritage.

None of this happened because of the influence of two men: the American President, Woodrow Wilson, and Lloyd George's imperial mentor, Field Marshal Jan Smuts, the future leader of South Africa. The moralising President was determined that the principle of self-determination of ethnic groups, enshrined in his 'Fourteen Points', should replace colonial partition of the Ottoman Empire. In his view, all the old-fashioned wartime secret treaties, like the Sykes–Picot Agreement between Britain and France, and McMahon's Agreement with the Grand Sherif, promising Arab independence, were null and void. The level-headed and practical Smuts bridged the gap between the old and new world concepts of international morality. He devised the ingenious 'Mandate' formula whereby there would be no annexation of former enemy territories, but the victorious powers would be made responsible for the tutelage of the new ethnically based, if backward, states under League of Nations' supervision.

Lloyd George's Government was more than happy to go along with the Smuts proposals and relatively clear as to which mandates Britain must claim to meet her own strategic requirements. Palestine was needed for three reasons: to give depth to the defence of the Suez canal; to honour the Balfour Agreement; and to satisfy a national urge, as the latest conquerors of Jerusalem, to administer the Holy Land. Iraq was needed to secure oil supplies from southern Persia and from the newer fields discovered at Mosul and Kirkuk; and to block the traditional overland approach to India through Persia and Afghanistan. As far as the rest of the non-Turkish provinces were concerned, the British view was that the Arabs should be left to rule themselves, except perhaps for the Lebanon, to which the French had a historic but tenuous claim as the self-styled protectors of the Christian communities on the Levant coast.

The French would have none of it: like Shylock, they demanded their pound of flesh under the Sykes–Picot Agreement, and were determined to have it. They started to pour French North African and Senegalese troops into Beirut, making themselves unpopular with the local Christians, hated by the Arabs and anathema to the British military staffs. They complained bitterly and with some justification about the pro-Arab stance adopted by British officers, most of whom supported the Arab cause and saw little reason why the French, who had provided an insignificant contribution to Allenby's victories, should have any slice of ex-Ottoman territory at all.

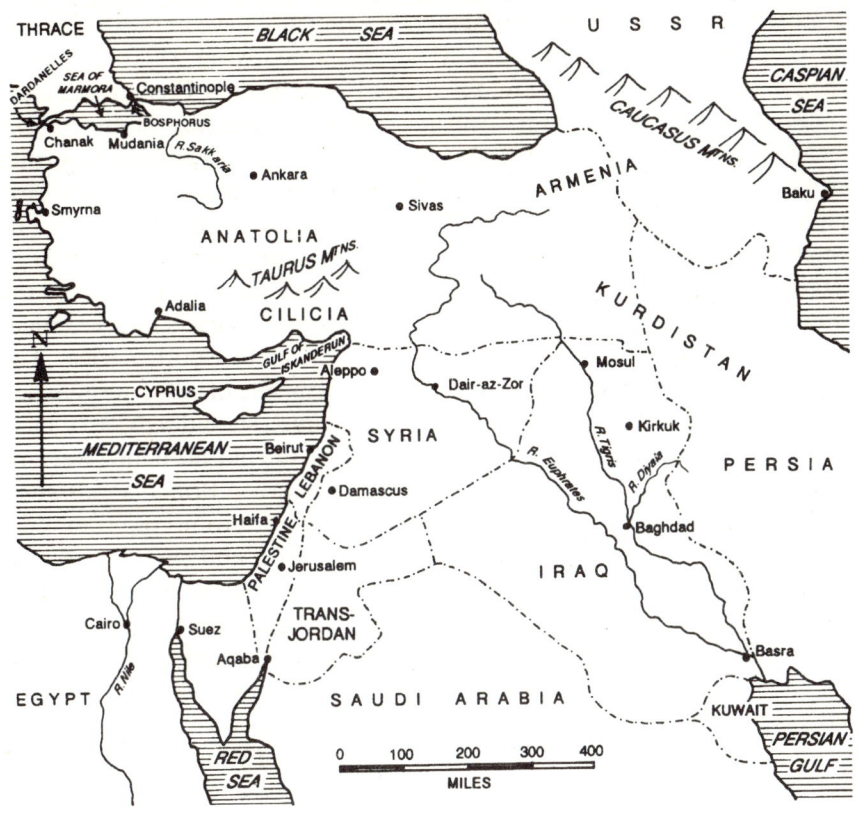

Map 1: The Turkish Peace Settlement: 1919–23

The United States interests in the Middle East had so far been philanthropic, educational and evangelistic. Led by the Congregational Church, American missionaries had established an extensive network of hospitals, clinics and schools in Turkey, the Lebanon and Palestine. Henry Morgenthau wrote of his tenure as United States Ambassador in Constantinople:

> I gave my chief attention to encouraging the work of Christian missionaries, and the spreading of the gospel of Americanism.[2]

It was the American missionaries, who brought the Turkish massacres of the Armenians to the world's attention, and gave Woodrow Wilson a keen interest in Turkish affairs. The 'Twelfth' of his 'Fourteen Points', quoted at the head of this chapter, spelt out the American view of the Turkish peace settlement: the hard-core Turkish provinces should be given a secure sovereign status as the new Turkey; and the inhabitants of their non-Turkish lands should be granted self-determination. Lloyd George proposed that the United States, as the only victorious power with its great resources left intact, should accept the mandate for the whole of Asia Minor, or, failing that, at least for the unhappy and destitute Armenian and Kurdish provinces in the Trans-Caucasus, which neither Britain nor France had the manpower, money or strategic need to undertake. He also suggested that, as an impartial power in Mediterranean affairs, America might take over the control of Constantinople and the Neutral Zone, which was to be set up around the Turkish Straits. The President dispatched a series of high-powered American investigatory teams to Asia Minor to advise him on these potential commitments. They reported favourably, but in vain. The isolationist-dominated United States Congress rejected the proposed mandates along with membership of the League of Nations. So it was that American interest in the Middle East would remain largely philanthropic until halfway through the Second World War.

The negotiations for the Turkish peace settlement naturally took a lower priority in Paris than the German, and within the Turkish peace process there were two distinct elements: settling the boundaries and future obligations of the new Turkey; and dividing up the Arab provinces between the victors as mandatory powers. Although the two went on concurrently and were interconnected, we will look at events in Turkey first and then turn to the complex Arab saga, the effects of which were to embitter Middle Eastern relationships for the rest of the 20th Century.

No Mediterranean victor power became more restive about delays in the Turkish peace negotiations than Italy, whose case for territorial aggrandisement at Turkey's expense was the flimsiest of all. Italy had been propped up by French and British forces since her disastrous defeat by Austro-German forces at Caporetto in 1917; she had contributed nothing to the defeat of the Turks; and even the much celebrated Italian victory in October 1918 at Vittorio Veneto was the result of Lord Cavan's 14th British Corps' hard fought crossing of the River Piave. Fearing that their claim to a slice of Asia Minor would be ignored, the Italians landed troops on the south-western coast of Anatolia around Adalia on 29 March 1919, intending to occupy the whole of the province of Smyrna. In so doing, they opened Pandora's Box, aborting all the preliminary negotiations for a Turkish settlement.

Woodrow Wilson reacted so strongly against this breach of his Twelfth Point, that the British and French prime ministers, Lloyd George and Clemenceau, pressed him to intervene as the only disinterested power by landing American troops and occupying the most important coastal regions to block any further European attempts to grab what was intended to be sovereign Turkish territory. However, faced with an isolationist Congress, the President had to refuse. Nevertheless, he agreed to Lloyd George's maverick pro-Hellenic decision to allow the Greeks to intervene instead, theoretically to protect the interests of their minorities in Asia

Minor. It was a mistake that ended any hope of a speedy Turkish peace settlement with an amenable Turkish Government.

As soon as the Greeks landed at Smyrna with the support of Allied warships on 14 May 1919, Mustapha Kemal, who was in eastern Turkey at the time, stopped all Turkish demobilisation, arrested and imprisoned the officers of the British control commission, who were supervising Turkish disarmament in the region, and raised the flag of Turkish nationalism.

In the weeks that followed, province after province in Asia Minor and the Trans-Caucasus fell under the control of Kemal's Nationalist Party, and veteran Turkish soldiers flocked from their villages to rejoin their regiments in a surge of patriotic frenzy. He organised a national assembly at Sivas, which, on 4 September, endorsed his 'National Pact'. It declared unilateral Turkish control of the Straits, relinquishment of the Arab provinces and retention of Turkish sovereignty over the rest of the Ottoman lands, and establishment of a new Turkish national capital at Ankara in central Anatolia. He secured his rear by allying himself to the newborn Soviet Union, whose leaders were only too willing to supply him with weapons and equipment to embarrass the British. By 5 October, the Turkish Government in Constantinople had fallen and had been replaced by a pro-nationalist Cabinet: Turkey was rising like a phoenix from the ashes of her defeat.

Kemal's successful nationalist revolution might not have been possible had it not been for the British electorate's demands for the speedy return of troops for demobilisation. Churchill, who was Minister for War at the time, had minuted the Prime Minister on 12 August:

> The strain of this [garrisoning the Middle East] upon our melting military resources is becoming insupportable. I hope, therefore, that it will be possible to arrange Peace with Turkey of a kind which will enable us to close down and bring home military establishments . . . [3]

Some relief from the military strain was found by handing the pound of Syrian flesh, demanded by the French, to them on a plate. British garrisons were withdrawn from the Lebanon and northern Syria, and were replaced by French troops in November 1919. The French grabbed a further slice of territory by occupying Cilicia – the land between the Taurus mountains and the sea on the northern side of the Gulf of Iskenderun, which they claimed was predominantly Christian. By this time, however, Kemal felt strong enough to challenge this third Western invasion of Turkey proper. In January 1921, two of his rebuilt veteran divisions descended on the French occupation force in Cilicia, which comprised some 13,000 troops largely recruited from Armenian refugees. He slaughtered half of them and another 20,000 Christian inhabitants as well.

Success breeds success, and Kemal's revolution began to snowball.

The Turkish Cabinet in Constantinople espoused his 'National Pact'. Allied protests about his attack on the French and other breaches of the Armistice were sullenly rejected, the blame being placed squarely and justifiably on the Italian, Greek and French invasions. With the Turkish peace treaty almost ready for presentation to the Turks, the Supreme Council of the victor powers decided enough was enough, and on 15 March 1920 ordered General Milne, the Commander-in-Chief of the British Army of the Black Sea, to occupy Constantinople and to arrest the nationalist leaders. Milne did his job extraordinarily well: without any bloodshed, his troops arrested most of Kemal's principal backers in the city, and packed them off to internment camps on Malta. The Sultan was cowed, but the real Turkish leadership went unscathed in remote Ankara, where Kemal was elected President of the 'Grand National Assembly'. Two months later, when the Allies presented their completed peace treaty to the Turkish delegation at Sèvres, they refused to sign it. Kemal, enraged by the Allied peace terms, which gave Smyrna to the Greeks and large zones of special interest to the Italians and the French, ordered his makeshift army to advance on Constantinople.

There was panic in the city. The small British occupation force was seen by the inhabitants as far too small to stop Kemal. Lloyd George turned to the only people who might be able to help: the Greeks, who had concentrated a well-trained army in their Smyrna enclave. They made short work of the Kemalist forces, and extended Greek occupied territory north to the Bosphorus, thus giving some additional protection to Constantinople. Their easy success was self-defeating. Greek ambitions to win a new empire, perhaps stretching to the Caucasus, were whetted with disastrous consequences. By January 1921, they had built up a force of 110,000 in their enclave and started their fatal advance on Ankara. Kemal's troops were, by then, far stronger, better equipped and motivated by bitter hatred of the Greeks. They drew the Greeks deeper and deeper into the Anatolian highlands and decisively defeated them on the Sakkaria river only 50 miles from Ankara at the beginning of September 1921. They then chased them back to their Smyrna enclave, inflicting heavy losses upon them as they withdrew.

It was almost a year before Kemal was ready to deliver the Greeks their *coup de grâce*. On 26 August 1922, he surprised them and threw them back to Smyrna itself with a slaughter of Armageddon proportions. By 9 September, the city and port were within his grasp and panic ensued. Three days later, the Christian quarters of the city were put to the torch in revenge for the Greek troops' wanton burning of Turkish villages. Allied warships tried to evacuate as many Greek soldiers and local Greeks and Armenians as they could from the wharfs. Those Christians who could not reach the ships in time were massacred. Over the next few weeks, Kemal solved the Christian problem in western Turkey with appalling brutality.

Most Greek and Armenian males were either conscripted into labour battalions destined for the Caucasus or slaughtered in cold blood. Allied warships, including American, took off half a million refugees, who had made their way to the coast from all over the Anatolian hinterland.

Kemal planned to cross the Dardanelles to destroy the Greek Army in Thrace, but was warned by the Allied High Commissioners in Constantinople that he would be infringing the internationally agreed Neutral Zone of Constantinople and the Straits, and would risk war with the victor powers if he tried to do so. In London, the Cabinet decided that further steps should be taken to deter Kemal from crossing into Europe and, more importantly, to stop him from re-establishing Turkish control of the Straits. Help was sought from the Balkan states and from British Commonwealth governments; the British Mediterranean Fleet was ordered to the Straits; and extra troops were sent from Malta and Egypt to reinforce Britain's meagre garrison at Chanak on the southern shore of the Dardanelles. Due to an unfortunate communications error in Downing Street, the Dominion governments heard of the British request for help from the press before the official cables from London reached them. This caused intense ill-feeling in Dominion capitals about lack of consultation and being taken for granted. In the end, New Zealand and Newfoundland offered help, while Canada and Australia huffily refused, and South Africa remained silent. To make matters worse, the French and Italians were not prepared to risk a new war with Turkey and withdrew their troops from the Neutral Zone. In Britain, some of the press, led by the *Daily Mail* and the Trades Unions, came out strongly against military action.

The British Cabinet and the Whitehall ministries were divided on the issue. Everything depended upon how quickly reinforcements could reach Chanak, and how determined Kemal was to cross the Dardanelles. Lloyd George and Churchill wanted to block Kemal, but even they doubted whether they could assemble forces quickly enough to do so. Others, like Lord Curzon, the Foreign Secretary, were even less sanguine about the chances of success. Field Marshal Lord Cavan, the Chief of the Imperial General Staff, recommended withdrawal to the north shore of the Dardanelles, thus reversing Kemal's role in 1915 by forcing him to attempt an amphibious crossing of the Strait to take the Gallipoli Peninsular. Only General Sir Charles Harington, Milne's successor in Constantinople and the man on the spot, never wavered in his belief that, given modest reinforcements, he and Admiral Sir Osmond Brock with the Mediterranean Fleet could hold Chanak.

Harington's assessment of Kemal's speed of movement proved correct. By the time Turkish troops approached Chanak on 23 September, he had a brigade, some 3,500 strong, dug in on a four-mile perimeter around the town, ready to face Kemal's 23,000 Turks; Brock had battleships offshore and a seaplane carrier providing air reconnaissance; a thousand airmen, destined for Iraq in the troopship *Braemar Castle*, were being diverted to Chanak as additional infantry; and three more battalions were on their way from Egypt. But the key to the situation lay in the relationship established by Harington through go-betweens with Kemal, whom he proposed to meet at Mudania on the southern shore of the Sea of Marmara.

Before the meeting could be arranged, the War Office panicked. The Turks had built up a large force around the British perimeter, and British Intelligence predicted a Turkish assault in overwhelming strength in a matter of days. Lloyd George sent for the Service Chiefs – Beatty, Cavan and Trenchard – all of whom tendered different advice on what should be done. They were peremptorily told by the Prime Minister to go away and produce an agreed military line. The advice they came up with was that the crisis should be brought to a head by the issue of an ultimatum to Kemal: the Fleet and Chanak garrison would open fire if he did not withdraw from the Neutral Zone by a time to be fixed by Harington. The Cabinet accepted their advice, and on 29 September Harington was instructed to issue the ultimatum forthwith with a very short time limit.

The Cabinet waited anxiously for 48 hours for Harington's acknowledgement and report of the ultimatum's effect. None came until the early hours of 1 October, bringing with it an annoying yet welcome sense of anti-climax. No ultimatum had been issued because Kemal had agreed to negotiate. The combination of Harington's diplomacy and the rapid build-up of British forces at Chanak had worked. On 2 October, Harington sailed from Constantinople in the Battleship *Iron Duke* to meet the Turks at Mudania. The British Cabinet was further irritated by Kemal not attending in person. Ismet Pasha, the future Prime Minister and President of Turkey, represented him. Nevertheless, the Chanak crisis ebbed away and the Mudania negotiations led on to the Lausanne Conference in November, at which the Turkish Peace Treaty was finalised and eventually signed on 24 July 1923 – four and a half years after the Turkish Armistice and longer than the war itself had lasted!

The Chanak crisis had indirect consequences in a quite different field. Lloyd George's frustration with the conflicting advice tendered to him by the professional heads of the three Armed Services led to the creation of the Chiefs of Staff Committee system, which was to direct British military strategy during the Second World War so successfully that it was copied in toto by the Americans, and remains the British and American system to this day.

* * *

In the non-Turkish provinces of the old Ottoman Empire, it was clear to Allenby, whose troops were in occupation of the whole of the western half of the Fertile Crescent, that reaching an equitable settlement with the Arabs without breaching Britain's promises to the French and the Jews would baffle the wisdom of Solomon. Added to the awkward British diplomatic duplicity of conflicting promises to the Jews, the French and the Arabs, was Woodrow Wilson's 'Twelfth point'. All the non-Turkish peoples of the Ottoman Empire interpreted this to mean that the British would soon be departing and leaving them to run their own affairs. The Arab nationalist leaders may have appreciated the subtlety of wording, which enabled the mandate principle to be applied by the League of Nations, but, if they did, they made sure that their followers did not. There was bound to be resentment and potential trouble where and whenever the Arabs felt let down. But neither Allenby nor anyone else had expected the first flare-up to occur in Egypt, Britain's main base and the key to her dominant position in the Middle East.

At the beginning of 1919, few people saw the Egyptians as a nation in the fullest sense of the word. All classes had prospered during the war: the educated land-owning and entrepreneurial Effendis had profited by the soaring price of cotton and contracts for services to the British base; and the fellahin had done well out of the sale of their produce and animals, and from the wages paid for service in the Egyptian Camel Corps and Labour Corps. But like anyone living in a house that has been mortgaged to the hilt, there is always a craving to regain ownership however co-operative and well-meaning the mortgagee may be. The status of being a Protectorate irked, but would not have caused a national rebellion on its own.

Three things had led to the revolutionary outburst all over Egypt in March 1919. The recently quiescent Egyptian nationalists had been energised by Woodrow Wilson's pronouncements about national self-determination, and they fortuitously found a charismatic leader to press their case. Moreover, all strata of Egyptian society had grievances of their own. The Pashas and Effendis felt insulted by Egypt not being invited to the Peace Conference, whereas the Arabs and other far less advanced people were allowed to send delegations to Paris. The semi-educated office workers were irked by post-war unemployment. The British educational system had produced an over-abundance of would-be government officials and lawyers, who resented Britons clinging to the more lucrative administrative posts as the wartime offices were run down. Those who had no jobs turned to politics, journalism and Anglophobe agitation. Amongst the fellahin, resentment had also been growing during the last two years of the war. Conscription of labour and compulsory purchase of produce had become necessary to supply Allenby's large army in Palestine. The mechanics of carrying them out had been left in the hands of Egyptian officials, who were far from even-handed, and the odium of compulsion fell on the British administration.

The leader who emerged, was Saad Zaghlul Pasha. He had been a supporter of Arabi Pasha, whose nationalist revolution in 1882 had led to the original British occupation of Egypt. Zaghlul had turned about after

Arabi's defeat at Tel-el-Kebir, and had become the first pure-born Egyptian to hold ministerial office in Cromer's time. Regrettably, his talents were more destructive than creative. Disillusioned by the vagaries of Anglo-Egyptian politics, he went into opposition and espoused the nationalist cause, bent on freeing Egypt from British tutelage. Unlike Arabi before him and Abdel Nasser later, he did not have the flair of true leadership. Inordinately vain and jealous of his reputation, he lacked hardness and singleness of purpose. Indeed, he only joined the Nationalist Party, or *Wafd* as it became known, in a fit of pique, when his nomination for a particular ministerial appointment was rejected by the Foreign Office. *Wafd* is Arabic for 'delegation' – the delegation formed by Zaghlul to demand independence for Egypt.

Shortly after the Turkish Armistice in October 1918, Zaghlul had led a small delegation of nationalists to call on Sir Reginald Wingate, McMahon's successor as the High Commissioner, claiming to speak in the name of the people of Egypt. They asked for the ending of the Protectorate now that the war was over, and that the delegation should be allowed to go to London to present Egypt's case. Wingate, who had over 20 years' experience on the Nile as Governor of the Sudan and then High Commissioner in Cairo, referred the request to London. The Foreign Office made two crass mistakes: they disregarded the advice of the man on the spot that the delegation should be received, and they refused to let Egyptian grievances be aired in any other way. When the Egyptian Prime Minister asked to lead a delegation himself, this too was refused on the grounds that nothing could be decided until the Peace Conference was over – the lack of an invitation to which lay at the very root of Egyptian discontent!

The Foreign Office's obtuseness gave Zaghlul the torch; all the tinder for his revolution was in place; every Egyptian from Prime Minister down to the poorest villager listened to his speeches with growing abhorrence of the continuing British presence. The country was still under martial law, so Zaghlul was warned by the military security authorities to stop his agitation. He was arrested on 8 March 1919 for disobeying and was deported to Malta with three of his nationalist colleagues. Egypt flared in spontaneous revolt. People from all walks of life from students to judges came out on strike in Cairo. Women too emerged to demonstrate, some of them unveiled for the first time. Riots spread to cities, towns and villages all over Egypt. The main material damage was mostly to communications with telegraph lines torn down and railway tracks torn up. European casualties were not heavy, but eight soldiers were murdered with great brutality on a train by a frenzied mob.

The General Officer Commanding British Troops, Egypt, was none other than Allenby's stout-hearted and level-headed 1st Corps Commander, Sir Edward Bulfin. He assembled a number of mobile columns to show the flag and restore order, which he did within ten days.

Wingate was recalled, and Allenby, who was giving evidence at the Peace Conference at the time, was appointed High Commissioner with a brief:

> to exercise supreme authority in all matters military and civil, to take all measures necessary and expedient to restore law and order, and to administer all matters as required by the necessity of maintaining the King's Protectorate over Egypt on a sure and equitable basis.[4]

Allenby was just the right man for the job. He had the strength and confidence of a successful military commander, but he was also politically aware, fair-minded and loyal to those he was sent to serve – the Egyptians. Within a fortnight of his arrival, he recommended the release of Zaghlul, which the Foreign Office consented to with ill grace, and the European community in Egypt considered a display of disgraceful weakness. It took him three tense, tortuous and difficult years to bring the Egyptian establishment, Zaghlul's nationalists and Whitehall towards a mutually acceptable *modus vivendi*. He fought to end the Protectorate and give Egypt the independence for which she craved, but subject to Britain retaining four reserved powers that he envisaged being enshrined in an Anglo-Egyptian Treaty: protection of Imperial communications, specifically the Suez Canal; the defence of Egypt against foreign aggression; protection of foreign interests and minorities in Egypt; and control of the Sudan.

Up to the very last moment, Whitehall fought his proposals, which were based on the simple thesis that the only way to keep the Canal secure was through partnership with a friendly Egypt. In the end, Allenby put a pistol to ministers' heads by tendering his resignation. All his principal advisers offered theirs as well. At his last meeting with Lloyd George and Lord Curzon on 15 February 1922, after five weeks of discussions in London, he seemed to be getting nowhere. In desperation, he said:

> I have told you what I think necessary. You won't have it, and it is none of my business to force you to.

The Prime Minister replied:

> You have waited five weeks, Lord Allenby; wait five more minutes.[5]

Lloyd George gave in, and the end of the Protectorate was announced on 28 February 1922. The Sultan became King of Egypt and hoped to be King of the Sudan as well, but control of the Sudan lay within the British reserved powers. Whilst a new constitution was successfully drafted and enacted, it took Allenby's successors another 14 years to conclude the Anglo-Egyptian Treaty, which he had envisaged; and it was only finalised in 1936 because of the obvious threat to Egypt posed by

Mussolini's invasion of Abyssinia, which sandwiched Egypt between the Italians' expanded East African empire in the south and their Libyan colony in the west. British garrisons and base installations were still in Cairo, Alexandria and the Canal Zone when the Second World War started in 1939.

* * *

The unrest in Egypt had few repercussions in the Arab world, which, in those days, did not include Egypt. The French take-over of the administration of the Lebanon, and their establishment of a sphere of influence over the Syrian interior, made a far greater impact upon the thinking of the Arab leaders in Damascus, and constituted the reason for growing Arab disillusionment with their British patrons. Feisal decided to look for other allies. He went as far as welcoming the Jews home to Palestine, and sought an alliance with them against the hated French. Secretly, he went even further, his advisers suggested to Chaim Weizmann, the Zionist leader, that a 'Semitic' Arab–Jewish entente would be preferable to a British mandate over Palestine. This approach foundered because Weizmann was not prepared to embarrass his friends in the British Government.

Palestine in 1919 was an impoverished country, thanks to Turkish pre-war neglect and the devastation wrought by the war. There were as few as half a million Arabs living there with a tenth of that number of Jews. With so sparse a population, there seemed little problem in absorbing those Jews who wanted to leave Europe for a land that did not flow with biblical 'milk and honey'. Allenby's military administration succeeded in restoring much of the Holy Land's infrastructure and bringing back a measure of prosperity. Most of the British officers, who worked through the existing local Arab and Jewish officials, were unashamedly pro-Arab. Nevertheless, it was the Palestinian Arabs who felt most threatened and insecure. As early as February 1920, they started raiding Jewish settlements, and in April that year there were three days of anti-Jewish rioting in Jerusalem, in which British troops had to intervene.

One result of these riots was the ending of the British military administration and its replacement with a provisional civil government to administer the League of Nations' mandate. Herbert Samuel, the eminent Liberal Party leader, former Cabinet minister and Jew, was appointed its first High Commissioner. He was determined to be, and was, fair and even-handed in dealing with Arab and Jewish affairs, but his task of setting up the promised Jewish National Home could not be achieved without alienating the very Arabs to whom Britain had already promised independence. Palestine became a further cause of Arab disillusionment with their British patrons.

The French take-over in the Lebanon was rigorously opposed by the local Arabs. Feisal, in Damascus, was unable to restrain their leaders, who launched an escalating but unco-ordinated campaign of terror against the Christian villages and French outposts. However, it was Feisal himself, who gave the French the excuse for which they were looking to establish direct rule over Syria. Foolishly, Feisal tried to embarrass them by refusing to allow French military traffic on the Aleppo railway, which they needed to supply their troops on the Turkish frontier.

On Bastille Day, 14 July 1920, General Maurice Gouraud, the French High Commissioner for Syria, sent Feisal an ultimatum: acknowledge the French Mandate over Syria; allow full French use of the railway; use French currency; end conscription; punish those responsible for anti-French terrorism; and reply within three days or take the consequences. Feisal timidly accepted these terms himself, but asked for more time to persuade the other Arab leaders to do so too. Gouraud gave him three more days, but despite Feisal's cabinet agreeing to the French terms, he set in motion a pre-planned advance by a French Senegalese division on Damascus, making the excuse that Feisal's second reply had arrived too late, which was palpably untrue. The Arab army stood no chance: it disintegrated under bombing by French aircraft. Damascus fell on 26 July; Feisal left for Italy; and the Mandated Territory of Syria became a centralised French state in all but name.

The loss of Syria to the French added to Arab disillusionment with Britain. Churchill as Secretary for War was very conscious of how let down the Arabs must feel. Writing to Lloyd George, he said:

> ... the [French] operations had been conducted very largely by black African troops, and it was extremely painful to British officers who had served the Arabs, to see those who had been our comrades such a little time before ... thrashed and trampled down ... However we have these strong ties with the French and they have to prevail ...[5]

As long as it lasted, Feisal's regime in Damascus had considerable influence in Iraq. Many former Iraqi officers in the Turkish Army, who might have raised an Arab revolt in Mesopotamia similar to the Hejaz revolt, had been cold-shouldered by General Marshall, who did not trust them. Instead, they had joined the Sherifian Army and provided Feisal with some of his best officers. They kept in close touch with Baghdad and hoped to return to positions of power when the British left. When the British did not do so, and, indeed, showed every sign of staying by allowing wives and families to join their husbands in Iraq, they became increasingly restless.

After the fall of Baghdad in 1917, Sir Percy Cox had assumed the role of Civil Commissioner to General Maude and then to General Marshall. His administration was on Indian imperial lines and carried out in the main by members of the Indian Civil Service, reinforced by wartime officers released from the Army, who were recruited in the time-honoured Indian style as

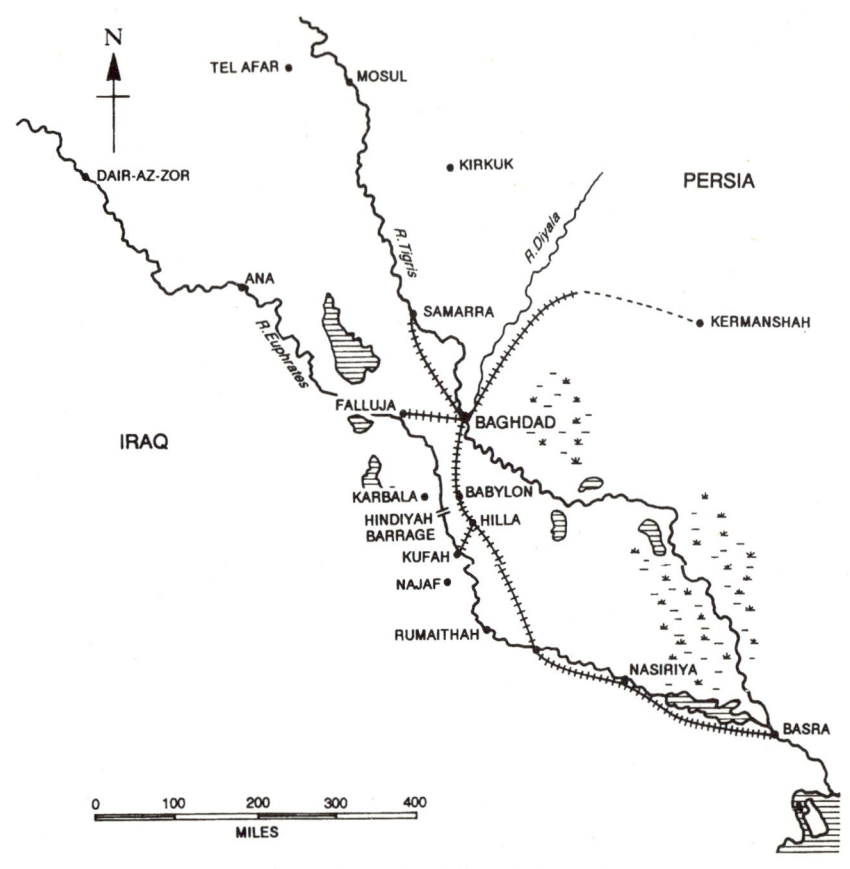

Map 2: The Iraq Revolt of 1920

'politicos'. Their self-denying efforts had brought a level of internal peace, stability and prosperity never known before in Iraq. Irrigation systems were repaired; new schools and hospitals built; streets widened and markets enlarged in most towns and villages, encouraging the restoration of trade disrupted by the war; and the frequent inter-tribal disputes and blood feuds were suppressed. But as in Egypt, the more politically minded Iraqis began to resent not running their own home. Moreover, the Anglo-Indian regime was alien to them in ways that Turkish rule had never been: non-Arabic speakers, non-Moslems, efficient and impartial, especially in tax collection, and lacking the lethargic approach characteristic of torpid Iraq. Each element of Iraqi tribal and urban societies had different grievances, but they were all united in their wish to oust the 'Infidel' administration despite its benefits. Into this pool of growing Arab resentment dived many disgruntled Iraqi officers of Feisal's defeated Sherifian Army, who had fled to Baghdad to avoid the French occupation of Syria.

Cox had left Baghdad to become British Minister at Tehran soon after the Turkish armistice, leaving his brilliant Oriental Secretary, Miss Gertrude Bell to work with his principal assistant, Lieutenant Colonel Arnold Wilson (later Sir Arnold), who took over as Acting Civil Commissioner for Iraq. The Iraqi Arabs had admired Cox, a tall imposing man, not the least for his silences – although by no means taciturn, he never talked for talking's sake. Wilson was also admired, but not as much as Gertrude Bell, whose knowledge of and devotion to the Arab peoples was every bit as deep as TE Lawrence's. She had a very similar background to Lawrence, and could be described as his intellectual equivalent in Iraq. In 1888, she had been the first woman to gain a First in History at Oxford. Slim, erect with auburn hair and piercing greenish-brown eyes set in a finely cut face, she was an intrepid traveller and mountaineer. She had climbed the Matterhorn in 1904; had journeyed extensively amongst the tribes of Arabia and Mesopotamia until 1914, when she joined the Red Cross in France; and had then joined the Arab Bureau in Cairo in 1915. Like Lawrence, her travels had been spurred by a fascination in archaeology. Her many years in the Middle East had given her fluency in Persian and Arab dialects, and a unique knowledge of Arab politics and personalities. She was a passionate believer in Arab independence and was a tower of strength to Wilson as Iraqi unrest gathered momentum in the spring of 1920.

As early as December 1919, a small Sherifian force, led by Iraqi dissidents, had raided and turned out the local British political officer with his small escort of Iraq Levies (armed police) from the frontier post of Dair-al-Zor on the Upper Euphrates, 300 miles from Baghdad. Dissident confidence rose when no attempt was made to avenge the insult. Anti-British preaching started in earnest in the mosques of Baghdad, and with greater virulence in the Shia holy cities of Karbala and Najaf on the Middle Euphrates. But it was not the feelings in the cities that mattered: the urban Iraqi could easily be roused to a pitch of political and religious excitement, but, when it came to action, he was not so keen to embroil himself or his family in the dangers of an armed uprising.

The key to the peace of Iraq lay with the nomadic and settled tribes of the Euphrates and Tigris flood-plains, who were fighting men and more often than not at war with each other. They had the ability to strangle British garrisons by intercepting their supply lines along the two great rivers, and by rooting up the railways upon which British military operations depended. They were not, however, so susceptible to religious or nationalist preaching as the townsmen. What did rouse them was the possibility of easy loot or of outsmarting rival tribes. Both played dominant roles in their acquisitive and competitive minds, which were always ready to exploit the least sign of weakness amongst their neighbours or the government, be it Turkish or British.

In February 1920, Churchill, as Secretary of State for both War and Air, had briefed the Commander-in-Chief (Designate) of Iraq, General Sir Aylmer Haldane, on the pressing need for financial retrenchment and hence for a rapid run-down of the Iraq garrisons. He pointed the finger of scorn at the Foreign Office's wide dispersion of British troops to back its political officers throughout Iraq, which in his view should never have been occupied in the first place. Putting on his Air Minister's hat, he declared roundly that the whole task would be better handled by the RAF. The political officers could be given sufficient air support to deter minor dissidence, allowing the soldiers to be held in reserve at a few strategic centres, ready to be flown in to deal with any really serious trouble.

Haldane, who had been a successful corps commander on the Western Front, may not have had the nimblest of minds, nor was he anything but orthodox, but he was not a man to be ruffled in a crisis and had the determination to win. His account of the Iraq Revolt of 1920 is written in a turgid Victorian style, but shows a man who knew what he was about. He took over as C-in-C in Baghdad on 24 March 1920, just two months before the revolt broke surface, and so he had little opportunity to test Churchill's theories. Rather than cutting back on the 60,000 British and Indian troops under his command, he was soon being compelled to call for reinforcements from India. He did find that his two RAF squadrons could do excellent work supporting isolated posts, provided – and this was crucial – they could find their targets, which was not always easy, particularly in towns and villages. There was no real substitute for men on the ground, who could flush out dissidents.

The tactical policy which Haldane inherited and which he wisely avoided changing in 'new broom' style, was to hold mobile columns at strategically important points in readiness to support political officers and isolated garrisons if they were in trouble. Movement of the columns could never be very quick at the best of times because the distances were so vast. In the summer heat it became a nightmare. Water in the rivers was low, making navigation hazardous; potable water for men, animals and railway locomotives was almost non-existent away from the rivers; and the scorching summer heat itself made marching by day well nigh impossible.

The Iraqi Revolt of 1920 was triggered by another Sherifian raid designed to show the tribes how easy it was to deal with the British now that all but two of their divisions had returned to India. They just did not have enough troops to support their political officers over the distances involved: isolated garrisons could be picked off with impunity almost at will. On 4 June, a force of 800 Sherifian horsemen, armed with Turkish weapons, descended on the assistant political officer's post at Tel Afar in the desert 50 miles west of Mosul, defended only by two armoured cars and a handful of Iraq Levies. The political officer and the armoured car crews sold their lives dearly, defending the post: the Levies deserted them. The Iraqi conspirators intended that Mosul should rise on the news of the capture of Tel Afar, but the revolt hung fire, its leaders being unable to persuade the pusillanimous townsmen to risk open rebellion without more obvious support from Syria. Their hesitation enabled the local British commander to assemble the pre-planned mobile columns, and by 9 June Tel Afar had been retaken by the 11th Indian Cavalry Regiment, which, supported by a small artillery detachment and a few aircraft, surprised and dispersed a gathering of 1,200 tribesmen bent on mischief. Thereafter, the Mosul area remained relatively quiet, but in London there was unseemly alarm and an immediate review of Iraq-government policy.

The causes of Arab unrest were rightly attributed to lack of Iraqi participation in their own government. On 16 June, Wilson was instructed to establish an Arab Council of State, and arrange for the election of a general assembly, but before much could be done, rebellion flared on the lower Euphrates where the garrison of Rumaithah was besieged on 4 July, followed by that of Samawah and of Kufah near Najaf. General Haldane reacted with stolid determination not to be rushed into unwise moves. He evacuated all minor posts which were in any danger; assembled mobile columns to relieve those garrisons which he could not withdraw; and called for reinforcements from India. He struck first at the dissidents on the lower Euphrates, containing them while he switched his main effort back to the area north-east of Baghdad where the route into Persia along the Diyala river was under rebel attack. Once free from worries in the north and with some 20 battalions arriving from India, he swung back to crush the rebellious tribes on the Lower Euphrates.

The rebel tribes only won successes when they managed to assemble overwhelming numbers against some isolated post, but they found such concentrations neither easy to achieve nor to sustain for very long. The prospect of loot drew them together, but tribal rivalry drove them apart. Losses suffered in engaging British units were heavy and discouraging. There were, nevertheless, many British tragedies in the searing heat of June and July while Haldane and his young troops – most of the older men had been sent home for demobilisation – were mastering their business. About a third of the 2nd Manchesters were lost in a poorly planned attempt to relieve Kifl on the Euphrates opposite Kufah. Losses were also sustained evacuating untenable garrisons, and a number of political officers were murdered in cold blood by Arabs, whom they trusted. Fortunately, most of the British women and children were brought to safety within secure garrisons.

The campaign is memorable for the extraordinary feats of railway repair and reconstruction that were carried out as armoured trains, escorting construction trains loaded with rails, sleepers and bridging materials, fought their way towards besieged garrisons. Miles of torn-up track were relaid as the trains worked their way forward, and were often cut off by the line being torn up again behind them, but they usually managed to fight their way to their objectives. Some trains were derailed and others were overwhelmed in tribal attacks, but railway repair work outstripped the Arab's ability to close vital lines. The worst railway disaster occurred in the evacuation of Khidhr station just south of the besieged garrison of Samawah. One armoured train ran into the back of another. Most of the troops managed to scramble onto a third train and made good their escape. Unfortunately, the Gurkha rearguard in the last truck of the rearward train did not receive its order to withdraw and was overrun by triumphant tribesmen. Their bleached skulls were found later laid out in a row in a nearby village.

By the time the first of the reinforcing battalions from India reached Baghdad on 10 August, the worst was over and Haldane was ready to carry out a series of operations to relieve his besieged garrisons on the Lower Euphrates and to punish the tribes that had raised their flags in revolt. He concentrated a major force at Hillah, near the ruins of Babylon, and first secured the great Euphrates barrage at Hindiyah, which enabled him to cut off river water from Karbala and Najaf – the hard-core centres of the rebellion. He then cleared his rear by finally crushing the rebels north and north-east of Baghdad, and succeeded in arresting most of the leading dissidents in the capital.

Haldane started his offensive against the Lower Euphrates tribes in the third week of September as the weather began to cool. Progress was slow at first due to the distances involved and the laborious business of having to repair long breaks in the railway tracks. As the columns advanced, they destroyed villages, in which they found tell-tale piles of sleepers and loot from stranded trains, in retribution for tribal hostility. By the beginning of October, the revolt was collapsing. Samawah was relieved on 14 October; Karbala submitted two days later; and the dissidents in Najaf followed suit soon after the besieged garrison of Kufah was reached on the 17th.

The revolt fizzled out at the beginning of November, but pacification took another three months to complete. The military measures were harsh: the destruction of villages proven to have been involved in attacks on British troops and installations; the summary execution of suspected ringleaders; and the imposition of fines on the dissident tribes, not in cash, but in surrender of rifles. By the end of January 1921 over 50,000 rifles had been handed over to the punitive columns, which re-established British hegemony throughout Iraq. Haldane was a general of the old imperial school. His military justice was rough but fair. In his account of the campaign, he remarks:

He [the Arab] must be made to understand that just as under Darius the statutes of the Medes and Persians were unalterable so also at the present time the demands of the British Government admitted no more favourable interpretation. Above all, it was to be remembered that we were amongst a people of whom it might be said with truth (I quote from memory):

> 'Use 'em kindly, they rebel;
> But be rough as nutmeg-graters,
> And the rogues obey you well.' [6]

In October 1920, Sir Percy Cox had been brought back from Tehran to resume his post as Civil Commissioner in Baghdad. As Iraqi enthusiasm for the revolt withered, he and Gertrude Bell set about forming an indigenous Iraqi government and drafting its constitution, but they needed a head of state. The Hashemite family of the Hejaz with its claim of direct descent from the Prophet Mohamed and its leadership of the Arab Revolt, seemed to be the right source upon which to draw. Gertrude Bell and Lawrence, who was fighting the Arab cause in London, favoured Emir Feisal. He had been driven out of Syria by the French in July and would be preferable to Abdullah, who was less dynamic. They could, however, only recommend Feisal. The decision lay with the British Government, Feisal himself and the people of Iraq; and within the first, only one minister mattered as far as Iraq was concerned – Winston Churchill.

* * *

Throughout the Iraq Revolt, Churchill had been irked by the plethora of ministries with fingers in the Iraqi policy-making pie. His War Office provided the troops and gave military direction; the Foreign and Colonial Offices handled political policy; the India Office watched over Delhi's political and military interests; and the Treasury screamed for financial cuts. He bombarded Lloyd George with papers suggesting the establishment of a Middle East Department to pull all the threads together into a coherent whole; and, above all, to make the rapid savings in troops being wasted in garrisoning Egypt, Palestine and Iraq. In his view, all Arab states should be given independence: British strategic interests would be secured by treaties with them. He was hoist with his own petard. On New Year's Eve 1920–21, the Cabinet agreed to set up a Middle East Department within the Colonial Office. Lord Milner, Colonial Secretary, refused the poisoned chalice and resigned. Churchill moved to the Colonial Office, but, as was his wont, only after securing from Lloyd George the plenary powers which he believed that he would need to sort out the Middle East shambles.

Churchill began work in the Colonial Office on 15 February 1921. His first decision was to go out to the Middle East to see for himself and to decide future policy with the men on the spot. In a whirlwind fortnight, he arranged a plenary conference in Cairo of some 38 British pro-consuls and their principal advisers. He took out a strong team from his new Middle East Department, which included TE Lawrence as his link with the Hashemites and Air Marshal Sir Hugh Trenchard (later Marshal of the Royal Air Force, Viscount), who was Chief of Air Staff and had a significant role to play in deciding future strategic policy. Sir Percy Cox and Gertrude Bell brought a team from Baghdad, Persia and the Persian Gulf, which included General Haldane. British Residents and Commissioners from the Sudan, Aden and the Arabian states came to seek direction, and Herbert Samuel arrived late with a team from Palestine. Allenby and General Sir Walter Congreve, the Commander-in-Chief, Egypt and Palestine, acted as hosts to this assembly of dignitaries in the Mena House Hotel on the banks of the Nile.

Churchill knew exactly what he wanted before he left London. Put starkly, it was to save money and manpower. He wanted to establish friendly independent Arab states in treaty relationships with Britain to protect her vital strategic and commercial interests in the Middle East. The use of Air Power rather than large garrisons on the ground was to provide the military underpinning for the Arab regimes in the cheapest possible way until they were able to look after their own internal security and external defence, hence Trenchard's inclusion in his Cairo team. Nothing was to be done, which would antagonise the French or the Turks.

Having clear ideas of what he wanted, which he refined during his voyage across the Mediterranean in the French liner *Sphinx*, was half the battle, and made the conference, which lasted from 12-22 March, an outstanding success. It established a political and military structure of the Middle East, which lasted until the Second World War.

The first decision to be taken was which Arab states should be established. Iraq was clearly a viable political entity within the mandate's boundaries, although some form of Kurdish self-government would have to be devised within Iraqi governmental structure – a problem, which remains unresolved in the last decade of the 20th Century. The future of Palestine was less easy to resolve. The promise of the Jewish National Home had to be squared with the British commitment to Arab independence. The Jews contended that their National Home should extend across the Jordan to at least as far as the Hejaz railway if not further east, although the Trans-Jordan lands were wholly Arab. The compromise suggested by General Congreve, made largely on grounds of saving British troops, was the division of Palestine into two separate states: Palestine and Trans-Jordan with the Jordan river as their boundary. Palestine would remain under direct British mandatory administration, and Trans-Jordan would become an independent Arab state like Iraq, tied by treaty relations to Britain. This solution seemed to square the circle of the two conflicting British promises.

The next step was to decide who should govern the two new Arab states, Iraq and Trans-Jordan. Lawrence and Gertrude Bell fought long and successfully for the two Hashemite princes, Feisal for Iraq, and Abdullah for Trans-Jordan. Both men agreed to stop anti-French hostility as far as they were able within their new kingdoms, and to allow the inhabitants of each state to signify their acceptance of the Hashemite dynasty. The success or otherwise of this elegant solution would depend upon the two Emirs making themselves acceptable to their future subjects.

These political steps would not have reduced British military garrisons very quickly had it not been for the persuasive powers of Trenchard and the Air Staff. The RAF had been established as an independent Service in 1918, but had had to fight for survival against not only the Navy and the Army, but also against the Treasury mandarins who saw attractions in saving the overheads of the new third Service if the fledgling could be strangled in the nest. Trenchard countered effectively with cogent economic arguments, suggesting that it was the two older Services that should find the savings demanded by the Treasury. He attacked the Navy for continuing the construction of battleships and heavy cruisers, which were so vulnerable to air attack; and he went for the Army, claiming that air squadrons could carry out imperial policing far more cheaply and efficiently than large Army garrisons tied down in uncomfortable and unhealthy overseas stations. He did not win the capital-ship argument, but he did persuade Churchill that he had everything to gain by allowing the RAF to prove its case for the assumption of imperial policing responsibilities by taking over from the Army in Iraq.

Churchill's decision to adopt 'Air Control' in Iraq did not go unchallenged. The Chief of Imperial General Staff, Sir Henry Wilson, ridiculed the idea, describing the RAF as 'coming from God knows where, dropping their bombs on God knows what, and going off again to God knows where.'[8] Haldane and Cox also objected strongly to the experiment being carried out in their territory. They had enjoyed useful air support from the two squadrons based in Iraq during the revolt, but, as Haldane explained, the airmen's Achilles heel was their inability to find all but the most obvious targets from the air. Most internal security problems arose in towns and villages where the airmen were blind. Their bombing had a useful demoralising effect, but even that wore thin after a time. Where the air could be useful was flying troops to trouble spots, thus enabling the Army to concentrate in fewer and larger garrisons. What was needed, in their view, were more air squadrons in support of the Army, which would help to reduce garrisons, but there should be no question of the RAF assuming overall command in Iraq where the successful handling of politico-military problems was so dependent on the presence of British troops on the ground, and on the long experience of the Army commanders in internal security operations.

Churchill, with Trenchard at his elbow, received support from an unexpected quarter. Colonel Wilson, who had been Haldane's Acting Civil Commissioner in Baghdad while Cox was in Tehran, came to the Cairo Conference as representative of the Anglo-Persian Oil Company. He tabled a paper pointing out that the motive power of an army was its men, who were exposed to fever, disease and exhaustion in the Mesopotamian climate. The RAF's strength lay in machines, which were less affected by the climate, and its men could be housed in relatively comfortable and secure accommodation on its main airfields. While Wilson's views may not have clinched the argument, Churchill found them a useful counterpoise to Cox's and Haldane's seemingly obtuse opposition to the modernisation of British imperial policing and to cuts in the Iraq garrison that were expected to flow from it.

There was more to Churchill's wish to impose 'Air Control' upon Iraq than just saving money on the army garrison, crucial though this was to Britain's economy. Trenchard and the British Air Industry were already envisaging an Imperial Air route to India, the Far East and Australasia. Ranges and carrying capacity of aircraft were still too limited for such a route to be established, but a start could be made and experience gained by developing an air reinforcement route from Cairo to Baghdad. This would be done by establishing a line of markers across the featureless Trans-Jordan desert with landing-strips and petrol dumps at 80-mile intervals, which would be guarded by the simple expedient of paying local sheikhs to look after them on pain of losing their subsidies if the dumps were tampered with in any way.

And there was another and less obvious facet to Trenchard's plan, which Churchill appreciated and the Army disliked intensely. If the RAF was to become an efficient fighting force, it needed operational training and experience, which, hopefully, it would not acquire nearer home in Europe. Giving the Air Force overall command in Iraq would give its senior officers experience in independent command, and provide the Service with an operational proving ground. For this reason, Trenchard insisted that the RAF in Iraq should have its own armoured car companies, river gun boats and armoured trains; and that the Army garrisons centred at Mosul, Baghdad and Basra should be under RAF overall command. In sum, responsibility for the internal and external defence of Iraq should be transferred from the War Office to the Air Ministry.

Churchill swept all opposition to 'Air Control' aside and by the end of the conference was able to report to Lloyd George that he had won over the men on the spot to making Iraq an RAF Command with the Army in a supporting role. A third of the Iraq garrison would be returned to India by the end of 1921. What was left would be halved again in 1922, if Iraq was not attacked and Feisal's regime proved a success; and eventually reduced to about four battalions supported by 15,000 British officered Iraq Levies. The RAF's strength would be raised to eight squadrons, including two twin-engined bomber squadrons, which could also be used as transport aircraft. The main air bases would be at Mosul, Habbaniya near Baghdad and Shaiba near Basra.

Map 3: The Campaign in Northern Iraq

Churchill went on from Cairo to Jerusalem where he met and persuaded Abdullah to accept the throne of Trans-Jordan, and settled the size of garrison for Palestine, which remained under Army command with the RAF in support. Feisal arrived in Baghdad on 23 June 1921, and was welcomed by many of the former Iraqi officers of his Sherifian Army. Thanks to Gertrude Bell's careful arrangements for his reception and for a series of whirlwind trips to meet the tribal leaders, the Hashemite dynasty was accepted in Iraq. Feisal was enthroned two months later, and the draft

Anglo-Iraqi Treaty was presented to the National Assembly in January 1922. After tortuous negotiations, typical of most Middle East political settlements, it was signed in October of that year. It was modelled on Cromer's Anglo-Egyptian Treaty, whereby the constitutional monarchy of Iraq was bound to accept the British High Commissioner's advice on external affairs and finance; and, in return, Britain accepted responsibility for the defence of Iraq's frontiers. The Iraq Army would be trained initially by British officers, and Britain would have free access to all road, rail, river and air communications.

* * *

The RAF took over responsibilities for the defence of Iraq on 1 October 1922. The first Air Officer Commanding-in-Chief was Air Marshal Sir John Salmond, who was later to become Trenchard's successor as Chief of Air Staff in 1930. He was faced almost at once with a military situation not envisaged when 'Air Control' was decided upon – an external threat to Iraq, which the British Government was now under treaty obligation to resist. Kemal's Turkish nationalists, victorious over the Greeks in the west, started to claim sovereignty over the provinces of Mosul and Kurdistan in the east on the grounds that they were not Arab lands. As the Chanak crisis deepened after the Greek expulsion from Smyrna, and an outbreak of war between the victor powers and a resurgent Turkey appeared increasingly likely, Cox and Salmond had to prepare for the defence of Iraq's ill-defined northern frontiers.

The omens were not good: a second Iraqi revolt against the 'Infidel' British, this time with Turkish support, seemed all too probable. Pro-Turkish agitation was smouldering in bazaars and mosques all over Iraq; both local Iraqis and Turkish agents could see and delight in the shrinkage of the British garrisons; wishful rumours were flying that Mosul and Kurdistan were about to be abandoned to the Turks; and those tribes, which had suffered British retribution during the first revolt, were readying themselves to seek revenge. There was one factor that the local agitators failed to take into account: the quadrupling of the RAF's striking power.

Salmond's appreciation of the situation, which he sent to the Air Ministry in November 1922, suggested that the Turks were concentrating some 18 divisions within 90 miles of Mosul. In true Napoleonic style, he deprecated any thought of acting on the defensive, although he did make highly secret contingency plans for a withdrawal from Mosul to Baghdad, and, if need be, right back to Basra. With Air Ministry agreement, he adopted an aggressive forward policy, concentrating a deterrent force of eight infantry battalions and a cavalry regiment with artillery and armoured car support at Mosul under Colonel Vincent, whom he backed with five RAF squadrons.

Vincent set about creating an atmosphere of great military activity with exercises around Mosul and marches towards the Turkish frontier, while RAF aircraft swept along it in daily demonstrations of air power. Bazaar rumourmongers did a fast U-turn, and started to exaggerate instead of denigrating British strength. The British were said to have an army corps concentrated at Mosul and an air force of immense strength ready to crush any foolish attempt by the Turks to invade the new Hashemite Kingdom of Iraq.

Most surprisingly, Salmond received full co-operation from the French in Syria under General Wedged, who provided intelligence on Turkish moves and agreed to attack any Turkish column that tried to cross north-eastern Syria, which they would have to do to reach Mosul. The Turkish threat, however, died away as the Turkish Peace Conference was resumed at Lausanne in March 1923. Salmond can be credited with the first successful use of air power as a deterrent.

While all this had been going on around Mosul, a Kurdish firebrand, Sheikh Mahmound of Sulimania on the Kurdish–Persian border, had started an intrigue with the Turks, hoping to acquire the kingship of an independent Kurdistan. When his disloyalty to Feisal came to light, he was summoned to Baghdad. As was to be expected, he refused to leave his mountain fastness. An ultimatum was dropped to him by the RAF together with a few delay action bombs, which exploded at six hourly intervals, to suggest the need for immediate compliance! He did send a delegation of tribal notables to Kirkuk, which made some insincere protestations of loyalty, but, unfortunately for him, correspondence between himself and the Turks was intercepted, pointing to the probability of a major Kurdish uprising if it was not quickly nipped in the bud.

Salmond did not have enough troops to tackle the Kurdish problem while still maintaining his deterrent force at Mosul. In pre-RAF command days, it would have been deemed too risky to use the Mosul force to deal with the dissident Kurds because it would have taken too long to bring it back if the Turks did decide to advance after all. Salmond calculated that, even with the limited airlift available to him to return troops quickly to Mosul in an emergency, he could still demonstrate the efficiency of 'Air Control' in Kurdistan without loosening his grip on Mosul. Intelligence from Ankara suggested that Kemal's interest in Mosul was temporarily in decline, which did reduce the risks.

On 18 March, two columns, each of about brigade strength set off from Mosul into the Kurdish mountains, partially supplied by air and with air patrols to reduce the time-consuming need to picket all the heights as the columns advanced. The southern column of British and Indian regular units made the main thrust towards Mahmound's stronghold at Koisanjak, while the northern column, composed of irregular Levy units, protected the northern flank from possible Turkish intervention by advancing on Rowunduz.

Both columns made rapid progress until the regular force was checked by a mixed body of Turks and Kurds, holding a strong defensive position, which would have been costly to storm. Salmond, whose advanced tactical headquarters was well forward at Erbil, and who was kept fully informed of both columns' progress by air reports, was able to direct the Levies to outflank the Turkish position far more quickly and with greater accuracy than had ever been possible in the past. The manoeuvre was gratifyingly successful. The Turks abandoned their well-fortified position and fled into Persia, where they were interned. By 17 May, the reoccupation of Kurdistan was complete, and the Turkish claim to the province was rejected at the Lausanne peace conference. The campaign, which without air support, would have taken perhaps two divisions six months and considerable casualties, had been accomplished by two brigades in a third of the time with minimal loss.

Salmond's successors developed and refined their 'Air Control' techniques while Iraq settled down under the British backed Hashemite rule and became the best administered mandate in the Middle East. The lid was kept on internal tribal rivalries and external cross-border raiding by the RAF supported Iraq Levies and the increasingly efficient Iraqi regular Army. Several minor campaigns were fought to stop incursions by Saudi tribes across Iraq's southern border, all of which were successfully dealt with by RAF aircraft and armoured cars, and the Levies.

Nine years later, in 1932, Iraq was granted full independence, including responsibility for external defence, and became the first Arab state to be accorded League of Nations' membership. A *modus vivendi* had been established to the mutual benefit of both Iraq and Britain. Feisal recognised Britain's continuing strategic need to protect her Middle Eastern oil supplies and to develop her imperial air communications. Under a new Anglo-Iraqi treaty, Britain was allowed to retain her Habbaniya and Shaiba air bases, which were to be guarded by the Iraqi Army at British expense; and Britain was to continue arming and training Iraqi forces, which eventually included a small Iraqi Air component. Despite these satisfactory trends in Anglo-Iraqi relations, elsewhere in the Middle East there was a continuing erosion of Arab gratitude for Britain's imperial patronage, and nowhere was this more evident than in Palestine to which we must now turn.

* * *

Throughout the 1920s, Arab resentment of Jewish settlement in Palestine simmered, but the Jews and Arabs were not yet irreconcilable. There were many Jews, who advocated friendly relations with the Arabs; and there were as many Arabs, who quietly welcomed Jewish investment, appreciating that Jewish expertise and Arab labour could be harnessed in tandem to create a prosperous Palestine. Such hopes were encouraged by a drop in Jewish arrivals: between 1926 and 1928 more Jews left than entered Palestine. The situation changed dramatically in the early 1930s with Hitler's rise to power in Germany and the consequential anti-Jewish *pogroms* in Europe. From 1933 onwards, the trickle of Jewish immigrants turned into a swelling stream; Arab resentment flared; and its flames were fanned by the Italian invasion of Abyssinia, accompanied as it was by blasts of Fascist propaganda about the decline of British power and the support that Arab nationalists could expect from Mussolini.

The Arab revolt in Palestine, which began in a small way in 1935, was essentially a peasant or fellahin rebellion in country districts where Jewish purchase of land was greatest and the Arab farmers felt most threatened. The outbreaks of violence were virtually spontaneous and carried out by gangs of men who felt dispossessed even though they had perhaps sold their land for a fair price. Their attacks were not directed solely against the Jews or the British mandatory authority, but against other Arabs, who were deemed to be collaborating with the Jews, and against rival Arab gangs as well. There was no plan, little co-ordination and only a shadowy idea of Arab nationalism as a cause for which to fight. Other more sophisticated Arab organisations were soon trying to exploit the weaknesses of the mandatory authority by politicising the fellahin violence.

In April 1936, the Arab Higher Committee, led by the Grand Mufti of Jerusalem, declared a general strike, aimed at stopping or at least reducing Jewish immigration. The gang warfare outside the towns, and terrorism and political assassination inside them increased; and the small Palestine garrison of three battalions had to be reinforced from Egypt and Malta to contain the situation until a political solution could be found. Further reinforcements to bring the garrison up to divisional strength were dispatched from England to crush the rebellion if need be. They were not required to do so immediately because the strike was called off in October, when the Peel Commission was sent out to review mandatory policy.

Obtusely, the Arab leaders boycotted the Commission, allowing the Jews to put their case almost unopposed. The Commission concluded that the partition of Palestine into three parts – Arab, Jewish and an international zone around Jerusalem – was the only political solution with any hope of success. When it published its findings in July 1937, the Jews accepted them with considerable reluctance because the land allocated to them fell far short of their aspirations: the Arabs rejected it out of hand as totally unacceptable. The gang warfare which had been spluttering in the background, burst into flame again in September 1937. The Arab Higher Committee was declared illegal in October, and the Grand Mufti made his escape to Damascus shortly afterwards.

The interrelationships between the British mandatory administration, the Police and Army were far from happy and ill-suited to dealing with the post-Peel upsurge in violence. During the first half of 1937, the Arab gangs had been largely taken over by soldiers of fortune or professional bandits from all over the Arab world, who paraded themselves as Arab nationalists, but were bent on self-aggrandisement and enrichment. They recognised no overall commander and had no political philosophy worthy of the name.

The Palestinian Arab was not renowned as a fighting man. The Turks had ruled the whole of Palestine with just two squadrons of cavalry. If there was trouble anywhere, a troop of horse would be sent to deal with it. Ringleaders, if caught, were strung up on the nearest olive tree; and if not, anyone else would do for the hanging as an example to others. Such methods were repugnant to the British in the 20th Century, and certainly would not have been tolerated by world opinion. Nevertheless, it should have been possible to deal with the sporadic and unco-ordinated outbreaks of violence quite easily had it not been for the weaknesses inherent in the Palestine Police, in the Mandatory Administration and in the security policy being pursued at the time.

The Police were largely Arab and hence subject to intimidation and divided loyalties; and their senior officers were not up to their jobs. Field Marshal Montgomery, who arrived out in Palestine as a Major General in 1938, wrote scathingly to the War Office about them:

> The basic root of the whole trouble is that the senior officers of the Palestine Police are utterly and completely useless.[8]

The standard of administration was far below that of Iraq or Egypt, many of its officers being low-calibre 'leftovers' of the Indian and Egyptian Civil Services. The judiciary was particularly jaded and ineffectual. General Sir John Dill, who was the GOC Palestine in 1937 and a future field marshal, complained:

> ... this very large increase [in the garrison] was not in my view due to the military requirements of the situation but rather to the disinclination of the civil authorities to make full use of their own powers and of the military forces at their disposal because they feared that strong repressive measures would leave bitterness.[9]

Security policy was decisively weakened by the British Government trying to avoid being pilloried in the League of Nations for using military repression to establish the promised Jewish National Home. Moreover, it was recognised British imperial policing policy in the 1930s, as it is today, that the Army should always operate in support of the civil power unless martial law has to be imposed. This was fine as long as there was an experienced and determined administration at the helm, but in Palestine in 1937 the Mandatory Government lacked both qualities. In consequence, the security situation deteriorated rapidly during the autumn and winter of 1937/38. The gangs grew larger and more confident; their attacks on rail and road communications, and on the Iraq–Haifa oil pipeline, were more frequent; and 'no-go' areas, from which the Police had been driven, presented an increasingly blatant challenge to the Mandatory Government.

Despite the pleas of General Sir Archibald Wavell (later Field Marshal, Earl), Dill's successor, that martial law should be imposed, the British Cabinet refused because its declaration would have been tantamount to a public confession of failure. Instead, General Sir Robert Haining, who succeeded Wavell in April 1938, was instructed to take over responsibility for restoring law and order from the civil administration, but using only the existing emergency powers. The garrison was doubled with the dispatch of an extra division from England. When it arrived in the summer of 1938, Haining divided Palestine into two divisional districts: Major General Bernard Montgomery with the 8th Division occupied the north, which was by far the most troublesome with the largest and most active gangs operating in Galilee and Samaria; and Major General Richard O'Connor, who in 1940 was to drive the Italians out of Libya, with the 7th Division in the south, looking after Jerusalem, Jaffa, Tel Aviv and Beersheba. The Police were placed in support of the Army, and District Officers became political advisers to the local army commanders.

Haining's force of two divisions would not be in place until October 1938, so in the meantime he took the offensive against the Arab gangs, which operated mainly by night, with specially trained shock-troops. They were led by Major Orde Wingate, a most unconventional British officer of Jewish origin, who was to win fame commanding irregular forces in Abyssinia in 1941, and later in Burma with his Chindit operations behind the Japanese lines. In Palestine his men were organised in 'Special Night Squads' (SNSs), each made up of picked British troops and members of the Jewish defence organisation, the *Haganah*. Fighting mainly by night under command of British officers, and using intelligence gathered by Wingate's own informers, they taught the gangs many salutary lessons, and began to exert what was to become intolerable pressure on them, depriving them of their freedom to operate with impunity by night.

While Wingate was taking the offensive, 3,000 British policemen were being recruited and sent out to replace the disaffected Arabs in the Palestine Police. Throughout the summer months, villages, which had been abandoned earlier by the police, were reoccupied by military units, and several of the worst 'no go' areas were re-entered. As more troops arrived, so the security framework was extended, cutting the gangs off from food supplies and the general support of the urban population. Arms supplies were cut by the construction and defence of the 'Tegart Wire' – a barbed-wire barrier on the Lebanon border, named after Sir Charles Tegart, the security expert sent out to advise Haining – and by the British officered Trans-Jordan Frontier Force controlling the crossings of the Jordan. All non-military movement on the roads outside urban areas was restricted to pass holders by day and stopped completely by night.

By November 1938, Montgomery and O'Connor were ready to search for and destroy the gangs, exerting unrelenting pressure on them by day and night. The gangs were allowed no respite and were driven relentlessly towards extinction: their morale slumped; many broke up into smaller disorientated bands, only interested in personal survival; and others were trapped and eliminated. In March 1939, the most successful and charismatic gang leader, Abdul Rahim el Haj Mohamed, was killed. His death symbolised the end of the revolt. Due to the ineptitude of the Grand Mufti and of the various Arab nationalist organisations, the struggle had never turned into a revolutionary war and remained a peasant revolt throughout. The ingredients for such a war were there, but were never properly exploited.

★ ★ ★

Well before el Haj Mohamed's death, events leading to the Second World War were casting their shadows before them. The Chiefs of Staff in London viewed the British hold on the Middle East as vital to imperial defence. The security of air routes had been added to the Canal and oil supplies as strategic reasons for dominating the region. This could only be done effectively through co-operation with the Arabs, and this would not be forthcoming unless the Peel Commission's proposals for the partition of Palestine were at least modified to meet Arab objections. With this in mind, the British Government called a major conference in London in February 1939, attended not only by the Jewish Agency and the Palestinian Arabs, but also by representatives of the principal Arab states – Egypt, Iraq, Trans-Jordan, Saudi Arabia, and the Yemen – to seek an alternative political solution to the Palestine problem.

Britain's chances of mending her fences with the Arab world over Palestine were fortuitously improved by the Woodhead Commission's report on the technical problems of partitioning Palestine, which suggested that the Peel Commission's proposals were impracticable. Nevertheless, the London Conference failed to agree on an alternative to partition, and so the British Government imposed its own solution, set out in the Palestine White Paper of 1939. This was usually referred to in discussions on the Jewish immigration problem as *the* White Paper. Palestine was not to be converted into a Jewish state against the will of the Arab population. Within ten years an independent sovereign state would be created, bound by treaty to Britain, in the government of which both Jews and Arabs would take part. Meanwhile Jewish immigration was to be restricted for five years, and thereafter would be subject to Arab consent. Land transfers were also to be regulated.

Neither side liked the plan, but both realised that the creation of a Jewish National Home in Palestine was, at least for the time being, dwarfed in the polarisation of the world into the pro- and anti-Axis camps. Dropping the Peel partition proposals was enough to keep Egypt and the Arab states faithful to their treaties with Britain. Arab extremists, like the Grand Mufti, were far from convinced that Britain would honour the White Paper proposals, and preferred to hitch their nationalist ambitions to Hitler's and Mussolini's ascendant stars. The Jews were despondent, but could not do otherwise than support Britain in her opposition to their German persecutors, and wait for better times. Their local extremists, however, took matters into their own hands, and the Palestine Police began to experience Jewish instead of Arab acts of violence – the harbingers of things to come.

CHAPTER 2

MUSSOLINI'S HOLLOW CHALLENGE

The Defence of Egypt and the British Riposte 1940-41

> *The eyes of the world were fixed on the fate of the British Island, upon the gathering of the invading German armies, and upon the drama of the struggle for air mastery. These were of course our main preoccupations. . . . Nevertheless the War Cabinet were determined to defend Egypt against all comers with whatever resources could be spared from the decisive struggle at home. . . . It is odd that while at the time everyone concerned was quite calm and cheerful, writing about it afterwards makes one shiver.*
>
> Churchill in his *The Second World War, Vol II*.[1]

It was in February 1938 that the British Chiefs of Staff gave their dire 'Three Power Enemy' warning to the Cabinet in London. The British Empire, they said, was faced with a military situation,

> fraught with greater risk than at any time in living memory, apart from the war years.[2]

The danger of simultaneous hostilities with Germany, Japan and Italy emphasised Britain's need for allies. No Mediterranean power, which stood athwart British communications with the East, should be estranged. In view of the growing menace of Germany and Japan, it was essential to improve relations with Italy by diplomatic means. This policy was partially successful although not through any brilliant footwork by the Foreign Office, but because Italy had exhausted herself militarily with her conquest of Abyssinia, her military support of Franco in the Spanish Civil War and her invasion of Albania. When Britain and France declared war on Germany in September 1939, Mussolini sat on the fence and declared Italy a 'non-belligerent'.

Mussolini's biased neutrality fooled no one in London or Paris. Anglo-French staff talks to concert plans for opposing his eventual entry into the war had been going on throughout 1939. The Anglo-French naval strategy was to sever Italy's sea communications with their troops in Libya,

Abyssinia, Eritrea and Somaliland by using their Mediterranean fleets in concert: the French fleet from Toulon and Mers-el-Kebir (near Oran), was to cover the Western Mediterranean Basin, while the British fleet, based on Alexandria, was to command the Aegean, the Eastern Basin, the Suez Canal and the Red Sea. Malta was only to be used by light naval forces and submarines because it was too near to the Italian airfields on Sicily. Their strategy on land was to clear the Italians out of Libya with advances by French troops from Tunisia and British from Egypt; to do the same in the Horn of Africa with British advances from the Sudan and Kenya, and the French from Djibouti; and the French troops in Syria and the British in Palestine were to be held in strategic reserve. The balance of forces favoured the Allies and Mussolini knew it.

Nor was the political balance in the Middle East unfavourable to the Allies. Mussolini's scant regard for the League of Nations, his brutal annexation of Abyssinia, and his puerile claim to be the new 'Defender of Islam', gave him a poor press in the Arab World. At the 1939 London Conference on Palestine, the Arab leaders were urged to maintain their treaty relations with Britain in spite of increasing German and Italian propaganda about supposed British military weakness and political decadence. All did so, believing that the moderate British 'devils they knew' were preferable to the bombastic Italians or ruthless Germans. The extreme nationalists and disaffected politicians naturally sought help from Italian and German agents to further their own aims, but they were in the minority.

The only real political disappointment was Turkey's determination to stay neutral, which was not unexpected. She had chosen the wrong side in 1914 and had paid a high price for her mistake. It might have been feasible to coax her onto the Allied side if it had been possible to rearm the Turkish forces and provide them with adequate logistic support, but neither Britain nor France could supply even Turkey's most pressing needs: the expansion of their own forces took all their armament production and more.

Germany's victory in the West in June 1940 brought Mussolini off the fence onto Germany's side, and the collapse of France left Britain to face the Italian challenge in the Mediterranean and Middle East with the military balance of power now tipped heavily against her. The numerically superior and faster Italian fleet, supported by numerous, although obsolescent, aircraft, was expected by the world's press commentators to clear the Royal Navy out of the Mediterranean; the large Italian Army in Libya would invade Egypt and cut the Suez Canal; and the Duke of Aosta, Italy's Viceroy in Abyssinia, would expand his East African Empire at the expense of Kenya and the Sudan. That none of this happened was due to the extraordinary leadership of Churchill, the sagacity of his Chiefs of Staff, and the professionalism of the British Commander-in-Chief in the Middle East: Admiral Sir Andrew Cunningham, General Sir Archibald

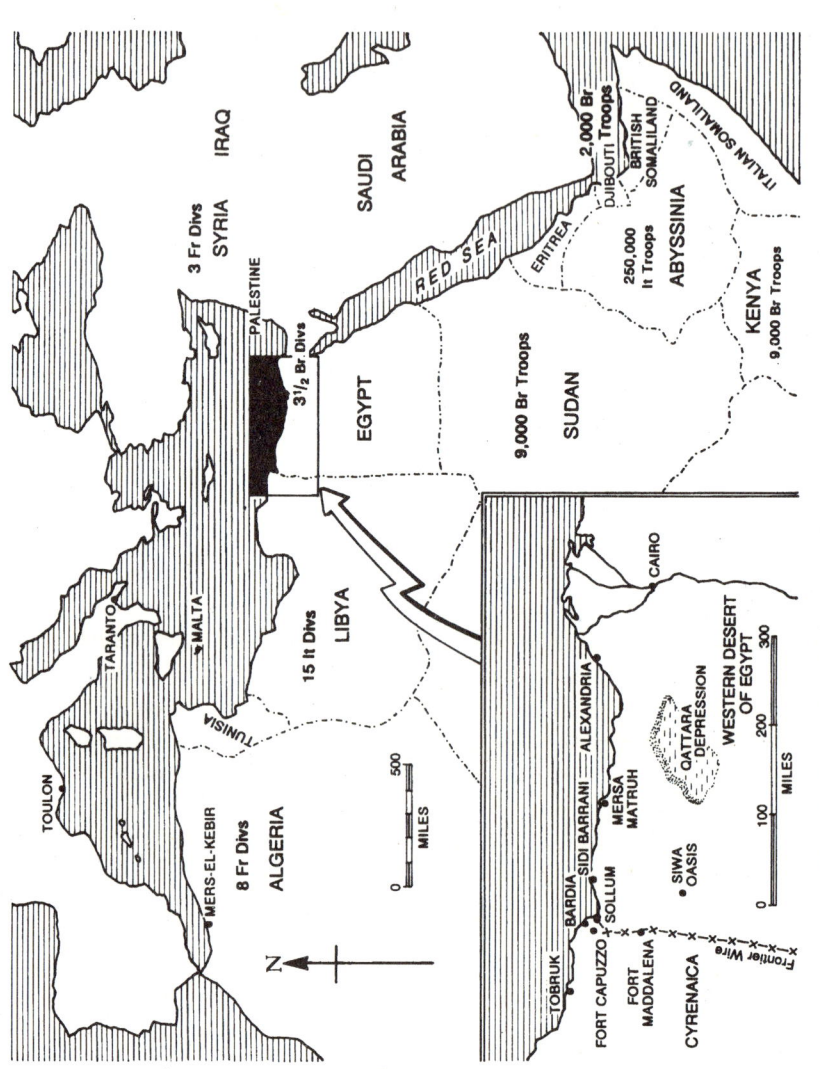

Map 4: Opposing Forces in the Middle East in June 1940

Wavell, and Air Chief Marshal Sir Arthur Longmore, all of whom had won their spurs during the First World War.

Italy was far from ready for war when Mussolini decided that he must jump off the fence to claim a share of the spoils of the French collapse. It was a futile gesture for which the Italian people, like the Turks in the First World War, were to pay a dreadful price. Their hearts were not in the war, and their naval, military and air forces were not equipped or trained to the standards needed for a major European conflict. The hollowness of Mussolini's challenge was revealed almost at once.

Cunningham, true to the Royal Navy's traditions, took his fleet to sea as soon as war was declared to seek out and destroy his opponents. Admiral Angelo Campioni, the Italian Naval C-in-C, stayed in harbour until the first week of July when he came out to cover a convoy destined for Libya. Cunningham tried to cut him off from his base at Taranto in the fleet action off Calabria on 9 July 1940. Campioni's flagship was hit and he used his superior speed to disengage his battle fleet under cover of smoke, escaping through the Strait of Messina. Thereafter, the Italian admiral showed a marked disinclination to engage, and by the end of 1940 had refused no less than three more opportunities to fight a fleet action.

Cunningham was faced with the constant problem of how to bring about a decisive engagement: he never succeeded, but he won most of the lesser naval encounters. About half Campioni's battle-fleet was crippled in Taranto on 11 November 1940 by the Royal Navy's aircraft, flown off the aircraft carrier *Illustrious*. Four months later, in Cunningham's brilliant night action off Cape Matapan on 28 March 1941, the Italians lost three heavy cruisers and two large destroyers. Subsequently, clashes occurred when one or other side was escorting an important convoy. The Italians, using their superior speed and making smoke, usually managed to escape from the larger and more destructive guns of the British ships. Massed squadrons of Italian bombers frequently attacked the British fleet – and sometimes their own ships by mistake – from high altitudes, but accuracy was poor and hits were few. The greatest danger posed to Cunningham's ships was from mines and Italian submarines: unlike the surface fleet, their submariners pressed home their attacks with great determination and some success.

On land, it was a similar story. Wavell's covering troops on the Libyan frontier surprised and took Forts Capuzzo and Maddalena, establishing an early dominance in the Western Desert of Egypt and Cyrenaica. In the first three months of the war, the Italians lost 3,500 men in frontier skirmishing at a cost of 150 casualties on the British side! The Duke of Aosta in Addis Ababa was better prepared to take offensive action and overran a number of British frontier posts on the borders of Sudan and Kenya, but he failed to exploit his initial advantages. His only real success was his occupation of the barren wastes of British Somaliland, which was evacuated temporarily in August 1940 and recovered in March 1941. Wavell's decision to abandon British Somaliland, since he did not regard its retention vital and he had no troops with which to reinforce its small garrison, brought yet another burst of recrimination from Churchill. Despite the fact that the withdrawal had been agreed by him when Wavell had visited England, Churchill, noting the few casualties incurred in General Godwin-Austen's masterly operation, sent a signal implying that the territory had been yielded with insufficient fight and demanding a court of inquiry. Wavell, infuriated by the charge, refused and ended his reply with the now famous phrase 'a big butcher's bill is not necessarily evidence of good tactics'. Churchill's rage at this thrust brought relations between the two men to a new low.

In the air, neither side had enough aircraft during the first months of the war in the Middle East to have any decisive effect on naval or land operations. Longmore's need was to conserve aircraft until an air reinforcement route could be established from Takoradi on the Gold Coast across Central Africa to Egypt. His opponent, General Francesco Pricoli, could be reinforced much more quickly across the Mediterranean, but fortunately for Longmore too many of the Italian aircraft were outdated and their crews inadequately trained.

The reinforcement of British ground forces in the Middle East followed much the same pattern as it had done in the First World War. India sent divisions to Egypt and the Sudan, and held a force in readiness to protect the Persian and Iraqi oilfields if need be. Australian and New Zealand divisions arrived for equipment and training in Egypt and Palestine. And South Africa sent troops to build up a striking force in Kenya. All this took time, so Wavell was forced initially to adopt a defensive strategy on land This was far from the liking of the impatient Prime Minister, who summoned him home in August 1940, just as the Battle of Britain was beginning, convinced that Wavell and Longmore were not using their resources to best advantage.

The Churchill/Wavell meetings in Whitehall resulted in one of Churchill's boldest decisions of the war. Wavell's paramount need was for new and more modern tanks to replace his antiquated and worn-out peacetime holdings. Despite the imminent threat of a German invasion of England and the dire shortage of weapons of all types after the Dunkirk disaster, Churchill, with the backing of the Chiefs of Staff, ordered an armoured brigade's worth of tanks – totalling 150 – to be shipped immediately to Egypt to enable Wavell to deal decisively with the Italians if they tried, as was generally expected they would, to invade Egypt in the autumn when the weather was cooler in the Western Desert.

Wavell made one point, which, seen in retrospect, was highly significant. He said that the thing he feared most was the surprise arrival of German armoured units at Tripoli or Benghazi. Both ports were beyond the RAF's reconnaissance range, and Britain's pre-war policy of not provoking Italy had hamstrung the development of an Intelligence network in Libya. It was thus difficult to detect what was being landed at either port. Unknown to British Intelligence, the Germans were, in fact, already training specially picked troops for operations in North Africa. Momentarily, these troops had been assigned to Plan *Felix*, the capture of Gibraltar, in anticipation of Franco agreeing to their passage through Spain.

The Churchill/Wavell meetings were, nevertheless, a personal disaster for both men. They had never met before, and, when they did, Wavell failed to win the Prime Minister's confidence. The two men were complete opposites in personality and style. Churchill thrusting, prying, criticising and cajoling, met the taciturn and verbally inarticulate Wavell, who saw no reason to make a special effort to please a politician, however eminent. Moreover, they were opposites in military experience. Churchill saw war in terms of his charge with the 21st Lancers at Omdurman, his service in India, and his work as a war correspondent during the Boer War. He could not or, perhaps, would not bring his romantic mind round to mastering the time-lags inherent in moving and providing logistic support for more modern fighting forces. Wavell had also served in minor wars, but his main experience had been on the Western Front and in Palestine under Allenby, where logistics could not be ignored. While he enjoyed taking well judged operational risks and using novel methods – as he was soon to demonstrate – he was no gambler and was a master of strategic timing. Churchill wrote later:

> While I was not in full agreement with General Wavell's use of the resources at his disposal, I thought it best to leave him in command.[3]

Wavell's subsequent victories never eradicated Churchill's doubts about him, with unhappy consequences.

Wavell's plan for the defence of Egypt, which Churchill dubbed as far too defensive, was to fall back from the Libyan frontier to a fortified, well-stocked base and railhead at Mersa Matruh, bequeathing to the Italians the unenviable task of supplying their troops across 150 miles of particularly arid desert with no railway and only a poorly maintained road behind them. He would destroy them when they tried to take or advance beyond Matruh. He had two divisions available to resist them if and when they did invade: the newly constituted 7th Armoured Division – the future Desert Rats – under Major General O'Moore Creagh, which was to fall back slowly from the frontier to join Major General Beresford-Peirse's 4th Indian Division dug in at Matruh. The two together comprised the Western Desert Force under Lieutenant-General Sir Richard O'Connor, whom we last met commanding the 7th Division, then an infantry formation, in southern Palestine. He was paradoxically a quiet, self-effacing but dynamic, fiery little man and an able commander, whose instructions were to ensure 'that if the enemy attacks Matruh, the greater part of his force will never return from it.'⁴

The Italian C-in-C in Libya had been Marshal Balbo, a much respected airman of international repute. He was shot down by mistake by his own anti-aircraft gunners over Tobruk, and was replaced by Marshal Graziani, a Fascist 'hero' of the Abyssinian campaign and a close friend of Mussolini. The Italian dictator ordered him to invade Egypt as soon as the first German troops landed on the south coast of England. Graziani demurred, demanding more time to make adequate preparations for what he saw as an idiotic attempt to advance 350 miles through waterless desert to Cairo so that his master could enter the city on a grey charger, emulating a Roman triumph. He had at his disposal in Cyrenaica General Berti's 10th Army of seven infantry divisions and the Maletti armoured group, and an air component of some 300 bombers and fighters. Most of Berti's men were European, either recruited in Italy or from Italian colonists in Libya. If he could master his logistic problems and muster the personal will to succeed, he had a chance of enhancing his reputation as a great Fascist general, but logistic mastery and personal willpower were to elude him.

Berti's 10th Army crossed the frontier on 13 September 1940 with a spectacular artillery display, which hit nothing but the empty barracks and unoccupied defences at Sollum. When the dust cleared, the waiting British covering troops of 7th Armoured Division's Support Group under Brigadier 'Strafer' Gott, who was to prove himself one of the outstanding desert commanders, saw the leading Italian formations advancing in closely packed columns in parade ground style, offering splendid targets for his highly mobile artillery and for the RAF. Gott fell back slowly as planned, inflicting a steady drain of casualties on the five Italian divisions that Berti was using – the other two had been left behind in reserve. On 16 September, the Italian advance guard reached Sidi Barrani – little more than a village with a mosque and a few white mudbrick buildings – to the acclaim of Radio Roma, which announced the fall of the city where the trams were still running in the streets! There Berti, much to Gott's surprise, halted and drew his troops into a ring of camps, which he proceeded to fortify with meticulous care. Graziani had deemed it unwise to go any further without a pause for logistic build-up, and for the construction of a metalled road and water pipeline from the frontier.

The autumn, winter and spring of 1940–41 can be said to have been Wavell's finest hour. Scarcely had he arrived back from his meetings with Churchill than he began planning counter-offensives not only in the desert but also in the Sudan, Kenya and Abyssinia. He was like a highly skilled juggler keeping four balls in the air at the same time. He gave the planning of the expulsion of Berti's 10th Army to Lieutenant General 'Jumbo' Maitland Wilson, the Commander of British Troops, Egypt. Recovery of the lost Sudan frontier posts and invasion of Italian Eritrea was the responsibility of Major General William Platt, the commander of the Sudan Defence Force, which was to be reinforced by Major General Heath's 5th Indian Division. The invasion of Italian Somaliland as a stepping stone to the liberation of Abyssinia from the south was to be planned by Lieutenant General Alan Cunningham, the younger brother of the Naval C-in-C, who would have East and West African troops and Major General Brink's 1st South African Division. And finally the return of the Emperor Haile Selassie to his throne in Addis Ababa was to be the task of Colonel Orde Wingate, leader, it will be remembered, of the Special Night Squads in Palestine. He was to infiltrate the Gojjam province of northern Abyssinia with locally recruited 'Patriot' bands to raise the country in a royalist rebellion against the Italians on behalf of the exiled Lion of Judah, who would accompany the expedition in nominal command. None of Wavell's four commanders were likely to succeed without reinforcement from one of his other fronts. The speed with which forces could be switched from one thrust to another was limited by the availability of shipping, so careful timing and refusal to be hurried by London would be the keys to Wavell's success or failure.

The principal requirement, as far as the security of the Middle East was concerned, was the expulsion of Berti's troops from Egypt. This was the one operation which Wavell kept close to his own chest. He appreciated that surprise was essential if Berti's five divisions were to be routed by the two divisions of O'Connor's Western Desert Force. Italian and German agents swarmed in Cairo, making it difficult to conceal preparations for any major operation, so only the closest personal staffs of Wilson and O'Connor were allowed to take part in the planning; nothing was committed to paper; and subtle deception measures were used to keep the British troops as well as the Italians and their agents in the dark.

For quite different reasons, Wavell did not even inform the War Office, and hence Churchill of his plans. He knew that if he were to do so, the Prime Minister would be unable to resist interfering and demanding action before training and logistic arrangements had been completed.

One special factor influenced planning. Amongst the 150 tanks sent out by Churchill was a regiment's worth of heavy 'Matilda' Infantry tanks destined for the 7th Royal Tank Regiment. The Matilda's armour could not be penetrated by the current Italian anti-tank guns. They were slow, but if they could be moved secretly over the desert from Matruh to Sidi Barrani, their surprise appearance might cause panic amongst the reluctant Italian invaders.

The plan for O'Connor's operation, code-named *Compass*, matured in stages. It was seen initially as a five-day operation to destroy as much of Berti's army as possible *in situ* at Sidi Barrani, and to chase the remainder back over the Egyptian frontier. The Italian fortified camps were in two

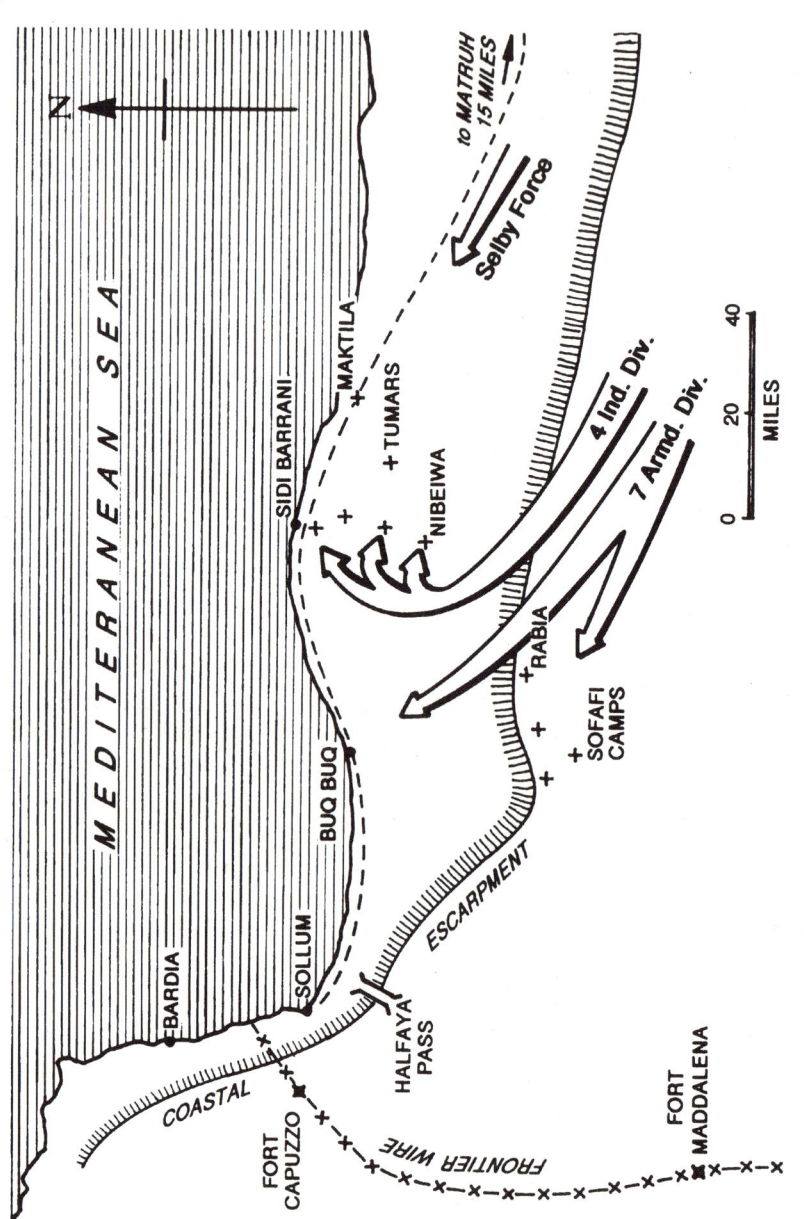

Map 5: The Battle of Sidi Barrani: 7–11 December 1940

distinct groups: six were on the coastal plain, and there were four more on the top of the coastal escarpment. A combination of air reconnaissance, air photography and careful patrolling on the ground revealed that there was a sizeable 15-mile gap between the most southerly camp on the coastal plain at Nibeiwa and the camps above the escarpment at Rabia and Sofafi. Moreover, there were practicable routes for wheels and tracks down the escarpment well to the east of Rabia. O'Connor decided it would be possible to pass his two divisions through this gap in the dark to attack the lower Italian camps in succession from the rear at first light.

His main problem was how to move and supply his troops in complete secrecy across the 75 miles of desert from Matruh. He calculated that his slow-moving Matildas (best speed 8 miles in the hour) would need at least two days. On Longmore's assurance that the RAF could neutralise their opponents' reconnaissance effort for that length of time, he decided to risk two days of daylight movement with his columns widely dispersed in the desert some 30 miles from the coast until they were within 25 miles of the Italian positions. The final lap would be by night: 4th Indian Division with its infantry in trucks driven by New Zealand drivers, and 7th Royal Tanks with their Matildas, would drive down the escarpment to reach the rear of Nibeiwa; 7th Armoured Division would continue along the top of the escarpment to mask the Rabia/Sofafi camps before also driving down the escarpment further west to cut the coast road at Buq Buq. Shortage of transport compelled him to risk setting up hidden stocks of petrol and supplies in the desert along his proposed route. The talkative gentlemen in the supply services were told that these were for the use of forces, which might be sent forward to harass the Italians when they tried to advance on Matruh.

Such a plan would not have been feasible but for two hidden factors. Ever since the campaign against the Senussi in the First World War, the Western Desert had held a fascination for successive generations of British officers stationed in Egypt. During the mid-1930s, when there were clear signs of Italian hostility due to the Abyssinian crisis, a handful of officers, led by Major RA Bagnall, had experimented with and mastered techniques for operating in the desert with motor vehicles rather than camels, horses and mules. They developed sun compasses, steel sand-channels for unsticking vehicles bogged in soft sand, radiator condensers to conserve water, special low pressure tyres, strengthening of vehicle suspensions, and a way of life for men operating in the desert. In short, they gave the British units in Egypt that indefinable quality known as 'desert sense' – the ability to move and fight by day or night in that lunar-like environment, making the desert their ally: to the Italians it remained an enemy.

The second hidden factor was that all commanders, staffs and troops in the Western Desert Force were professional long-service regulars, who understood the need for thorough training and meticulous planning.

Nevertheless, it was not easy to train and rehearse the troops without them becoming aware that something was afoot. O'Connor staged a series of training exercises designed to study desert operations in general, which happened to include, amongst many other things, attacks on fortified camps, for which replicas of typical Italian camps were set up near Matruh. The exercise programme extended well beyond the target date for the attack. Everything was done to make the whole period seem routine, as if time was being usefully filled while waiting for the Australian and New Zealand divisions to complete their training in the new year. Wilson went as far as taking Colonel Bonner Fellows, the US military attaché, up to Matruh, to see 'some training'.

Mussolini came close to killing *Compass*. Much to Hitler's fury, he invaded Greece on 28 October. Churchill, knowing nothing of *Compass*, demanded that the Cs-in-C, Middle East, should send immediate help to the Greeks. Longmore had to send aircraft earmarked to support O'Connor's planned offensive, and Wavell had to find troops to occupy Crete at the Greeks' request. Fortunately, Anthony Eden, the Secretary of State for War, was touring the Middle East at the time. Wavell decided that in order to prevent further diversion of aircraft and troops to Greece, he must let Eden into the *Compass* secret so that he could brief the Prime Minister on his return to London before any more damage was done. Churchill, when he received Eden's report on 8 November, wrote:

> Here then was the deadly secret which the generals had talked over with the Secretary of State. This was what they had not wished to telegraph. We were all delighted. I purred like six cats. Here was something worth doing.[5]

Churchill's impatience, as Wavell foresaw, soon got the better of him, and he was goading Wavell into striking earlier than he planned on the grounds that the Italians had suffered an unexpected reverse in Greece; the Italian fleet had been crippled at Taranto; the Italian airmen had made a poor showing during the battle of Britain; and Intelligence reported a marked deterioration in Italian civilian morale. All this pointed to German intervention to prop up Mussolini: time might be all too short before German aircraft and, perhaps, troops were sent to the Mediterranean.

Wavell refused to be hurried. He appreciated as much, if not more, than anyone in Whitehall that he was faced with a race against time in which he must destroy Graziani's forces in Libya and the Duke of Aosta's in the Horn of Africa before the Germans intervened, but he was faced with physical difficulties of time and space. The limiting factor became the speed with which Whitehall could replace the RAF squadrons sent by Longmore to Greece, since, without them, he could not cover the Western Desert Force's advance on Sidi Barrani.

Wavell reported to London that he could not mount *Compass* until the end of the first week of December when the moon would be in its last quarter, which was needed for the final advance by the Matildas on Nibeiwa. This drew a thoroughly vindictive minute from Churchill to Eden about Wavell's dilatoriness, ending 'Anyway all his troops, except the barest defensive minimum, will be drawn from him before long [for Greece].'[6] But more importantly, the Prime Minister changed the aim of *Compass*. Cabling Wavell on 26 November he demanded to know what plans were being made to exploit success at Sidi Barrani with a rapid advance along the Libyan coast to destroy all Graziani's forces in North Africa before the Germans could intervene as he was now sure that they would. *Compass* ceased to be a five-day operation: success, if it came, was to be exploited *à outrance*. Whether the Prime Minister appreciated it or not, it was too late to build up the logistic resources needed for an advance into Libya: Wilson and O'Connor would have to improvise as best they could.

Neither Wavell nor Wilson warned O'Connor, because they thought it would worry him, that 4th Indian Division was to be shipped off southwards to the Sudan to reinforce Platt for the invasion of Eritrea as soon as the battle of Sidi Barrani was over. The timings were tight because the ships to be used were part of a convoy leaving for England via the Cape. The next convoy would not be sailing for another six weeks. The Indians would be replaced in the Western Desert Force by Major General Mackay's 6th Australian Division, which was just completing its training.

On 5 December, Wavell sent Wilson the executive order attack on the 9th. Churchill was not informed, but his impatience was again frothing over. A hastening cable to Wavell received the curt reply 'Actual date dependent on weather conditions'.[7] However, 24 hours later, Wavell relented, giving the dates and adding:

> ... feel undue hopes being placed on this operation which was designed as a raid only. We are greatly outnumbered on the ground and in the air, have to move over 75 miles of desert and attack enemy who has fortified himself for three months ... [8]

This produced another Churchillian explosion. Minuting the CIGS, he wrote:

> If, with the situation as it is, General Wavell is only playing small, and is not hurling on his whole available force with furious energy, he will have failed to rise to the height of the circumstances. I never worry about action, but only about inaction.[9]

During 7 and 8 December, as the Western Desert Force was advancing undetected through the desert towards its objective, Wavell was seen with his family around Cairo on normal social routine. He gave a dinner party for 15 on the evening of 8 December. None of his guests noticed anything unusual!

Compass was one of those rare battles that did go according to plan. It was fought to professional standards, which were never to be achieved again by the British in the Western Desert until Montgomery was given command of the 8th Army almost two years later. The expansion of the British Army in the Middle East brought with it an over-dilution of experienced officers and men, which lowered standards and weakened the close co-operation between infantry, armour, gunners and sappers, upon which so much depends in battle and was to be so evident in the battle of Sidi Barrani.

On 7 December, the RAF surprised the Italian Air Force and destroyed a substantial number of its aircraft on the ground. Thereafter, they maintained tactical air superiority over the battlefield, and O'Connor's two-day desert march went unseen by the few Italian aircraft that did manage to fly over the area. By dusk on 8 December, the attacking formations had reached their rendez-vous 15 miles south-east of the gap in the Italian line of camps. As a diversion, a small force from the Matruh garrison under Brigadier Selby advanced along the coast road with a number of dummy tanks, and was ready to exploit a naval bombardment of the camps nearest the sea. It was hoped that the noise of naval gunfire, which was to start soon after midnight, would help to mask the noise of the Matildas churning their way towards Nibeiwa. For some nights previously, the RAF had been flying a routine of harassing bombing sorties over the camps, and these were continued to maintain a feel of normality as well as adding further distractions for Italian look-outs.

The night was clear and bitterly cold. Navigation through the gap was remarkably accurate. Although the Maletti Group in Nibeiwa seemed alert during the first half of the night, everything was quiet by midnight when the naval diversionary bombardment started 20 miles away to the north. The Maletti Group were the élite of Berti's Army, but their long boring sojourn at Nibeiwa, where nothing ever seemed to happen, had blunted their inquisitiveness. It should not have been possible for Brigadier Savory's 11th Indian Brigade Group in trucks, the 7th Royal Tank Regiment with 48 Matildas, and 72 guns of the Divisional Artillery to form up undetected in the rear of Nibeiwa ready to attack at first light, but that is what happened.

At 5am, one Indian battalion launched a feint attack on the eastern side of Nibeiwa, which woke the Italians up and drew their attention away from Savory's force in their rear. By 6am, all was quiet again and the Italians settled down to their normal early morning routine. As dawn broke, a slight haze covered the desert, conveniently shrouding the assembled assault force. At 7am, the Divisional Artillery registered its targets, and fifteen minutes later, started to drench the camp with high explosive. The Matildas approached the back entrance of the camp where they found and destroyed 20 unmanned Italian tanks before crashing their way into the camp. The 2nd Queen's Own Cameron Highlanders and the 1st/6th Rajputana Rifles debussed from their New Zealander-driven trucks and followed in the Matildas' wake. Some of the Italians fought well, particularly their gunners, but most were caught cowering in their dugouts. The sudden realisation that the Matildas were impervious to Italian anti-tank weapons, and the death of General Maletti, who was cut down by a burst of tank machinegun fire as he scrambled out of his command post, induced a spontaneous wave of surrenders. By 10.30am, all was over in Nibeiwa. Two thousand prisoners and 35 tanks were in Savory's hands, and the Matildas were churning their way to support Brigadier Lloyd's 5th Indian Infantry Brigade Group in his attack on the next camp to the north, Tumar West.

Surprise was now gone and Tumar West did not surrender quite so easily. Six Matildas were mined; and the weather deteriorated with sandstorms, making target acquisition difficult. The camp's gunners again fought the hardest, but were demoralised by seeing their anti-tank shot ricocheting off the Matilda hulls. The surrender came at 4pm and, as the dusk was gathering, Lloyd went for the next camp, Tumar East. The tanks broke into the camp, but it was not finally cleared until daylight next day.

While 4th Indian Division had been rolling up the camps on the coastal plain, 7th Armoured Division had used its Support Group to mask the Rabia/Sofafi camps on the top of the escarpment, and had sent its 4th Armoured Brigade down it to cut the coast road near Buq Buq, isolating Sidi Barrani and creating panic in the Italian rear areas.

During 10 December, the battle developed into a series of dogfights with Italian formations as they tried to escape, helped by further sandstorms. Twenty-four hours later, all the Italians in Egypt, except for a small rearguard at Sollum, were either dead or amongst the 38,300 prisoners in British hands. O'Connor's casualties were 624 killed, wounded and missing! Alan Moorehead, the highly respected war correspondent, who entered Nibeiwa as it fell, recorded:

> Extraordinary things met us wherever we turned. Officers beds laid out with clean sheets, chests of draws filled with linen and an abundance of fine clothes . . . uniforms heavy with gold lace and bedecked with medals . . . dressing tables in officers' tents strewn with scents and silver mounted brushes . . . and never did an army write and receive letters as this one did. For five miles around, the landscape was strewn with their letters . . . There the whole thing was; the explanation of this broken savaged camp . . . The British brigadier in this action had not for many weeks or even months lived as the Italian non-commissioned officers were living.[10]

Count Ciano, Italy's Foreign Minister and Mussolini's son-in-law, records in his diary the Italian Dictator's wry comment on hearing that one Italian general had been killed and five captured:

This is the ratio of Italians who have military qualities and those who have none.[11]

Berti was sacked after the battle and replaced by Graziani's chief of staff, General Tellera.

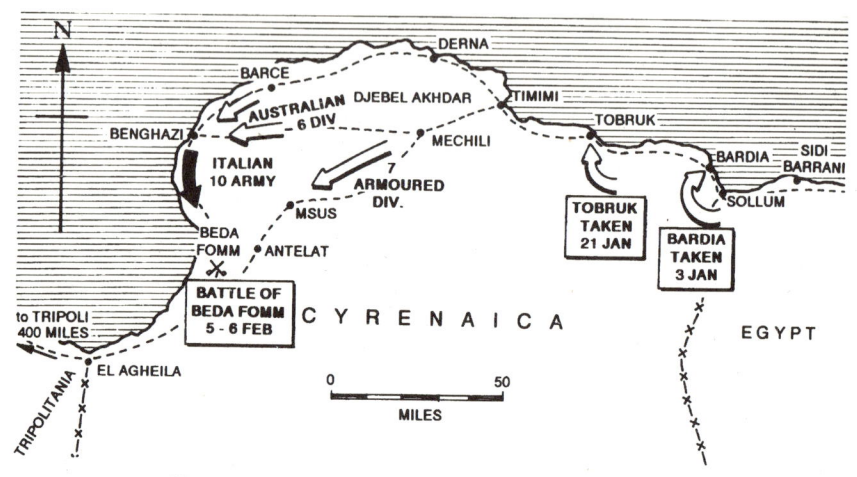

Map 6: O'Connor's Seizure of Cyrenaica in 1941

The battle of Sidi Barrani was barely over before 4th Indian Division was on its way back to Suez to embark for Port Sudan to join 5th Indian Division for the invasion of Eritrea. Their place was taken by Mackay's 6th Australian Division, which had barely completed its training as a division in Palestine. The Western Desert Force was renamed the 13th Corps.

7th Armoured Division pursued the remnants of Tellera's 10th Army into the strongly fortified port of Bardia, investing the northern third of the perimeter while the Australians came up to take over the rest. Probing patrols soon found that the Italian garrison, which had not experienced fighting the British at Sidi Barrani, was far from demoralised, and the fortifications were new, strongly built and well manned. British Intelligence estimated that there were some 20,000 fresh Italian troops in Bardia. They were under command of a notorious eccentric, Lieutenant General Bergonzoli. He was a tall, spare man with long twirled and waxed moustachios, and a silvering forked beard. He was known to both sides as 'Electric Whiskers'.

Wavell hoped that if he offered Bergonzoli an escape route by leaving only an obviously weak observation screen in the northern sector, and if he also made life too uncomfortable for him in Bardia by continuous naval and air bombardment, there was a chance that he might make a flamboyant gesture by breaking out. He would then be set upon by 7th Armoured Division as he tried to reach the relative safety of Tobruk. When it was clear that Bergonzoli had every intention of staying put, Mackay recommended a set-piece attack to breach Bardia's defences with the help of the surviving Matildas.

Mackay's preparations took until the end of December, and on 3 January his Australians went forward in an old-fashioned First World War style attack. It was another bitterly cold night and the men were weighed down, wearing greatcoats and carrying all the paraphernalia needed for cutting the wire, crossing the anti-tank ditch and clearing the minefields. In spite of these handicaps, which were never to be repeated by the Australians, a breach was made and the Matildas entered the fortress with the Australian infantry and supported by the fire of 120 out of the 154 guns belonging to 13th Corps. Again it was the Italian gunners who put up the stiffest resistance, which lasted late into the afternoon of the second day of the battle, when Mackay's men took the port almost intact. Bergonzoli escaped on foot to Tobruk, leaving four divisional commanders and 40,000 men in Australian hands, making the British Intelligence estimate of a garrison strength of 20,000 look a little foolish, and the Australian feat all the greater.

* * *

In Berlin, December had been the month in which Hitler's plans for 1941 had been finalised and issued. Everything revolved around his decision to invade Russia at the beginning of June – Operation *Barbarossa*. In the meantime, he decided he must help Mussolini after his crass decision to invade Greece on his own. The Italian disaster at Sidi Barrani was the last straw as far as Hitler was concerned, but it was Cunningham and the Royal Navy, who were the first to suffer the consequences of his frustration. Hitler ordered the immediate transfer of *Fliegerkorps X*, which was specialised in anti-shipping operations, from Norway to airfields in Sicily to challenge British naval dominance of the Central Mediterranean; and he issued Plan *Marita* for the invasion of Greece, which was timed for the end of March, in order to clear his southern flank before his invasion of Russia two months later. Plan *Felix*, the attack on Gibraltar, was cancelled and the troops earmarked for it reverted to training for operations in North Africa.

The British high command knew little of these plans and could only guess at Hitler's next move. This guessing brought on another Churchill/Wavell clash. Anthony Eden, now Foreign Secretary, minuted the Prime Minister on 6 January:

Salutations and congratulations upon the victory at Bardia. If I may debase a golden phrase, 'Never has so much been surrendered by so many to so few' ...

A mass of information has come to us over the last few days from divers sources, all of which tends to show that Germany is pressing forward her preparations in the Balkans with a view to an ultimate descent on Greece. The date usually mentioned for such a descent is the beginning of March ... [12]

Wavell was sceptical about Eden's deductions. Cabling the CIGS, General Sir John Dill, Wavell said:

Our appreciation here is that German concentration is more a war of nerves designed with object of helping Italy by upsetting Greek nerves, inducing us to disperse our forces in the Middle East and to stop our advance into Libya. Nothing we can do from here is likely to be in time to stop the German advance if really intended ... [13]

Churchill reacted venomously in defence of Eden's view and directed:

... Nothing must hamper capture of Tobruk but thereafter all operations in Libya are subordinate to aiding Greece...

We expect and require prompt and active compliance with our decisions for which we bear full responsibility ... [14]

In the Western Desert, O'Connor had already surrounded Tobruk and lost no time in instructing Mackay to make preparations to repeat his Bardia breaching operation. The Tobruk defences were just as strong as Bardia's, but twice the length to be manned by a garrison of half the size. This time British Intelligence estimated correctly that General Mannella, the Fortress Commander, had 25,000 troops and 200 guns in the fortress. O'Connor's most difficult task was to stock-pile enough ammunition at his guns to give the assault adequate artillery support. Bardia was not yet open as a port, and it took a fortnight to move forward the 1,000 tons of gun ammunition needed by truck from the frontier. 21 January was set as the target date for Mackay's assault.

In the meanwhile *Fliegerkorps* X had settled on the Sicilian airfields and had started to show its prowess at sea. On 10 January, Admiral Cunningham was off Malta with his battle fleet, covering the passage of an important convoy through the Sicilian Channel, when he was attacked ineffectively by Italian bombers from high level. The aircraft-carrier *Illustrious* was just recovering her fighters when her radars detected a raid coming in at a much lower level than usual. She had barely time to scramble more fighters when a formation of 30 to 40 German dive bombers appeared and pressed home attacks at close range, hitting her six times. After circling for three hours out of control, she limped back to Malta under further German attacks, receiving one more hit. For the next fortnight she was pounded by the *Luftwaffe* in the dockyard while the British and Maltese engineers struggled to make her seaworthy. At dusk on 23 January, she slipped away to Alexandria and thence to the United States for repairs.

Although *Illustrious* survived to fight another day, the balance of naval power in the Central Mediterranean had been tipped temporarily in favour of the Axis. The change could hardly have come at a worse time for the British and a better time for their opponents. Two more months of freedom from German intervention would have enabled Wavell to clear the Italians out of Africa: but those two months, during which *Fliegerkorps* X dominated the seas between Italy and Libya until it was flown off to take part in *Marita*, gave Hitler the chance to ship German troops across to Tripoli, which he seized with both hands and persuaded Mussolini to do so as well. On 11 January he ordered Operation *Sonnenblume*, the dispatch of his specially trained and equipped troops to Tripoli as the 5th Light Division. Mussolini agreed to send two of his best divisions as well: the Ariete Armoured and the Trento Mechanised Divisions.

★ ★ ★

Just before dawn on 21 January, Mackay's Australians assaulted Tobruk, using all the experience that they had gained at Bardia to simplify their breaching techniques. Although the weather was still cold, the men went forward unencumbered by greatcoats or jerkins, and unburdened with too much ammunition and equipment. Breaching the anti-tank ditch, wire and minefields was completed by early afternoon when 18 Matildas crunched their way forward and destroyed the Italian medium tanks sent by Mannella to check the Australian infantry. Mannella, himself, was captured when his headquarters was overrun just before dusk. The Australians settled down for the night with half the fortress in their hands. All resistance collapsed next day and another 25,000 Italians became prisoners of war. The port was so little damaged that supply ships were berthing within two days, easing O'Connor's logistic problems.

Wavell flew from Cairo to Tobruk to discuss the practicability of meeting a demand from Churchill for an immediate advance on Benghazi. Creagh's 7th Armoured Division was down to about 50 serviceable tanks, but Major General Gambier-Parry's 2nd Armoured Division from England was arriving to relieve it and would reach the forward area by the end of the February, by which time other supplies needed for the advance would have arrived as well. 10 February was fixed for the start of a plan, which had been developing in O'Connor's mind for some weeks and owed much of its inspiration to Allenby's battle of Megiddo in 1918.

To the west of Tobruk, the coast of Cyrenaica bulges northwards around the relatively fertile and easily defended hill country of the Djebel Akhdar. The main road to Benghazi runs through the Djebel, but there is a short-cut across the desert south of the Djebel via Mecheli and Msus, leading to the coast road 80 miles south of Benghazi near Beda Fomm. It was not much more than a camel track about which little was known. O'Connor's plan was for the Australians to press the Italians back through the Djebel, where they seemed to be fighting with unusual determination, while 7th Armoured Division, reinforced by Gambier-Parry's regiments as they arrived, cut across the desert to encircle and destroy the remains of Tellera's 10th Army. Lack of water and the unknown hazards of the track made it a high risk operation, but both Wavell and O'Connor judged the risks worth taking to achieve the decisive victory they needed before Churchill's desire to give priority to helping Greece halted their operations.

Much to their surprise, air reconnaissance and Australian infantry patrols on 1 and 2 February reported clear signs of a major Italian withdrawal taking place, including the evacuation of Benghazi and the destruction of its port. Graziani had panicked, and had recommended to Mussolini that Cyrenaica should be abandoned until the Germans could arrive with anti-tank weapons capable of defeating the British tanks. O'Connor threw caution to the wind and set Creagh's 7th Armoured Division off across the desert track to its destiny at Beda Fomm without waiting for Gambier-Parry's 2nd Armoured Division to arrive.

The advance, which began on 4 February, was led by a wheeled column of all arms, based upon Lieutenant Colonel JFB Combe's 11th Hussars in armoured cars. The first 50 miles were agonisingly slow. The rock strewn track and steep sided wadis delayed and damaged trucks and tanks, the wheeled column making slower progress, at first, than the tanks. Later the going improved and Combe's armoured cars reached Msus by mid-afternoon. The Italian garrison did not stay to argue, and Combe reached Antelat, only 20 miles from the coast, by dusk. The main body of the division struggled on through a clear starlit night and was at Msus by dawn.

Air reconnaissance reports confirmed the continuation of the Italian withdrawal, and so Creagh ordered Combe to block the coast road near Beda Fomm, while the rest of the division closed up ready to attack the inland flank of any Italian columns trying to escape into Tripolitania. Combe was in position by midday when the first Italian column hove in sight. It was thrown into confusion and stopped by Combe's gunners. During the afternoon the block was strengthened by the arrival of the 2nd Rifle Brigade, and the 4th Armoured Brigade's tanks came into action on the flank. By dusk, 1,000 prisoners had been taken and the coast road was strewn with burning vehicles. Further air reports showed much larger columns were moving south from Benghazi. The British block was absurdly weak to stop the withdrawal of Tellera's 10th Army, which still had four unbroken divisions as well as the flotsam of the rest of his force.

The second day of the battle was a struggle by small groups of Italian tanks and infantry to break through in an unco-ordinated way, while the rest of Tellera's army piled up on the roads and tracks behind them, offering the British gunners and tanks excellent targets. Most of the heaviest fighting fell to the cruiser tanks 2nd Royal Tank Regiment. By nightfall, none of the Italians groups had broken through, although at times it had been, like Waterloo, 'a close run thing' with British tank strength dropping all the time as inevitable mechanical failures rather than enemy action took their toll. Nevertheless, signs of Italian demoralisation were showing in their total inability to organise a successful breakthrough attempt, despite their gross numerical superiority in men, tanks and guns.

At daybreak on 7 February, the Italians launched what was to be their last attempt to escape, using 30 medium tanks against the 2nd Rifle Brigade's position astride the coast road. They almost succeeded and might have done so had the British artillery not been asked and received permission to bring down fire within the battalion's position. This fire, and the execution done by the anti-tank gun crews, stopped the attack just short of the battalion's officers' mess truck!

After this failure, white flags began to appear along the coast road as Italian morale slumped into apathetic acceptance of defeat. General Tellera had been mortally wounded; Bergonzoli, who had escaped from Bardia, and all the 10th Army staff surrendered; and another seven Italian generals and 25,000 men became prisoners of war. Mackay's Australians entered Benghazi on 6 February to find the port installations largely intact apart from the damage done by previous RAF bombing. O'Connor signalled Wavell:

Fox killed in the open . . . [15]

* * *

Unbeknown to O'Connor or Wavell, another 'fox' of a very different calibre was on his way to North Africa. Hitler had appointed Lieutenant General Erwin Rommel to command the *Sonnenblume* force, which would develop into the famous *Deutsches Afrika Korps* – the DAK for short. The pre-war British regular army had fought its last battle in the Western Desert. A very different army was to face Rommel in a few weeks' time.

O'Connor made immediate plans to advance along the Libyan coast to Sirte by 20 February, and then to Tripoli about 650 miles from Benghazi by the end of the month. Even Rommel, who arrived in Tripoli on 12 February, considered that there would have been nothing to stop him driving the Italians out of North Africa before German help became effective. He recorded:

> On 8 February, leading troops of the British Army occupied El Agheila [on the Tripolitanian frontier] . . . Graziani's Army had virtually ceased to exist . . . If Wavell had now continued his advance into Tripolitania, no resistance worthy of the name could have been mounted against him. [16]

Map 7: The 1941 Campaign in East Africa

O'Connor never had the opportunity to prove the point. The highly controversial decision was taken by the Cabinet in London to go no further. O'Connor's request for permission to advance on Tripoli was refused; the defence of Cyrenaica was to be consolidated; and the bulk of Wavell's available troops in Egypt and Palestine were to be dispatched to Greece with the hopeless task of trying to help the exhausted Greek Army defeat *Marita*.

Mussolini's Hollow Challenge

It is still difficult to understand how sensible men like Churchill, Eden, Wavell, and Smuts together with the governments of Australia and New Zealand could have expected an expeditionary force of four lightly equipped British divisions to stem the onrush of von Weich's 2nd German Army through Yugoslavia and von List's 12th German Army through Bulgaria when they descended on Greece at the beginning of April. However, the story of the disastrous three-week campaign in Greece in April 1941, like that of Gallipoli in 1915, lies outside the scope of this book on the Middle East. Only its consequences matter: the forces, which should have made the whole of the Middle East secure in British hands for the rest of the war, were squandered as Churchill tried to act the 'White Knight' in the Balkans without the resources to do so!

* * *

While Wavell was assembling forces under General 'Jumbo' Maitland Wilson for probable deployment to Greece, he did not relax his efforts to destroy the Italian East Africa Empire. The build-up of British forces, which he had engineered in the Sudan and Kenya, despite Churchill's opposition, was well advanced; and his victories in Cyrenaica had so lowered Italian morale in Eritrea, Abyssinia and Somaliland that the moment was right to strike.

The Duke of Aosta had discerned the three likely British thrust lines with some accuracy. He had given the task of opposing Platt's advance from the Sudan with the 4th and 5th Indian Divisions to General Frusci, his ablest and most energetic general, to whom he assigned the largest force, amounting to four colonial divisions to check any British attempt to reach Massawa, his vital port and base area on the Red Sea coast upon which the survival of the Italian Abyssinian Empire largely depended. General Nasi with a much smaller force of four colonial brigades was to suppress any Patriot revolt engineered by Wingate in the Gojjam. General de Simone with ten colonial brigades was to oppose Cunningham's advance northwards from Kenya. And Aosta, himself, held two of his very best European divisions, the Savoia and 'Africa', under his own hand in central reserve at Addis Ababa.

Platt had to open his offensive earlier than he planned, because Frusci withdrew from the flat plains of the frontier area to the more easily defended hill country of western Eritrea. 4th Indian Division was only just arriving, flushed with its victory at Sidi Barrani, when Platt set off in pursuit of Frusci on 11 January. The advance of 4th and 5th Indian Divisions was far quicker than Platt expected or Aosta would have liked, but Frusci knew what he was about. By the end of January, Platt's men were scanning the apparently impenetrable wall of the Keren escarpment, blocking any attempt to advance on Massawa by land. There was only one way through that escarpment – the Dongolaas Gorge, which carried the road and railway to Massawa and was as narrow, steep and difficult as any of the worst gorges on the North West Frontier of India with which the sepoys of 4th and 5th Indian Divisions were so familiar. Air photographs showed that the way through the gorge was blocked with piles of rock brought down by major cliff-side demolitions.

The battle of Keren was fought in two fiercely contested spasms: from 3–13 February, and from 15–27 March. Full of confidence, 4th Indian Division set about its task of clearing the high ground either side of the gorge on 3 February, but was met with unexpectedly savage counter-attacks each time an important feature was scaled. The Italians held the reverse slopes, immune to British artillery fire, whereas every move made by the Indian battalions could be seen by the Italian artillery observers. But what mattered most was the extraordinary fighting spirit with which Frusci was inspiring the Italian defenders. After ten days' fighting with no success, Platt decided to pause while efforts were made to find another way through the barrier, and to stockpile ammunition for a two divisional set-piece battle for the Dongolaas Gorge if none could be discovered.

There was, indeed, no way round, and while the search was being made, Aosta sent the Savoia Division to reinforce Frusci. Platt reopened the battle on 15 March with both his divisions and 750 rounds per gun available to their divisional artilleries. The key to the position appeared to be Fort Dologorodoc on the eastern side of the Gorge, which was 5th Indian's objective, while 4th Indian tried to clear the dominant features on the west side. Both divisions failed on the first day, but 5th Indian managed to take and hold the fort during the night, only to find, when daylight came, that it did not command the block in the gorge below, as had been hoped.

Night attacks with carefully limited objectives, mounted over the next few days, enabled the Indian Sappers and Miners to reconnoitre the block which they found was less extensive than had been feared. Platt paused again until 25 March to make careful preparations for a final assault to break through the gorge. This time Italian resistance began to crumble and he succeeded in uncovering the block. His Sappers worked non-stop all night and by dawn his few Matildas were grinding their way through the gorge. Frusci had realised that he was powerless to stop the block being cleared and had started to fall back. Part of his force withdrew into Massawa, which fell on 8 April, while he and his main body slipped away south-eastwards to join Aosta at Dessie. Platt had used 100,000 rounds of gun ammunition, and had lost 500 killed and 3,000 wounded in his two attempts to break through. Frusci had indeed fought well.

★ ★ ★

Wingate's force, which he called 'Giddeon', made a slow and difficult start. Giddeon was based on one regular Sudanese battalion and a battalion of Abyssinian exiles. He used a number of what he called 'Operational Centres', supervised by British officers and NCOs, to raise and help 'Patriot' bands to spread revolt from district to district in favour of the dethroned Emperor. Wingate was the ideal man for the job with all the attributes of a successful guerrilla leader: determinedly original and unorthodox, but also politically aware and able to inspire potentially rebellious tribal chiefs and their followers. Initially he had a supply train of 15,000 camels, but these proved to be a wasting asset once he had struggled up the main escarpment onto the Abyssinian plateau. Thereafter, he was dependent on local draft animals, which General Nasi tried to stop him acquiring without much success.

Like most successful rebellions, Wingate's snowballed, helped by exaggerated rumours of Italian defeats and British victories elsewhere. A mixture of audacity, endurance, tactical skill and masterly use of deception, enabled Wingate to outwit those hostile chiefs, who were opposed to Haile Selassie's return to power and were still counting upon an Italian victory. The RAF helped with bombing raids on Italian forts, which raised tribal morale and worried the Italians. A unique use of loud-speakers by a special propaganda section, set up by Wingate, increased tribal defections, and increasing numbers of chiefs decided it might be politic to espouse the Lion of Judah's cause. By the beginning of April, Wingate had established the Emperor at Debra Markos, the principal city of northern Ethiopia, 100 miles north of Addis Ababa. Ras Hailu, who was Haile Selassie's principal rival for power, had submitted, and Nasi had withdrawn to Dessie, leaving the road to Addis Ababa open.

* * *

Cunningham started his offensive from Kenya on 11 February. His three divisions – Brink's 1st South African, Wetherall's 11th African and Godwin-Austen's 12th African Divisions – made short work of de Simone's colonial brigades. Kismayu fell on 14 February, and Mogadishu, the capital of Italian Somaliland, was in Cunningham's hands by the 26th. Wetherall's 11th African Division then started its epic march on Harar with its Nigerian brigade leading. Supply was his principal limiting factor.

The snowballing of Wetherall's success was even more marked than in Wingate's operations. His West African battalions were mainly impeded by mines and demolitions. Whenever the Italian commanders decided to fight a delaying action, their determination evaporated as soon as the first clash came. Wetherall covered the 750 miles to Jijiga at an average speed of 65 miles per day, taking the town on 17 March. Nine days later, he entered Harar, having frightened the Italians out of the Marda and Babile

Passes, which were every bit as formidable as the Dongolaas Gorge at Keren.

By this time, Wavell was becoming increasingly worried by German arrivals in Tripolitania, and the Italian commanders in Abyssinia were beginning to fear for the safety of their women and children if a general Abyssinian uprising were to occur, which seemed all too likely. Wavell directed Cunningham to cut the Addis Ababa railway at Diredowa so that Brink's South Africans could be shipped as quickly as possible to Egypt through Red Sea ports; and to advance up the railway to take Addis Ababa as soon as possible for humanitarian rather than military reasons, instead of waiting for Wingate to escort Haile Selassie back to his capital from Debra Marcos.

Wetherall's 11th African Division completed its historic march by taking Diredowa on 29 March and entering Addis Ababa on 5 April. Aosta had left his capital the day before and headed to join the bulk of his surviving forces at Dessie. He then withdrew to a natural stronghold, fortified by the faithful Frusci, at Amba Alagi, where he hoped to hold out until Germany won the war. He was encircled by a mobile force from 5th Indian Division from Massawa and 1st South African Brigade from Dessie, where it had just taken 8,000 Italian prisoners. He would not agree to an armistice, but, after his outer defences had been stormed, he was eventually persuaded to surrender on 16 May to save more of his men from falling into Patriot hands. The last Italian provincial commander, General Gazzera, did not surrender until 3 July.

The spotlight of world interest had long since lifted from events in East Africa. On 6 April, Hitler launched *Marita*. The Anglo-Italian War in Africa was over. The British were about to face the second German challenge to their vital interests in the Middle East.

CHAPTER 3

DEFEATING HITLER'S CHALLENGE

Rommel versus Wavell, Auchinleck and Montgomery 1941–42

Hitherto the Bosphorus has provided the world with embarrassment enough; now you have created a second, and more serious, source of anxiety. For this defile not only connects two inland seas, but it acts as a channel of communication to the oceans of the world. So great is its importance that in a maritime war everyone will strive hard to occupy it. You have thus marked the site of a future great battlefield.

From a speech of welcome by Ernest Renan to Ferdinand de Lesseps on entering the French Academy in 1884.[1]

Ernest Renan's prophecy of 1884 did not come true for over half a century. The first German challenge to British dominance of the Suez Canal, made by supporting Turkey in the First World War, did not turn it into a great battlefield as he predicted. Kress von Kressenstein's attempts to cut the Canal were hardly more than skirmishes compared with the fighting for the Dardanelles, and hence for the Bosphorus. The second German challenge, nominally in support of Mussolini's Italy, was quite another matter. Renan was to be proved right beyond all reasonable doubt, not only by Rommel's brilliant performance in the Western Desert, which brought him within striking distance of the Canal in the summer of 1942, but also by the development of the Axis grand strategy of enveloping the British position in the Middle East with three encircling thrusts: Rommel's across the desert from the west; Japan's across the Indian Ocean from the east; and von List's from Russia through the Caucasus from the north. Although the Canal itself was never reached, it became the strategic focus of the war in the Mediterranean and Middle East in 1941–42 as Renan foretold.

The British obtained their first positive identification of German troops in Tripolitania on 24 February 1941, when an RAF pilot, flying over the Tripolitanian frontier, sighted an eight-wheeled armoured car, a type only used by the German Army. On that day, Wavell had reluctantly accepted the War Cabinet's plan to send an expeditionary force to help the Greeks to repel a probable German invasion of their country. The RAF report worried Churchill, who demanded an immediate appreciation from Wavell of the new situation.

Wavell's reply was over-sanguine. He knew that two new Italian divisions had been landed at Tripoli, together with some German armoured troops, estimated at one brigade group at the most; and his logistic staff calculated that supply difficulties would prevent the Germans reaching Cyrenaica much before May at the earliest. Even then, with only one poorish road, which was devoid of water for 400 out of the 670 miles from Tripoli to Benghazi, the enemy force would be not be large.

With hindsight it is possible to dub Wavell's appreciation as wishful thinking, but the German High Command held exactly the same view, but for rather different reasons. They did not plan to open an offensive to retake Cyrenaica until mid-May, by which time they hoped that the *Deutsches Afrika Korps* (the DAK for short) would have two divisions – Streich's 5th Light and von Prittwitz's 15th Panzer Divisions – ashore and partially acclimatised, and their supply problems lessened by the efficient German logistic staffs. But neither High Command, British or German, appreciated the thrusting impatience and tactical abilities of Rommel, who had arrived in Tripoli on 12 February to take command of the DAK. He cajoled General Gariboldi, who had taken over from the demoralised Graziani as the Italian Commander-in-Chief, to authorise not only the advance of the leading elements of Streich's division to the Tripolitanian frontier to deter a further British advance, but also to send the newly arrived Italian *Ariete* Armoured Division forward in their support. Moreover, he persuaded Gariboldi to allow *Fliegerkorps X* to bomb the port at Benghazi despite the risk to Italian life and property. The initial *Luftwaffe* attacks were so successful that the British had to abandon Benghazi as an advanced base and revert to the long haul of supplies by truck from Tobruk.

By the second week of March, evidence of a more immediate German threat to Cyrenaica was growing apace. On 5 March, Brigadier John Shearer, Wavell's Director of Intelligence, had sent his C-in-C an appreciation, written from the point of view of the, as yet, unidentified German commander in Tripoli. Shearer suggested that the Germans were moving forward far quicker than the logistic experts anticipated. He envisaged them planning their operations in three phases: securing Tripolitania against British attack; reoccupying Cyrenaica; and finally invading Egypt, aiming for Cairo and the Canal. In his view, the first phase was complete; and the second might start at any time after 1 April. Wavell, however, preferred the judgement of his logistic staff and was to pay the price for his misjudgement.

Rommel was identified as the commander of the DAK three days after Shearer had presented his appreciation of German plans. Rommel was well known in military circles for his pre-war book on infantry tactics, and for the aggressive part played by his 7th Panzer Division in France in 1940, but Wavell saw no reason to think that he could beat the logistic difficulties facing him. There was time in Wavell's view to bring the 4th and 5th Indian Divisions back from Eritrea and the 1st South African Division north from Abyssinia before Rommel could strike. In the meantime, General 'Jumbo' Maitland Wilson would leave for Greece with the Commonwealth Expeditionary Force, made up of Freyberg's 2nd New Zealand Division and Mackay's 6th Australian Division, refreshed after its victorious campaign in Cyrenaica. They would be supported by 1st Armoured Brigade and a large slice of the Support Group of Gambier-Parry's 2nd Armoured Division, and Laverack's 7th Australian Division would follow in reserve. All that would be left in Cyrenaica for the time being would be Gambier-Parry's novice 2nd Armoured Division less one of its two armoured brigades and half its support group, and Morshead's partially trained and equipped 9th Australian Division from Palestine. 7th Armoured Division was back in Egypt refitting, and O'Connor was there as well, having taken over command of British Troops, Egypt, in place of 'Jumbo' Wilson.

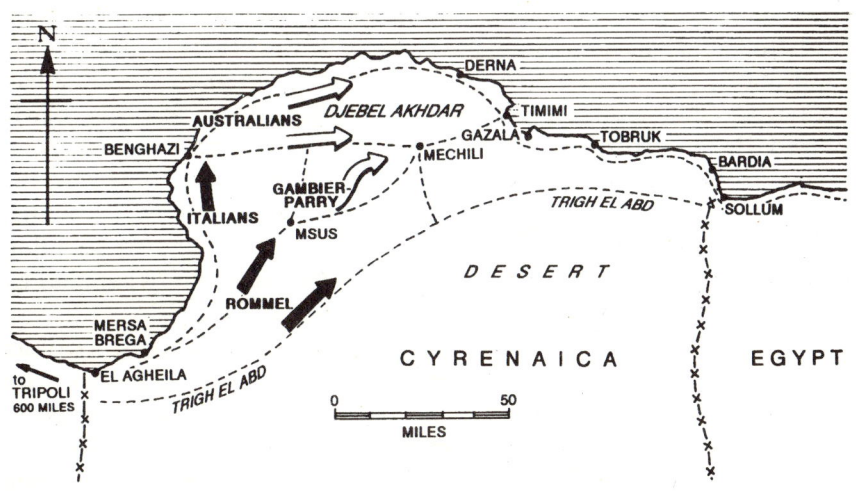

Map 8: Rommel's First Invasion of Cyrenaica: April 1941

The worst feature of this scratch force holding Cyrenaica until more experienced troops could be brought back from East Africa was that it was established as a garrison rather than a fighting formation. O'Connor had been replaced by Lieutenant General Philip Neame VC from Palestine. His headquarters, called Cyrenaica District, was not mobile and had minimal communication equipment; Neame, himself, was a Sapper with no experience of desert or armoured warfare; and Gambier-Parry's 3rd Armoured Brigade had a motley collection of tanks left over after his 1st Armoured Brigade had taken the best to Greece. One of its regiments was equipped with captured Italian medium tanks. Worse still was the paucity of air cover left for Cyrenaica after the RAF had met its Greek commitments.

In stark comparison, Rommel had the highly trained 5th Light Division with 150 of the latest German tanks, supported by a panoply of anti-tank, anti-aircraft and field artillery with which to defeat Gambier-Parry's scratch division, and up to five Italian divisions to hold Morshead's Australians. Furthermore, *Fliegerkorps X* had the punch to spare with which to support the DAK. Militarily, there would be no contest if Rommel struck before Wavell could bring troops back from East Africa.

Rommel, of course, had his problems too. His supply difficulties were just about overcome by the hard work and ingenuity of his logisticians, but his worst headaches stemmed from the attitudes of the Italian and German High Commands! In theory, he was under the command of Gariboldi, who was directed by the Italian *Commando Supremo* in Rome: in practice, his real direction came from Hitler's *Oberkommando der Wehrmacht* (OKW) and von Brauchitsch, the C-in-C of the German Army, at *Oberkommando der Heeres* (OKH), both in Berlin. Rommel could dominate Gariboldi without much difficulty; he was one of Hitler's favourites; but he was no friend of von Brauchitsch. He was not a member of the General Staff and so his organisational abilities were suspect; and he had been chosen specifically by Hitler, which made his appointment suspect too in OKH. He was so much of an outsider that he was not briefed on the planned invasions of Greece and Russia, which would absorb all available German resources in the spring of 1941. In consequence, he could not understand von Brauchitsch's reluctance to allow him to attack as soon as possible. If he attacked too soon and went too far, there would be no reinforcements available to get him out of trouble. His job was seen by von Brauchitsch as helping the Italians to hold Tripolitania and no more for the time being.

Irritated by lack of direction from Berlin, he flew back to place his plans for an early invasion of Cyrenaica before Hitler and von Brauchitsch. The latter was unimpressed, but authorised him to probe the British defences at El Agheila on the Tripolitanian frontier, and warned him not to go beyond Benghazi. Hitler was much more amenable. After investing him with 'Oakleaves' to his Iron Cross for his services with 7th Panzer Division in France, he seems to have encouraged him to ignore the caution of the General Staff. When he arrived back in Tripoli on 23 March he ordered von Wechmar's 3rd Reconnaissance Unit to drive the British covering troops out of El Agheila, which it did without much difficulty next day.

Rommel paused for a week at El Agheila while he reconnoitred the next British defensive position in the coastal defile at Mersa Brega, and while he brought up troops and supplies for what he intended would be a reconnaissance in force into Cyrenaica. Gariboldi sanctioned 'the raid' with the proviso that Rommel was not to advance 'round the corner' into Cyrenaica without his express authority.

Rommel's 'raid' was in two phases: before and after he decided on 3 April to disobey Gariboldi by attempting the reverse of O'Connor's Beda Fomm operation. After suffering two defeats at Gambier-Parry's hands, Streich's 5th Light Division broke through the Mersa Brega position on 31 March, thereby uncorking the Cyrenaica bottle and enabling Rommel to use his numerical superiority once he was through the defile. Gambier-Parry reported that he was down to 22 medium and 25 light tanks, and was losing an average of one tank every ten miles of his withdrawal. He proposed to Neame that he should block O'Connor's old desert route through Msus and Mechili, while Morshead's Australians looked after Benghazi and the Djebel Akhdar.

Neame might have accepted this plan had not Wavell arrived and insisted that Gambier-Parry join the Australians in the defence of Benghazi because he calculated that Rommel would soon run out of logistic steam and would need the port before he could go any further. Wavell also felt that Neame was out of his depth and sent O'Connor from Egypt to take over command. Unfortunately, O'Connor was too much of a gentleman to do so straightaway. He recommended to Wavell that he should stay with Neame for some days to help and advise him and should then become responsible for the preparation of a firm base at Gazala, covering Tobruk, to which Neame could fall back if need be. Neame should continue to command in the forward area. This was a recipe for disaster: dual commands never work in war. Order, counter-order led to constant confusion, which was exacerbated by poor radio communications.

Rommel's experienced eye was quick to detect the confusion behind the British front. Since their firm showing at Mersa Brega, the British had been falling back too easily, doing too little fighting and abandoning too much equipment. He decided to throw caution to the wind and go for Tobruk across O'Connor's desert route plus a route across the desert even further south – the Trigh el Abd caravan route – which led more directly into Egypt. In those early days of his desert campaigns, he could not count on the loyalty of his officers and men who scarcely knew him. Streich, for instance, was awkward about heading off into the desert without adequate preparations, and the Italians were equally reluctant to advance on Benghazi. Grabbing reliable commanders whom he could trust, he formed *ad hoc* battle groups and drove them relentlessly towards Mechili.

Gambier-Parry's orders to fall back on Benghazi did not reach him until his columns were already committed to the Msus-Mechili route. He tried to swing them north towards the Australian flank in the Djebel. Some units heard the orders transmitted by radio, others did not, and by the end of 3 April Gambier-Parry had virtually lost control of his hopelessly dispersed division. To make matters worse, rumours of German columns appearing far behind the front – many of them, in fact, British units that had gone astray – resulted in fuel and supply dumps being destroyed prematurely.

Rommel did not lose control of his equally widely dispersed columns as they forged their way across the desert tracks through Msus and along the Trig el Abd. Flying from column to column in his light *Fieseler Storch* communications aircraft and using his efficient radio network, he drove and inspired his column commanders with his ruthless personal dynamism. His aim was to get behind the Australians, and such elements of Gambier-Parry's division as had joined them, by cutting the coast road near Timimi, just west of Tobruk, with his DAK while the Italian divisions pinned them in the Djebel country.

Morshead's withdrawal from Benghazi through the Djebel had started on 4 April and went as well as could be expected of any forced retreat. He was not particularly hard pressed by the Italians, and had a brigade in position at Timimi by 6 April, ready to cover the withdrawal of the rest of the Cyrenaica garrison into a new defensive line organised by O'Connor at Gazala, which was between Timimi and Tobruk. But bad luck, which usually plagues armies in retreat, struck with a vengeance. Neame was driving back in the dark to Gazala in his staff car, accompanied by O'Connor, when they ran into a German reconnaissance force, probing towards the coast, and were both captured. Gambier-Parry and Morshead were the only British generals left in the field: and soon there was to be only one!

Gambier-Parry reached Mechili with little more than his headquarters on 6 April. It was garrisoned by the 3rd Indian Motor Brigade, which had been rushed up from Egypt to help form a new front. Rommel soon had Mechili surrounded and summoned it to surrender twice on 7 April, but Gambier-Parry refused and planned to break out that night. It was a bungled affair. Most of the Indian units escaped, but Gambier-Parry started too late and was captured in his command vehicle!

Morshead took the only course open to him. He withdrew into the defensive perimeter of Tobruk and prepared to stand siege, reinforced, he hoped, by troops sent by sea from Egypt. Rommel, still with his whip out, made straight for the fortress, hoping to break in before Morshead could man its extensive defences properly. He made three attempts between 11 and 30 April to no avail. Morshead's Australians, manning captured Italian guns, which they called 'bush artillery', proved unbeatable. Rommel's 'raid' was over: out of supplies, his men exhausted and their equipment worn out, he settled down to besiege Tobruk while awaiting the arrival of 15th Panzer Division and the replenishment of his resources.

He did push flying columns on to the Egyptian frontier, but they were stopped by a new force, based on 22nd Guards Brigade, under Brigadier 'Strafer' Gott's command.

Set in the context of the great events which were already unfolding in the Balkans and Eastern Europe, the loss of Cyrenaica was little more than a preliminary skirmish. Neame had lost about half of the novice 2nd Armoured Division and had abandoned a vast area of desert, but Rommel had been presented with the problems of much longer supply lines and with a strongly held enemy fortress on the flank of his route towards Egypt and the Suez Canal. He realised that he must take Tobruk before he could go any further.

* * *

Marita had started on 6 April 1941 with the German bombing of Belgrade and the invasion of Yugoslavia, which was followed immediately by their invasion of Greece. A fortnight later, the evacuation of the Australian and New Zealand divisions from Greece had begun. Losses in men were not as heavy as might have been expected, but most of their heavy equipment was left behind. The worst effect of the failure to hold Greece was the loss of the Greek islands from which the *Luftwaffe*'s anti-shipping aircraft could operate to cover Rommel's trans-Mediterranean supply lines; to close the Mediterranean to British convoys; and to interdict the British coastal supply route to Tobruk. These threats, however, still lay in the future because the *Luftwaffe* was already leaving the Mediterranean to play its part in *Barbarossa*.

Much was still to happen in the Middle East before 22 June when Hitler invaded Russia and turned the Russians into Britain's allies. Wavell, standing at the eye of the storm, had to face in four directions: northwards to Crete, where Freyberg's New Zealanders had been dropped off on their way back from Greece to prevent its use as a German base; westwards to Rommel's activities around Tobruk and on the Egyptian frontier; southwards to Abyssinia, where the Duke of Aosta had yet to surrender at Amba Alagi on 16 May; and eastwards to Iraq and Syria where German influence amongst nationalist opposition leaders was growing. It was in Iraq that unexpected and unwelcome trouble first arose.

Apart from the Vichy French in Syria, all the established regimes in the Middle East had so far remained neutral to the extent that they were not actively hostile to Britain. Their political opponents, of course, were pro-Axis and as German successes mounted so would their internal political support grow. In Iraq, an Arab state created by Britain, there had always been a love-hate relationship between the efficient Christian British and the *laissez-faire* Moslem hierarchy, which could veer unpredictably either way with the political winds.

The experienced Feisal had died in 1933; his successor had been killed in a car accident soon afterwards; and his son Feisal II was still a minor in 1941 with his uncle Abdullah exercising the powers of Regent. Within the Iraq regular army of four fully equipped infantry divisions there were four over-influential anti-British and rabidly nationalist Iraqi officers, called the 'Golden Square', who were in close touch with German agents. A new British High Commissioner, Sir Kinahan Cornwallis, was just taking over in Baghdad when they mounted a successful *coup d'état* on 2 April. The Regent, who was considered incorrigibly Anglophile by the rebels, fled disguised as a woman to the American Embassy, and was spirited away to safety at the RAF base at Habbaniya, hidden under a blanket in the back of the US minister's car. The 'Golden Square' installed a time-serving politician, Rashid Ali, at the head of the rebel government in Baghdad.

Although the new regime took no immediate hostile action against British interests, Churchill decided that the whole British position in the Middle East would be undermined if the Regent was not restored to power. He asked Wavell and General Sir Claude Auchinleck, Commander-in-Chief India, what intervention forces they could provide. Wavell, quite understandably, ducked, pointing out that he had too much on his hands, and thereby started the first of three calamitous confrontations with Churchill, each of which added another nail to his coffin as far as the Prime Minister was concerned. While Wavell showed a lack of immediate willingness to co-operate, Auchinleck quickly offered to dispatch the 10th Indian Division to Basra, quite unwittingly acquiring correspondingly greater merit in Churchill's competitive mind. Cornwallis, however, advised from Baghdad that no troops should be landed until Rashid Ali had provided a *casus belli* by refusing Britain's rights under the Anglo-Iraq Treaty to pass troops through Basra to Palestine and Egypt.

Rashid Ali, as was to be expected, did refuse to sanction 10th Indian Division's landing at Basra, which started on 17 April and was unopposed because the 'Golden Square' thought that they had easier prey quite close to Baghdad – the RAF base at Habbaniya on the west bank of the Euphrates (*See Map 3*). On the base, which was primarily used as a flying training school, Air Vice-Marshal Smart had some 78 obsolescent training aircraft, 1,000 British airmen, 1,200 Iraq Levies and 9,000 civilians, including British and Iraqi servicemen's families. He improvised the arming of his aircraft, and set everyone on the base to digging, wiring and generally preparing for its defence.

On 1 May, a reinforced Iraqi brigade arrived and started digging in and deploying artillery on the higher ground overlooking the base from the south. Three hundred men of the 1st Kings Own Royal Regiment of Lancaster were flown in from Basra, accompanied by Colonel Ouvry

Roberts, a Sapper officer on 10th Indian Division's staff (later to become General Sir Ouvry and Quartermaster General of the Army), who was to command the land defence of the base. In Baghdad, Cornwallis demanded the withdrawal of the Iraqi brigade, and when there was no sign of compliance, he authorised Smart to attack.

Before dawn on 2 May, all Smart's aircraft took off with their maximum bomb load, and eight Wellington bombers, flown from Egypt to Shaiba, arrived over Habbaniya to add weight to Smart's attack. Two hundred sorties were flown against the Iraqi positions that day by the instructors and pupils of the flying school. The Iraqi artillery replied but did far less damage than expected. The cost of the first day's fighting was five aircraft lost to Iraqi fighters, and 13 killed and 29 wounded in the base. Smart kept up his attacks for four more days, while the Wellingtons from Shaiba destroyed the Iraqi Air Force on its airfields. At dawn on 6 May, British patrols found the Iraqi positions overlooking Habbaniya deserted. The rebel force had apparently withdrawn in some haste to be clear of the position by daylight when British bombing would begin again. They left large quantities of equipment and ammunition behind as they withdrew to more distant blockading positions. Part of their force went eastwards and dug in around the Falluja bridge over the Euphrates to cover Baghdad. Others went west to Ramadi to block any relief column which might arrive from Palestine.

The close siege of Habbaniya had been lifted, but the rebellion was far from over; nor was the first of Churchill's three fatal confrontations with Wavell. The Prime Minister, while applauding Smart's brilliant defence of Habbaniya, demanded that a relief column be sent from Palestine as the Iraqis expected. Wavell demurred, saying that it would be too weak and too late. He recommended diplomatic action, using Turkish good offices. He was overruled and had to dispatch a scratch force drawn from the 1st Cavalry Division, which was in the throes of exchanging its horses for mechanical transport, and from the Transjordan Frontier Force. 'Habforce', as it was called, left Palestine on 13 May, mounted in trucks with no tanks and little artillery. Ominously, it was attacked by German aircraft flying from Syria when it was half way across the Transjordan desert, and was attacked again when it brushed aside the Iraqis at Ramadi to reach Habbaniya on 18 May.

The German threat was clearly growing, but they had problems too. Like Rommel, the 'Golden Square' had struck too soon, and were an embarrassment to Hitler, who wanted nothing to divert resources away from launching *Barbarossa*. He had, however, reluctantly agreed to give the Iraqis limited air support with 14 fighters and seven bombers but, much to his fury, Iraqi anti-aircraft gunners shot down and killed his emissary, Major Axel von Blomberg, son of the Field Marshal, as he was trying to land on Baghdad's airfield!

The commander of the 1st Cavalry Division, Major General Clark, decided to waste no time at Habbaniya and to advance on Baghdad straightaway, despite the knowledge that the Iraqis could muster a very considerable force against him from their four regular divisions. Taking the risk paid off handsomely. He took the Euphrates bridge at Falluja without loss on 19 May, and beat off two unexpectedly determined Iraqi counter-attacks on the bridge. German aircraft again made an appearance, but exaggerated bazaar rumours of British strength far outweighed the effect of German air support on Iraqi morale, and Clark was able to enter Baghdad on 30 May, hindered more by flooding than by sporadic Iraqi resistance. Rashid Ali fled and the Regent re-established the Hashemite Government.

★ ★ ★

Wavell had been proved wrong: firm action by improvised forces had succeeded. Usually, all's well that ends well, but not in Wavell's case – far worse was to come. An 'Ultra' intercept was the cause of the second near fatal flare-up with the Prime Minister. During the Iraqi affair, Rommel had attacked Tobruk for a third time on 30 April and had been repulsed by Morshead's Australians, but this success had not been matched by the Royal Navy's efforts at sea. Wavell reported that the Germans had managed to land von Prittwitz's 15th Panzer Division almost unscathed at Tripoli, and warned Whitehall that, on its arrival in Cyrenaica, the DAK would take some stopping if Rommel lunged for Egypt and the Canal. Churchill's pugnacious reaction was to insist, despite Admiralty misgivings, on the despatch of tank reinforcements to Wavell in a fast and heavily escorted convoy through the Mediterranean. The Tiger Convoy, as it was code-named, left England at the end of April, carrying 300 precious tanks, purloined from the defence of the British Isles, which Churchill fondly called his 'Tiger Cubs'. His whole being was engaged in their successful passage to Alexandria; their unloading and modification for desert operations; and their manning by 7th Armoured Division, which had been without battle-worthy tanks since Beda Fomm.

While Churchill was straining every sinew to reinforce Wavell, OKH was doing the opposite for Rommel. General von Paulus, who was later to surrender to the Russians at Stalingrad, was sent out to Tripoli at the end of April 'to head off this soldier gone stark mad', as General Halder, the Chief of Staff to von Brauchitsch at OKH, recorded in his diary. Von Paulus arrived just in time to witness Rommel's last abortive attack on Tobruk. He was not impressed and reported to OKH that Rommel was in an operational and logistic muddle. He recommended that attacks on Tobruk should stop; that Rommel should confine himself to the defence of the western half of Cyrenaica, building a reserve defensive position at

Gazala (*See Map 8*) on which he could fall back if the British took the offensive; and that no more troops should be sent to him until his supply position could be improved. He also reported that Rommel was short of ammunition and fuel; his tanks were worn out; and he lacked medium artillery and needed more anti-tank guns.

It was von Paulus's report, which, intercepted by the highly secret 'Ultra' communications interception system, caused the second Churchill/Wavell confrontation. Armed with this evidence of Rommel's over-stretch, the Prime Minister demanded that Wavell should probe the German positions on the Egyptian frontier in preparation for a major offensive, which was to be mounted as soon as the 'Tiger Cubs' arrived. Wavell acquiesced and gave Beresford-Peirse, who had arrived back from Eritrea with 4th Indian, command of a reconstituted Western Desert Force with which to carry out the probing operation, code-named *Brevity*.

Brevity lived up to its name. The force deployed was little more than a reinforced brigade group under 'Strafer' Gott's command, and was directed to seize Sollum and the Halfaya Pass in the Sollum escarpment. Gott took both on 15 May, but Rommel intervened next day with a force containing two panzer battalions from 5th Light Division from near Tobruk. Gott was forced to withdraw, leaving a small force holding Halfaya, which Rommel overran ten days later. Gott did not lose many men, and his tank losses were caused more by mechanical failure than German action.

Brevity had one unforeseeable effect upon the Anglo-German desert war. Rommel decided that he must create a stronger defensive line in the frontier area if he was to stop Wavell raising the siege of Tobruk. As von Paulus had reported to OKH, Rommel was short, by German standards, of anti-tank guns. As he had done in France in May 1940, when repelling the British counter-attack at Arras, he decided to sacrifice some of his air defence and use his powerful 88mm anti-aircraft guns in a ground mode to give depth and punch to his anti-tank defences on the frontier. He emplaced these unwieldy guns, unbeknown to the British, in camouflaged gun pits at Halfaya and behind the Hafid Ridge to its north-west, blocking the most direct route to Tobruk. Only the gun barrels were just visible above the desert surface. This improvised use of 88mm anti-aircraft guns was to prove a battle winner.

Churchill was not upset by Gott's failure to hold Sollum and Halfaya, because he was elated by the safe arrival of most of his Tiger Cubs at Alexandria on 12 May. Only one ship had been sunk with the loss of 50 tanks. He expected Wavell to launch his main offensive, code-named *Battleaxe*, almost immediately, totally underestimating the time needed to make the tanks desert-worthy and their crews familiar with them. Two other factors stoked his impatience: Crete was lost in the last week of May, opening up the eastern Mediterranean to the *Luftwaffe*'s shorter range dive bombers, which could only be neutralised by the RAF if Rommel was driven out of Cyrenaica; and pro-German activities of the Vichy French regime in Syria, abetted by the machinations of the Grand Mufti of Jerusalem in exile in Damascus, were beginning to pose a threat to Palestine. In Churchill's view, Wavell had quite enough troops and aircraft to relieve Tobruk and to settle matters with General Dentz, the French High Commissioner for Syria, simultaneously if need be.

Relations between Cairo and Whitehall became more and more acrimonious in the latter half of May as Wavell and Longmore tried to persuade the War Cabinet not to take on Rommel and Dentz at the same time. Cabling the CIGS, Wavell said:

> Hope I shall not be landed with Syria commitment unless absolutely essential. Any force I could send would be painfully reminiscent of the Jameson raid and might suffer a similar fate . . . [2]

This cable was seen by Churchill, who informed the CIGS that he had decided to get rid of Wavell. He and Auchinleck, the apparently more co-operative C-in-C India, would change places. A few days later, Wavell, stung by what he saw as Free French intrigue in Whitehall for an attack on Syria, unwittingly offered his resignation to the CIGS, if his judgement was not trusted. Churchill, however, recoiled momentarily: Wavell was too large a public figure to be dismissed over an argument with de Gaulle's unpopular clique. Nevertheless, Churchill couched his reply in terms that forced Wavell to milk his *Battleaxe* order of battle to build up a force for an invasion of Syria, code-named *Exporter*, which the War Cabinet insisted should be launched on 8 June; just a week before *Battleaxe*.

Longmore was not so lucky. He had been even more outspoken than Wavell about lack of resources and the ludicrously wide dispersion of his aircraft. He was summoned home to report and was never allowed to return to Cairo. His controversial deputy, Air Marshal Sir Arthur Tedder, succeeded him as Air Officer Commander-in-Chief, Middle East.

Exporter was, indeed, launched on 8 June, ending the second Churchill/Wavell confrontation in the Prime Minister's favour. 'Jumbo' Wilson, just back from the Greek fiasco, was given command of the *Exporter* force, consisting initially of Laverack's 7th Australian Division, a brigade from 4th Indian Division, and a Free French division of two brigades. There were no tanks available and air support was minimal, but the Royal Navy provided a cruiser squadron and a commando landing-ship to operate along the Syrian coast. Some help came from 10th Indian Division and Habforce in Iraq, the former advancing up the Euphrates into northern Syria to threaten Aleppo, and the latter recrossing the Transjordan desert to help the Free French take Damascus. The 6th Division, which had been training for amphibious operations in the

Dodecanese Islands, was sent later from Egypt to speed up operations. The Vichy French fought back with commendable spirit against the Australians, and with expected bitterness against the Free French. It took Wilson five weeks' hard fighting to persuade Dentz that further resistance was futile since he could not be reinforced from France, nor were the Germans in a position to help him. Armistice negotiations started on 11 July. The Vichy troops in Syria were given the option of joining the Free French or being shipped back to France: only 5,700 out of 38,000 opted for de Gaulle.

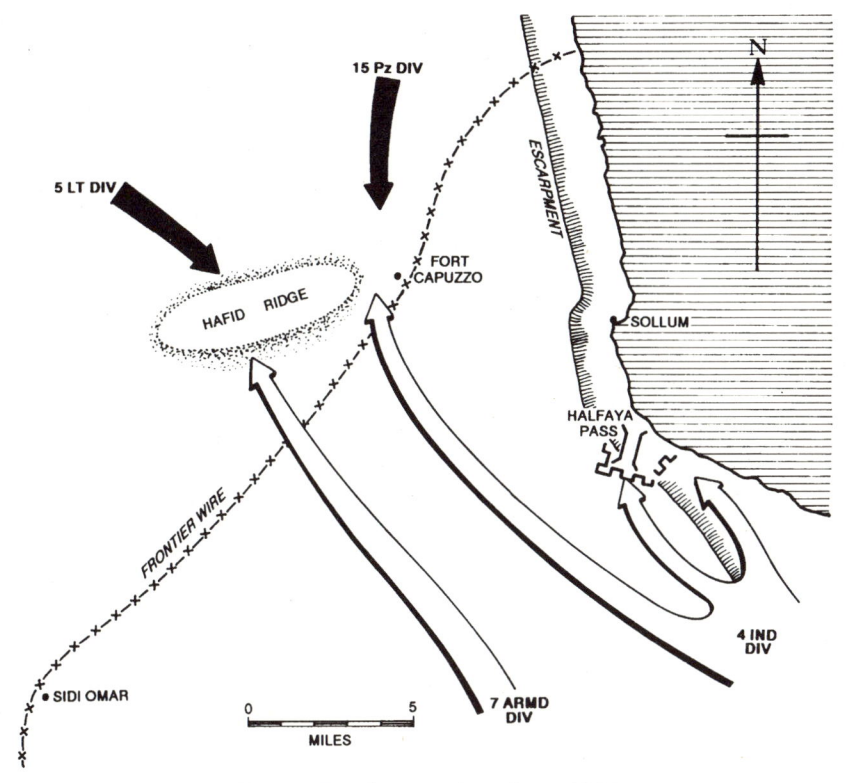

Map 9: Battleaxe: 15–17 June 1941

★ ★ ★

Battleaxe was the cause of Wavell's final and disastrous confrontation with Churchill in the Middle East. Beresford-Pierse's Western Desert Force was far from ready to take the offensive, but Churchill's conviction that Rommel was in dire logistic difficulties brooked no delay. Its two partially equipped divisions each had only two brigades. 4th Indian Division, now under Major General Frank Messervy, supported by the Matilda tanks of

4th Armoured Brigade, was to attack along the coast, retaking Sollum, Halfaya and Fort Capuzzo, and ultimately Bardia. He had only one of his own brigades, the 11th Indian Brigade, and the 22nd Guards Brigade, which had been on the frontier since Rommel reached it in April. His 5th Indian Brigade was in Syria, and his 7th was not yet back from Eritrea. Creagh's re-equipped 7th Armoured Division was to operate on the desert flank to protect Messervy from German armoured interference, and attempt the relief of Tobruk if the battle on the frontier went well. He had only Gott's 7th Armoured Brigade with two instead of three regiments, one in reconditioned cruiser tanks and the other in the new 'Crusader' cruisers brought out by the Tiger convoy, totalling no more than 100 tanks all told. His crews had barely enough time to get a feel for their new equipment, and he had had no time to carry out a divisional exercise to give them the training they needed.

What Churchill did not understand about German generals was their propensity to 'cry wolf' over lack of resources as a means of winning larger allocations to their own front, and to provide a documented excuse if things went wrong. Von Paulus's intercepted report conveyed a far worse situation in the DAK than actually existed for the additional reason that it was written to denigrate Rommel, who was to be brought to heel. The investment of Tobruk was in the hands of the Italians, corseted by German detachments. 15th Panzer Division under Major General Neumann-Silkow with 100 new tanks was watching the frontier, and 5th Light Division, under Major General von Ravenstein, with another 90 tanks was refitting in reserve between Tobruk and the frontier. The Sollum–Halfaya area was strongly fortified and garrisoned by a mixed German and Italian force under command of Major Bach, an ex-Lutheran priest turned soldier, who knew how to inspire men militarily as well as spiritually! 15th Panzer's string of posts, which ran south-westwards along the frontier from Fort Capuzzo to the Hafid Ridge were an unknown quantity to British command.

Battleaxe began on 15 June and lasted for three hard-fought days, in which the fortunes of both sides fluctuated to an extent that kept the outcome uncertain until the very end. It was important not only because it was the first battle between evenly matched British and German forces in the desert – about 200 tanks on each side – but also because it held within it the secrets of German success, which, if properly analysed by the British, might have saved them much of the blood, sweat and tears of the next year and a half of the desert fighting.

Before the battle began, the RAF had managed to achieve a tolerable air situation over the battlefield. Most of *Fliegerkorps X's* squadrons had been withdrawn for *Barbarossa*, leaving the Italians largely responsible for Rommel's air cover. Bombed on their airfields, they put up a poor performance in the air during the land battle.

On the first day, Messervy took the Capuzzo area, but was thwarted by Major Bach's sterling defence of Halfaya. Creagh was not so fortunate as he executed his flanking movement through the desert to the west, which brought him up against the well concealed Hafid Ridge positions. 7th Armoured Brigade made three abortive attempts to clear them, but were stopped by what they thought was tank gunfire. In the last attempt, two British tank squadrons in new Crusaders were lured into attacking what looked like a German supply column's leaguer. The hidden German anti-tank gunners, including a few 88mm crews, destroyed 11 Crusaders in quick succession and damaged six more. By the end of the day, Creagh's tank strength had dwindled to 37, although the figure was raised to 48 by dawn next day through the hard work of his recovery and repair crews. Beresford-Pierse decided that his operations had gone as well as could be expected, and decided to persevere next day, making only one significant change: the Matildas of 4th Armoured Brigade would join Creagh to deal with the Hafid Ridge positions.

On the German side, Neumann-Silkow's 15th Panzer Division had been severely mauled and Major Bach had suffered heavy casualties as well. It was with some relief to both men to see the leading regiment of von Ravenstein's 5th Light Division approaching as dusk fell. Rommel was not in the least put out by depressing reports from the front. His radio intercept unit had given him a remarkably accurate picture of the British dispositions and the state of their units, because their radio security discipline at regimental level at that time was abysmally lax. He decided to seize the initiative by ordering Neumann-Silkow to counter-attack Messervy in the Capuzzo area while von Ravenstein worked round Creagh's open desert flank.

The second day's fighting was a draw, slightly favouring Rommel. Neumann-Silkow failed against Messervy, but his attacks prevented Messervy from releasing 4th Armoured Brigade to Creagh at the Hafid Ridge. Messervy for his part again failed to drive Bach out of Halfaya. Without 4th Armoured Brigade's help, 7th Armoured Brigade just managed to counter von Ravenstein's outflanking moves in a series of running battles, which zig-zagged south-westwards along the frontier wire to Sidi Omar, where both sides leaguered for the night. Creagh was down to 21 fit tanks. Twenty-five of the 27 tanks that he lost that day were thought to have succumbed to superior German tank guns, whereas, in fact, the damage had been done, as on the Hafid Ridge, by hidden anti-tank guns.

During the night, Beresford-Peirse again decided to persevere. Messervy was thought to be secure enough at Capuzzo to release 4th Armoured Brigade for Creagh to deal with von Ravenstein when dawn came. The German divisional commanders were depressed by the day's fighting: Neumann-Silkow had suffered further losses; Von Ravenstein had failed to outflank Creagh; Bach was almost out of ammunition; and the RAF was playing havoc with the German supply columns. Again Rommel reacted with characteristic determination not to be beaten. Piecing the evidence together as it came in, he concluded that Beresford-Peirse would reopen his offensive with an attack northwards from Capuzzo, and decided to forestall him with pre-dawn moves of his two divisions round the desert flank, aiming to cut in behind the British when they plunged northwards.

17 June was the decisive day. Wavell had sensed this and had flown up to Beresford-Peirse's headquarters so as to be on hand for any major decisions that might be needed. Messervy again fended off Neumann-Silkow's 15th Panzer Division as it tried to move round his open flank, but he had to keep 4th Armoured Brigade in order to do so. Creagh was out-manoeuvred by von Ravenstein, whose 5th Light Division slipped past him and appeared in Messervy's rear at about 8am. Both British divisional commanders recognised what was happening and called for Beresford-Peirse to come up to decide what should be done. Accompanied by Wavell, he reached Creagh's headquarters at 11.45am, only to find that Messervy had already been forced by shortage of ammunition to pull 22nd Guards Brigade back from Capuzzo, opening Neumann-Silkow's route to join von Ravenstein. Wavell quickly recognised that the battle was lost and ordered the Western Desert Force's disengagement.

Wavell flew back to Cairo that afternoon and penned an apology to Churchill for wasting his precious Tiger Cubs, shouldering all the blame. Churchill had the excuse, which he had wanted for some time. On 21 June, he wrote to Wavell, saying:

> I have come to the conclusion that the public interest will best be served by the appointment of General Auchinleck to relieve you in command of the Armies of the Middle East . . . the victories which are associated with your name will be famous in the history of the British Army, and are an important contribution to our success in this obstinate war. I feel, however, that after the long strain you have borne, a new eye and a new hand are required in this most seriously menaced theatre. [3]

★ ★ ★

Wavell showed no rancour at his dismissal, commenting in cricketing terms that he agreed 'it was time for a change of bowling'. There were three reasons why *Battleaxe* had failed, none of which could be laid at Wavell's door. In the first place, he had been forced to attack too soon due to von Paulus's intercepted report, which grossly exaggerated Rommel's difficulties. Secondly, in equipment terms, there is little doubt that the British tanks were far less reliable and their anti-tank guns inferior to the German equivalents. The villains of the piece were the German towed 'long' 50mm anti-tank guns and the formidable 88mm anti-aircraft guns used against tanks, neither of which the British could begin to match until their own 6 pounders entered service in 1942 and their 17 pounders appeared a year later.

Thirdly, and most crucial of all, the DAK had mastered the techniques of armoured warfare quicker than their British opponents. The German Army, having started afresh after the First World War, found close co-operation between tanks, infantry and artillery easier to achieve than the tribal British, who stuck to the traditions of yesteryear. It was to take the British another year to match the German tactical philosophy: use anti-tank guns to kill tanks, tanks to kill infantry, and artillery to kill anti-tank guns and infantry. If the British had appreciated that the real damage was being done by the German anti-tank guns and not by the guns in the German tanks, they would have used their highly skilled artillery to neutralise them. In 1941 and for two-thirds of 1942, the British tank regiments tended to see themselves either as fighting naval battles on land, in which Nelson's dictum that no captain can go far wrong, who lays his ship alongside his enemy; or as cavalrymen of old, who placed their faith in the impact of the charge. Neither tactic was much use unless the artillery had rid the battlefield of the hidden but vulnerable towed anti-tank guns.

During *Battleaxe* both sides lost about a thousand men. The British lost half their tanks, and the Germans a third of theirs, but, as they held the battlefield, they could recover tank casualties from both sides, and, indeed, they used several recovered Matildas in the siege of Tobruk. Fortunately for the British, however, the DAK was in no fit state after the battle to invade Egypt. It would also take many months to rebuild 7th Armoured Division. In the meantime, the approaches into Egypt were covered by a screen of 'Jock' columns, named after Brigadier Jock Campbell, the commander of 7th Armoured Division's Support Group, who was given the task of watching the frontier without any tanks. The 'Jock' columns consisted of a battery of field guns, a troop of anti-tank guns, a troop of light anti-aircraft guns and a company of mechanised infantry. They could not hold ground and depended on their mobility for offensive raids and ambushes, but they appealed to the buccaneering spirit of the officers and men of the Western Desert Force. On each occasion when British armoured forces suffered serious losses in subsequent desert battles, the 'Jock' columns were to emerge as a temporary tactical panacea in the disorganisation caused by defeat.

* * *

Auchinleck replaced Wavell in the last week of June as the German armies thrust deep into Russia at the start of *Barbarossa*. Whitehall and Cairo reacted in diametrically opposite ways to the news of Hitler's Russian adventure. To Whitehall, it seemed that the opportunity for throwing Rommel out of North Africa while Hitler's back was turned must be snatched without delay. Russia would probably collapse by the autumn, opening the way for the German armies to drive through the Caucasus into the Middle East. Auchinleck must clear his Libyan flank as quickly as possible so as to be able to swing all his resources northwards to meet this new threat in conjunction with the Indian forces already in Iraq and now under Wavell's command as C-in-C India. To Cairo, *Barbarossa* was seen as a god-sent opportunity to pause; to absorb the flow of reinforcements from Britain and Lend-Lease equipment from the United States; and to train thoroughly before seeking a decisive confrontation with Rommel. In brief, while Cairo craved time to refit and retrain to meet the Germans on more equal terms, London demanded immediate action to take advantage of Hitler's fatal strategic error.

Auchinleck sent his first appreciation of the situation in his new command to Whitehall on 1 July. He insisted that Syria and Iraq must be secure before any fresh attempt was made to relieve Tobruk and to expel the Axis forces from Libya. For the latter, he would need at least two, preferably three, armoured divisions and a motorised division to insure success. Moreover, he needed a 50 per cent reserve of tanks – 25 per cent to cover those in workshops and 25 per cent to replace battle casualties. This demand drew Churchill's famous quip:

> This was an almost prohibitive condition. Generals only enjoy such comforts in heaven. And those who demand them do not always get there! [4]

As we have seen, 'Jumbo' Wilson had forced the Vichy French to capitulate in the second week of July. A new 9th Army was created under his command to start preparations to meet a German threat through the Caucasus. The British Embassy in Tehran had been worrying for some time about the increasing size of the German colony in Persia, which was ostensibly working on development projects. The need to establish an overland supply route from the Persian Gulf to the Caspian Sea to help satisfy Russia's voracious demands for material help from the Western Allies increased the need to rid Persia of this potential 'fifth column' of over 5,000 German agents. A joint Anglo-Russian demand for their immediate expulsion was delivered to the Shah's Government on 17 August 1941.

The Persians prevaricated, and so on 25 August the Russians invaded north-western Persia; 8th Indian Division landed at Basra and started occupying the southern Persian oilfields; the Indian Navy occupied Bandar Shahpur, the Persian Gulf terminal of the railway to Bandar Shah on the Caspian; and 10th Indian Division returned from Syria to Baghdad and advanced into Persia to meet the Russians south of the Caspian Sea.

After only offering trifling resistance for three days, the Shah's Government ordered a cease-fire. The armistice terms gave the Allies control of, and the right to develop, all practicable supply routes to Russia, a right which was to be used to the full, first, by British railway and road construction engineers, and then, in a much bigger way, by the Americans after the United States entered the war at the end of the year.

Meanwhile argument between Whitehall and Cairo over the timing of the next British attempt to relieve Tobruk was becoming increasingly acrimonious. Churchill wanted it launched by September at the latest. The Cs-in-C, Middle East – Cunningham, Auchinleck and Tedder – brought matters to a head by sending a blunt statement of their views as the responsible commanders. Provided 150 new cruiser tanks arrived by mid-September, air superiority was maintained and Rommel was not reinforced in the meantime, they should be able to mount an offensive to relieve Tobruk in November!

Churchill's heart sank: had he exchanged a tired Wavell for an obstinate Auchinleck, and an over-demanding Longmore for an equally rapacious Tedder? Auchinleck and Tedder were summoned back to Whitehall 'for consultation', much as Wavell and Longmore had been in 1940. Unlike the taciturn Wavell, who had refused to humour the Prime Minister, Auchinleck dominated the scene, putting his case with lucidity and winning agreement to a November date for his offensive, code-named *Crusader*. By that time it was hoped that the leading armoured brigade of 1st Armoured Division would have reached the desert with the rest of the division arriving soon afterwards; and the RAF's strength would have been raised from 34 to 52 squadrons.

Auchinleck's plan for *Crusader* was a scaled-up version of Wavell's *Battleaxe*: corps replaced divisions and the area of operations was expanded southwards to Fort Maddalena on the frontier wire, 50 miles south of Sollum. The Western Desert Force became the 8th Army under Admiral Andrew Cunningham's brother, Alan, the recent conqueror of Abyssinia. Messervy's old role of destroying the Axis defences in the coastal sector, was given to the 13th Corps, commanded by Godwin-Austen, also from East Africa. It consisted of Messervy's 4th Indian Division, Freyberg's 2nd New Zealand Division and the 1st Army Tank Brigade in Matilda and Valentine infantry tanks. Creagh's armoured flanking role went to Norrie's 30th Corps with 7th Armoured Division, now under Gott, Brink's 1st South African Division from East Africa, the 4th and 22nd Armoured Brigades, and, to confuse matters, the 22nd Guards Brigade. While Godwin-Austen's task was to hold the Axis forces in the coastal area, Norrie was to seek out and destroy Rommel's armour, and then relieve Tobruk.

★ ★ ★

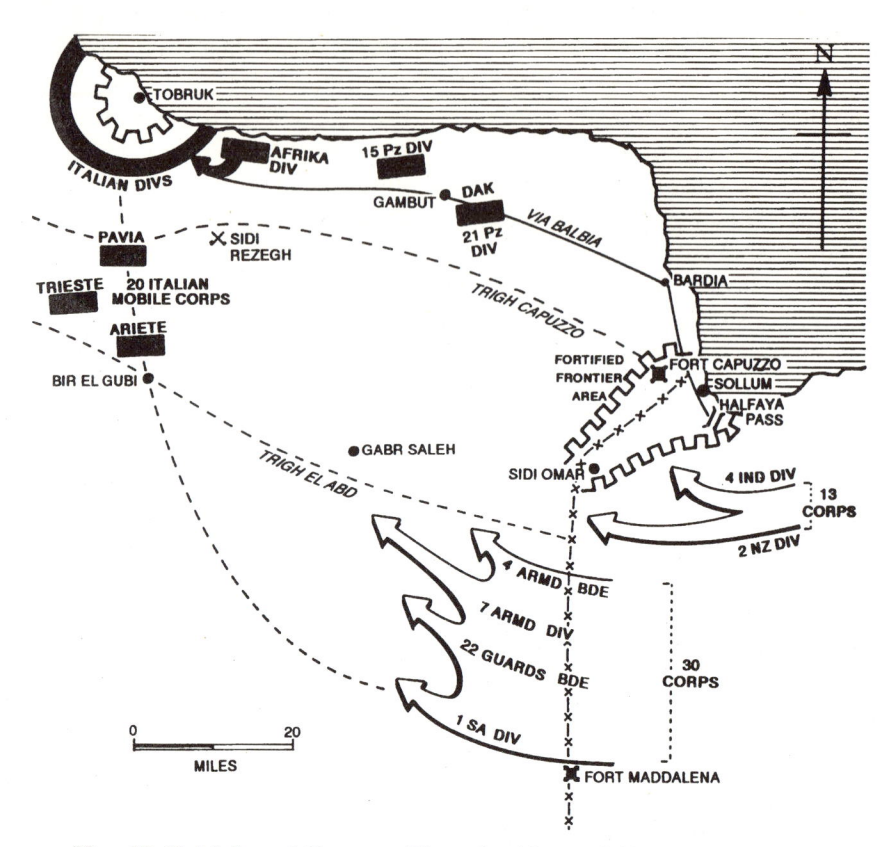

Map 10: British and German Plans for 'Crusader': November 1941

Rommel's attention was firmly fixed on Tobruk, which he was preparing to storm at about the same time as Auchinleck was to attempt its relief. He had four Italian Divisions and Major General Summermann's newly arrived German 'Afrika' Infantry Division (soon to be reorganised as the 90th Light Division) deployed around Tobruk; Cruwell's DAK with 15th and 21st Panzer Divisions (the 5th Light Division became 21st Panzer Division after *Battleaxe*) lay in reserve between Tobruk and the frontier, covering the main coastal routes east of Tobruk; and Gambara's Italian 20th Mobile Corps, consisting of the *Ariete* Armoured and *Trieste* Motorised Divisions, covered the desert approaches south of the fortress.

In mid-September, Rommel decided that he must find out what was going on behind the British lines. He mounted a major reconnaissance in force, code-named *Mid-Summer Night's Dream*, with von Ravenstein's 21st Panzer Division, which he accompanied himself, to seize and carry off the contents of a major supply dump, which his Intelligence sources told him existed some twenty miles inside Egypt to the south-east of Sidi Omar. The raid was a disaster: harassed by 'Jock' columns and the RAF, his tanks ran out of fuel and were lucky to be found by their resupply vehicles in time to withdraw successfully; he found nothing pointing to an imminent British offensive – not even the major supply dump or any other installations of interest; and he, himself, had a narrow escape after his captured British ACV (Armoured Command Vehicle), in which he was travelling, became detached from the main column, having lost a tyre during an RAF attack. He was lucky to escape back over the frontier before daybreak. But the greatest disaster as far as Rommel was concerned was the false impression it gave him of the chances of the British pre-empting his assault on Tobruk, which he concluded were so low that he could concentrate almost exclusively on his own preparations. He was, therefore, caught off balance when *Crusader* started on 18 November, three days before the date he had fixed for his own attack on Tobruk.

★ ★ ★

Auchinleck may not have had all he asked for, but he had parity in numbers of men, a two to one advantage in tanks and slightly less in aircraft. The only thing he lacked was a team of experienced commanders who could handle large formations in a swirling, mobile armoured battle, which was about to take place and last for two months of the most intense fighting yet seen in the Western Desert. Regrettably, Auchinleck was a consistently poor judge of character.

The British concentration for *Crusader* was a masterpiece of deception. The German radio intercept units did detect a change in the pattern of British signals traffic, but could pinpoint nothing that would rid Rommel of his delusion that he was free to attack Tobruk without worrying about his back. Norrie's 30th Corps plunged across the frontier in arrow-head formation, seeking a decisive tank battle, with Gott's 7th Armoured Division leading. 4th Armoured Brigade was echeloned back on his northern flank, watching for any move by the DAK and covering the flank of Godwin-Austen's 13th Corps as it thrust its way round the Axis coastal defences, which had been extended from Halfaya to Sidi Omar. 22nd Armoured Brigade was echeloned back on his southern flank, and Brink's 1st South African Division, which had barely completed its desert training, was further back on the same flank well out of harm's way. Surprise was so complete that for the first day Gott only encountered German reconnaissance units. When Cruwell alerted the DAK that evening on his own initiative, Rommel refused to allow him to move south to engage, assuming that the British were carrying out a *Mid-Summer Night's Dream* of their own. He insisted on beginning the preliminary moves for his assault on Tobruk.

The decisive armoured battle, which Cunningham and Norrie sought, proved a will-o'-the-wisp affair. The November days were still stiflingly hot, but the nights unpleasantly cold. Dust storms often reduced visibility;

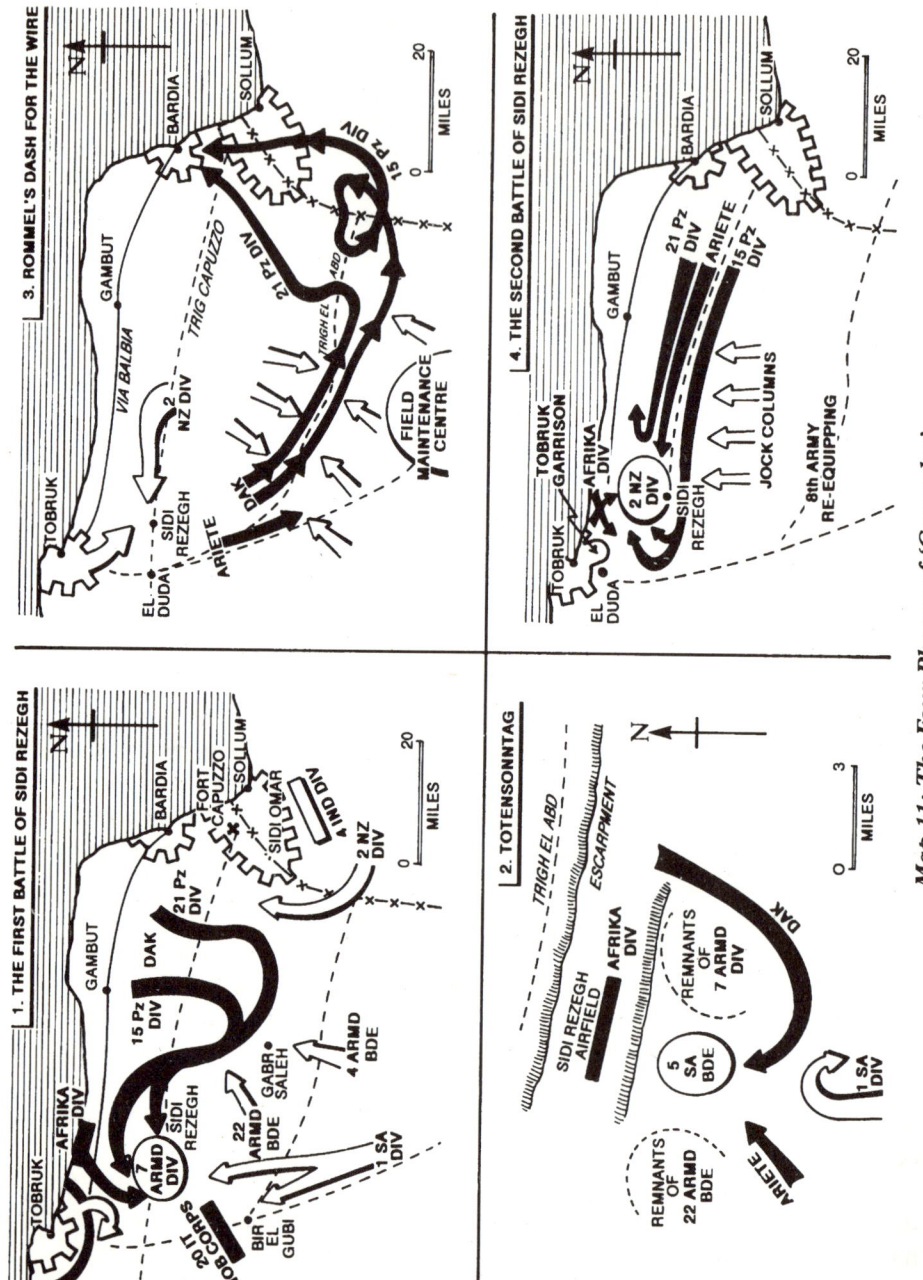

Map 11: The Four Phases of 'Crusader'

radio communications were unreliable and made worse by electronic storms; navigation was difficult due to lack of landmarks; and identification of friend and foe at a distance was far from easy as both sides were using vehicles captured from the other. These peculiarities of desert warfare in the early 1940s, and the great distances involved, created an all-pervading uncertainty of what was happening and what had actually happened on the battlefield. Dust thrown up by bursting shells; black billowing oily smoke from burning vehicles; and the natural desert haze made tactical control a matter of battle-instinct. Nothing was ever clear-cut. The successful desert commanders acquired the 'feel of the battle'; the less successful never did so. In November 1941, the new British 8th Army had much to learn at all levels.

On the second day of battle, the new 22nd Armoured Brigade suffered quite unnecessary losses at the hands of the Italian *Ariete* Division near Bir el Gubi, half-way to Tobruk, but Gott reached Sidi Rezegh airfield, just south of Tobruk, from which he hoped to join hands with the fortress's garrison when he called for it to break out next day. The fog of war was perhaps thickest on the German side: neither Rommel nor Cruwell realised that a serious British attempt to relieve Tobruk was in train. Cruwell's two panzer divisions probed southwards in an uncertain way and fought a series of indecisive actions with 4th Armoured Brigade around Gabr Saleh where it was protecting Gott's flank and supply line along the Trigh el Abd. That evening, the truth dawned on Rommel: his inflexible determination not to be distracted from his assault on Tobruk was converted into an equally fixed resolve to prevent Auchinleck from relieving it. Cruwell was ordered to smash Gott at Sidi Rezegh with his two panzer divisions and the 'Afrika' Division, which was to have led Rommel's assault on Tobruk.

The first battle for Sidi Rezegh raged for two days. The Tobruk garrison started to break out, but was stopped by Gott, who was having to fend off the three German divisions, and realised that he would be unable to cover the last few miles to Tobruk. In the end the German pressure became too great and Gott was forced to abandon the airfield and fall back southwards towards Brink's South Africans after some of the fiercest fighting of the desert war, in which the British gunners fended off panzer attack after attack, using their 25 pounders as anti-tank guns, and Brigadier 'Jock' Campbell won his Victoria Cross, leading the 4th Armoured Brigade's final attack, which enabled Gott to disengage successfully during the night of 22–23 November.

Neither Rommel nor Cunningham knew really what had happened that day. The British had, in fact, lost tank superiority. Their tank strength had dropped to 144, whereas the DAK reported still having 173 fit tanks left. Not knowing the extent of his tank losses, Cunningham ordered Godwin-Austen to leave 4th Indian Division to mask the Sidi-Omar defences and to hurry Freyberg's New Zealanders westwards along the

Trigh Capuzzo to Sidi Rezegh, where his 13th Corps would take over the task of breaking through into Tobruk from Norrie's 30th Corps. Rommel did not know much about the state of his tanks either, but his 'feel of the battle' told him that Norrie's 30th Corps must be in a bad way. He ordered Cruwell to attempt the encirclement and destruction of Gott's 7th Armoured Division south of Sidi Rezegh with his DAK and Gambara's Italian 20th Mobile Corps.

23 November was the Lutheran *Totensonntag* (All Souls Day). Cruwell celebrated it with a day of brilliant manoeuvre. Gott was facing north, reorganising and awaiting the arrival of the New Zealanders along the Trigh Capuzzo. He was supported by the 5th South African Brigade from Brink's 1st South African Division, which was still well to the south of the battlefield. Cruwell led the DAK in a wide sweep round Gott's eastern flank, linked up with Gambara and attacked Gott from the rear. The DAK's attack fell upon the 5th South African Brigade, which was overrun in a massed panzer attack before Gott could help them, but the DAK suffered crippling losses at the hands of the South Africans before their defence collapsed. Cruwell lost 72 tanks and more commanding officers and other key personnel than any army could stand for long. *Totensonntag* had lived up to its name.

While the *Totensonntag* battle was in progress, Cunningham became aware of the scale of his tank losses, and, like Beresford-Peirse during *Battleaxe*, asked his C-in-C to come up to decide whether to break off the battle before the defence of Egypt could be jeopardised by the loss of 8th Army. Luckily only his personal staff knew of his agony of mind, and, even more fortunately, he gave no orders that would suggest withdrawal before Auchinleck arrived by air from Cairo that afternoon. Auchinleck found both Corps Commanders and 8th Army's Chief of Staff adamant that Tobruk could be relieved. Tank recovery work and the delivery of new tanks to regiments was going well, and the DAK would soon be trapped in the Sidi Rezegh area between the two British corps. Auchinleck gave Cunningham orders to

> continue to attack the enemy relentlessly using all your resources even to the last tank.[5]

* * *

Auchinleck flew back to Cairo a worried man, not because he thought that the battle might be lost but because he feared that Cunningham was buckling under the strain: indeed, he should never have been given command of the 8th Army. He was a chain smoker, who lived on his nerves, and the Abyssinian Campaign had already over-strained them. But who could be found to take over in the midst of the battle? 'Jumbo' Wilson, whom Churchill had always wanted to command the 8th Army, was too far away, watching the dangerous Caucasus approach with his 9th Army in north-eastern Syria; Norrie and Godwin-Austen were too deeply embroiled in fighting their own corps battles, and, in any case, neither was showing real aptitude for higher command. Auchinleck decided that the only man available was his own Deputy Chief of General Staff, Neil Ritchie, a relatively junior major general, who had done most of the *Crusader* planning in Cairo. He was the principal operations officer in GHQ and was *au fait* with the current state of the battle. Rightly or wrongly, he sent Ritchie forward to take over 8th Army temporarily: again he had misjudged his man, but this was not to be revealed for another seven months. Cunningham accepted his supercession almost gratefully and retired exhausted to hospital in Cairo.

Rommel, in the meantime, was living up to Halder's description of him as a soldier gone mad. Overestimating the British losses and underestimating their staying power, he decided to deliver the *coup de grâce*. During the morning of 24 November, he set off at the head of the DAK's two panzer divisions down the Trigh el Abd on his famous 'Dash for the Frontier Wire' with the Afrika Division, reorganised as the 90th Light Division, following in his wake to scoop up the spoils of what he hoped would be a disrupted British logistic system. He scattered the miscellany of British headquarters and supply units located along the Trigh, but missed the main supply dumps of the Field Maintenance Centre to the south of it. The panic that ensued amongst the British rear echelons did no credit to those who took part in the 'Matruh Stakes' as the ignominious rush for safety in Egypt was rudely called by the fighting formations, which set about hammering the German columns with artillery fire from either flank.

Rommel reached his frontier garrisons that evening, but his divisions had been losing tanks and vehicles all day and he had alienated most of his subordinate commanders, who knew that their units were already too exhausted to succeed unless the British collapsed, which they were showing no sign of doing. Quite the opposite was happening: the RAF and quickly assembled 'Jock' columns had begun eroding his strength. For the next two days, he lunged about in the frontier area, achieving little for the loss of more tanks and men. After refuelling at Bardia, he set off back for Tobruk on the 27th along the Trigh Capuzzo. Cries for help from his rear headquarters near Tobruk told him that the New Zealanders had reached Sidi Rezegh. Whilst he had been away, the New Zealand infantry, led by the Matildas of the 44th Royal Tank Regiment of 1st Army Tank Brigade, had broken through at El Duda to link up with the Tobruk garrison in a bold night attack.

Harassed constantly by 'Jock' columns and attacked by partially re-equipped British armoured brigades, the DAK fought its way to Sidi Rezegh, growing ever weaker by the hour. Ritchie, who was now in command of 8th Army, thought he detected clear signs of an imminent Axis withdrawal from Tobruk, but this was the last thing Rommel actually had in mind. He felt he still had the tactical initiative and could yet win by destroying Freyberg's New Zealanders in a second battle for Sidi Rezegh. Whether his logisticians could keep the DAK replenished for much longer seemed increasingly doubtful.

The 2nd Battle of Sidi Rezegh was a New Zealand epic. Cruwell attacked them viciously for three days, eventually forcing Freyberg to extricate his division and break his links with the Tobruk garrison, but this time Cruwell's losses were too great even for Rommel to ignore. Confessing to the Axis High Command that he had lost 142 tanks and 14,600 German troops, including one divisional commander (von Ravenstein was captured by the New Zealanders) and 16 commanding officers, he demanded reinforcements and supplies to enable him to withstand the growing pressure from 8th Army, which was reappearing in the desert like a many headed hydra as its tanks were replaced from reserves. By 7 December, it was made clear to him by Gariboldi that no reinforcements were likely to reach him for some time. With a heavy heart, he ordered the evacuation of Cyrenaica to begin. New Year's Day 1942 saw the last German units retiring across the Tripolitanian frontier.

Auchinleck had won a pyrrhic victory. Rommel was quite clear why Cunningham and Ritchie had failed to destroy his Panzer Group, Afrika, despite their numerical superiority in tanks. Talking to a captured British officer, he is reported to have said:

What difference does it make if you have two tanks to my one, when you spread them out and let me smash them in detail?[7]

Crusader was a disappointment to Churchill: it had taken longer and the losses had been heavier than expected. The casualty figures, however, show that Auchinleck's victory, although far from decisive had inflicted severe losses on Rommel: the Axis lost 32 per cent of their troops engaged compared with 15 per cent on the British side (both had committed just short of 120,000 men during the battle).

By the beginning of 1942, Auchinleck was back where Wavell had been after O'Connor's victory at Beda Fomm a year earlier, and the dispatch of the Commonwealth Expeditionary Force to Greece had stopped him advancing on Tripoli. This time it was the Japanese attack on Pearl Harbor on 7–8 December which stopped a British pursuit along the North African coast. Every British naval, army and air force unit that could be spared from the Middle East, was soon on its way to the Far East. Even desert-hardened formations like 7th Armoured Brigade left for the jungles of South East Asia, as did the 6th and 7th Australian Divisions. Auchinleck feared that he would also lose the 9th Australian and 2nd New

Zealand Divisions. Like Wavell, he was forced onto the defensive with a very depleted 8th Army garrisoning Cyrenaica.

★ ★ ★

On the Axis side, the opposite was happening. The *Luftwaffe* had returned in great strength to the Mediterranean as flying conditions deteriorated in Russia, and German U-boats were dispatched to challenge Andrew Cunningham's grip on the Axis sea routes to North Africa. Field Marshal Albert Kesselring – 'Smiling Al; a soldier turned aviator – arrived with his *Luftflotte 2*, and was appointed by Hitler to be the German C-in-C, Mediterranean, nominally under the Italian *Commando Supremo*. As soon as *Luftflotte 2* had re-established a tolerable air situation in the Central Mediterranean, the rapid reinforcement and resupply of Rommel's defeated Panzer Group, Afrika, went ahead almost unhindered by British naval and air forces, much as had happened when Rommel had first set foot in Tripoli the year before, and *Fliegerkorps X* was operating from Sicily. By mid-January, Rommel was ready to open his second campaign to recover Cyrenaica, again conceiving it as a major raid rather than a renewed invasion.

Rommel recrossed the Tripolitanian frontier on 21 January. What happened next was almost an exact replay of the first half of his 1941 'raid'. Godwin-Austen's weakened 13th Corps was garrisoning Benghazi and the Djebel Akhdar bulge of Cyrenaica with 4th Indian Division, while the novice 1st Armoured Division under Major General Herbert Lumsden, which had been arriving from England during *Crusader*, had been made responsible for the frontier and covering the desert flank. As in 1941, the British higher command was caught off balance and was at sixes and sevens within itself. Benghazi was abandoned again on 28 January after an altercation between Ritchie and Godwin-Austen; and on the desert flank, Lumsden's division was thrown into chaos by the DAK and scrambled back to Mechili, losing most of its tanks on the way. The only sensible thing done on the British side was to move forward Norrie's 30th Corps from the Egyptian frontier, where it had been refitting, to prepare a new defensive position, running from Gazala on the coast to Bir Hacheim in the desert 50 miles to the south. The Gazala Line, as it was called, covered Tobruk.

By the time Rommel had reoccupied Benghazi, he realised that his logistics would not allow him to do more than close up to the Gazala Line into which Godwin-Austen had withdrawn. Both sides settled down to make preparations for what they believed would be the decisive battle in a few months time. By then, however, both Rommel's and Ritchie's plans had become entangled in Axis and Allied grand strategies for 1942 and they were not entirely free agents.

In Berlin, Hitler was intent on closing the strategic pincers around the British in the Middle East before the Americans could intervene. When the spring thaw was over, his armies in southern Russia were to cross the Don and swing down through the Caucasus while Rommel advanced on the Suez Canal across the Western Desert. To give Rommel the necessary logistic support, Grand Admiral Raeder, Hitler's naval chief of staff, wanted to take Malta in order to secure the Axis hold on the central Mediterranean. Kesselring, however, believed that his airmen could suppress the island sufficiently by bombing so as to avoid a costly amphibious and airborne operation to take it. Rommel sided with Kesselring, suggesting that the capture of Tobruk meant more to him than Malta: with Tobruk in his hands as a forward supply base, his chances of reaching the

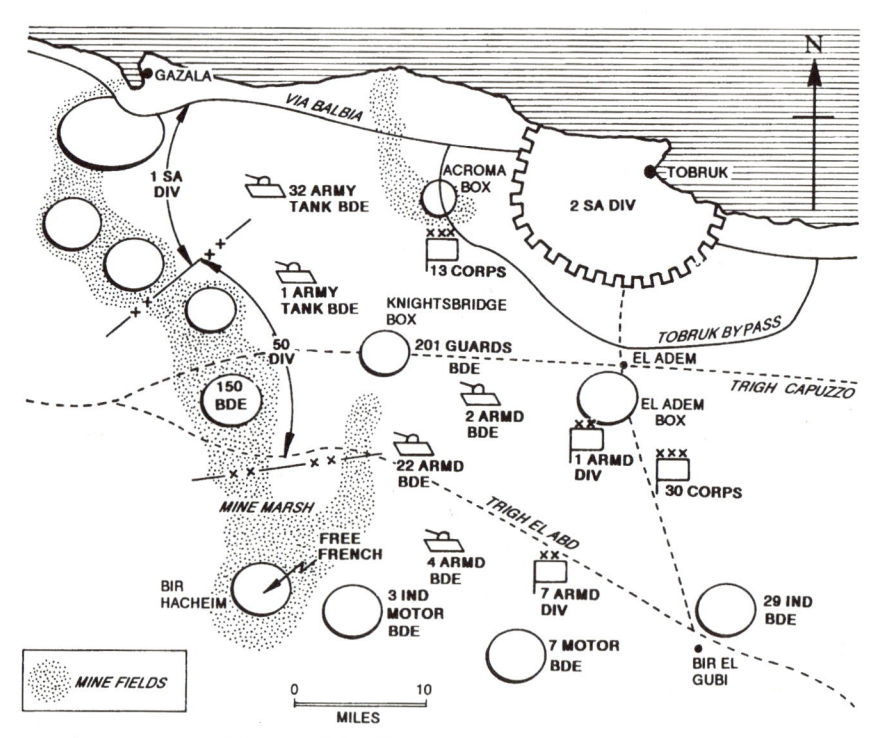

Map 12: The Gazala Line in May 1942

Canal would be greatly enhanced. Kesselring and Rommel won the argument: the former was authorised to suppress Malta by air action and the latter was directed to attempt to take Tobruk before 20 June when a large proportion of the *Luftwaffe* units in the Mediterranean would start flying back to Russia for Hitler's summer offensive of 1942.

★ ★ ★

Defeating Hitler's Challenge

In Whitehall, there had been dismay at 8th Army's poor performance in letting Rommel push it back so easily to the Gazala Line. General Sir Alan Brooke (later Field Marshal Viscount Alanbrooke) had just taken over from Field Marshal Sir John Dill as CIGS. He was a harder man than the gentlemanly Dill and had no sympathy for military failures. He started rooting out officers about whom he had his doubts. He forced Auchinleck to sack his Director of Military Intelligence, who had consistently underestimated Rommel's abilities, and his Chief of Staff, who was worn out. Godwin-Austen went of his own accord after being overruled by Ritchie during the withdrawal from Benghazi, but Brooke failed to persuade Auchinleck to replace Ritchie in command of 8th Army. Gott took over 13th Corps much to everyone's delight, but Auchinleck then made the gross error of appointing a new Chief of Staff, whom all GHQ knew was not up to the job. Thus, he faced the coming battles with an Army Commander of doubtful quality, whom he tended to treat like a puppet, showering him with instructions and personal letters of advice, and a Chief of Staff in whom only he had any confidence. Both were to let him down.

As usual, Churchill was soon pressing for a renewal of the offensive in the Western Desert, firstly to recover the airfields in Cyrenaica from which Malta-bound convoys could be given air cover; and secondly, to dispense with Rommel before a Russian collapse could open the Caucasus back door to the Middle East. Calculating that Auchinleck should have numerical superiority in men and tanks by May, he called for his plans, and was aghast when he received a detailed appreciation from Auchinleck explaining why he could not attack before June at the very earliest.

The reverberations of the consequential Prime Ministerial explosion were not to die away until Auchinleck was dismissed six months later by his exacting master. Brooke only just managed to stop Churchill sending him a savage reply, littered with such barbs as 'soldiers are meant to fight' and 'armies are not expected to stand around doing nothing'! Instead, Auchinleck was summoned home for consultation, but, much to the dismay of his many friends, he refused to leave his embattled theatre. He countered by inviting the Chiefs of Staff to visit Cairo and the Western Desert to see the conditions under which his soldiers and Tedder's airmen were fighting. His invitation was refused. However, Sir Stafford Cripps, who was on his way to India for political negotiations with the Congress Party, was asked to break his journey at Cairo to explain the War Cabinet's position to the Cs-in-C Committee. Much to the Prime Minister's chagrin, Cripps, like Balaam, sent out to curse, could only bless. He reported strongly in Auchinleck's favour.

The whole tiresome wrangle had been based upon the assumption that 8th Army would be attacking Rommel at a time and place of Auchinleck's choosing. Early in May, 'Ultra' decrypts revealed that Rommel was likely to attack first and probably by the end of May. Ritchie's plans for a June offensive were thrown into reverse, and improvements to the defences of the Gazala Line became his priority task. Unfortunately, the Gazala Line had been chosen originally as a temporary position to cover the construction of a series of major defensive lines in great depth, protecting Cairo and the Canal. The first was on the Egyptian frontier; the second at Mersa Matruh; and the third, it should be noted, was at El Alamein (*See Map 14 on page 96*). The Gazala Line had three principal weaknesses as a position on which to fight a major battle: lack of natural anti-tank obstacles, for which extensive minefields had to be substituted; an open desert flank; and being too close to the large reserve stocks of supplies built up in Tobruk, which would become hostages to fortune if anything went wrong at Gazala.

The 8th Army was organised much as it had been for *Crusader,* with two corps. 13th Corps, under Norrie, was the mobile corps with the 1st and 7th Armoured Divisions, manning British Crusader tanks, the light American 'Honey' and some of the new American Grants. The latter, designed and built in the United States in close co-operation with the British, gave the Eighth Army its first long-range tank gun – a 75mm mounted in a hull sponson. It was not an ideal tank but, at long last, they had a dual purpose weapon, firing both armour-piercing and high explosive ammunition, and could tackle the Germans on equal terms. Indeed, until the Germans introduced their long 75mm on their Mark IV tanks in the middle of 1942, Grant outgunned anything they had to offer. It was responsible for the southern half of the front and meeting any attempt by Rommel to drive around the desert flank, held by General Koenig's Free French Brigade at Bir Hacheim. 30th Corps, now under Gott, was largely infantry and commanded the 1st South African Division and the newly arrived 50th (Northumbrian) Division. They were supported by 1st and 32nd Army Tank Brigades in Valentines, the Matildas' successors as Infantry support tanks. Major General Klopper's also newly arrived 2nd South African Division garrisoned Tobruk, reinforced by a brigade from the veteran 4th Indian Division.

One major organisational change had been made, which was to spell disaster in the coming battles. The brigade group rather than the division was made the principal tactical unit. Each was given its own gunners, sappers and administrative units, leaving divisional commanders with only a broad co-ordinating role and no reserves, particularly of artillery, with which to influence the battle. This would have been fine under conditions of wide dispersal over vast areas of desert in which concentration was the exception rather than the rule; and if the Germans had been playing the 'Jock' column game as well. They had no intention of doing so. They had mastered the techniques of concentration of armoured forces: the British had not.

Gott held the main front with a series of brigade 'boxes'. These were all-round and self-contained defensive positions with integral artillery and tank support within a mined and wired perimeter. Three South African boxes covered the northern end of the line; then came three 50th Division boxes in the centre with the Free French box at Bir Hacheim in the south. The South African 'Boxes' were relatively close to each other, but the gaps between 50th Division's boxes became progressively wider towards the south. Its most southerly box lay between the Trigh Capuzzo and Trigh el Abd, and was held by 150th Brigade. It had a five-mile gap to the north, and a ten-mile gap between it and the Free French box, which was obstructed with an undefended 'mine marsh'. There were additional brigade boxes in depth behind the front, covering such key features as the Acroma position, the 'Knightsbridge' cross-tracks, and the El Adem airfield and supply depots.

Norrie's armour was disposed to defeat either of the two possible German plans, which Auchinleck and Ritchie deemed most likely. Auchinleck thought that Rommel would feint in the north and try to burst through the centre somewhere near the 150th Brigade box to avoid the long, fuel-consuming drive around the desert flank. Ritchie thought the reverse to be more likely: Rommel, in his view, would feint in the northern sector, and then go round the desert flank with his main striking force. Lumsden's 1st Armoured Division with two armoured brigades was deployed behind the centre of the front in case Rommel followed Auchinleck's hunch; and 7th Armoured Division, now commanded by Messervy, with one armoured brigade and three motor brigades, was given the task of dealing with any German attempt to drive round Bir Hacheim as Ritchie predicted.

On the German side, the Panzer Group, Afrika, had been re-styled Panzer Army, Afrika, with Rommel promoted to Colonel General. Unlike Ritchie, he was his own man, brooking no interference from above, and demanding and being given total loyalty by his subordinates. Unlike his two previous offensives, which had been planned as raids, he was now preparing a major set-piece battle designed to carry him through to the Suez Canal once he had taken Tobruk. Although a great tactician, Rommel was no strategist. His approach was cavalier and he made a bad plan, which was only salvaged by his tactical skill, by the extraordinary endurance and fighting qualities of his troops and by the incompetence of the British higher command, which still lacked a winning command team able to concentrate its forces at the right time and place.

★ ★ ★

Rommel's plan was to do exactly as Ritchie expected. He gave responsibility for the feint in the northern sector to Cruwell, who had been on leave in Germany and came back only just in time to take command of the German and Italian troops assigned to the task. Rommel, himself, was to lead the striking force, consisting of the DAK and the 90th Light Division under the DAK's new commander, General Nehring, and the Italian 20th Mobile Corps. He aimed to drive round the southern flank to attack the British position from the rear. Once British resistance started to crumble, he would lunge for Tobruk.

As long as he could throw the British off balance, as he had done at the start of his two 'raids' into Cyrenaica, all would be well; but, if they stood fast, he would find it almost impossible to refuel his 560 tanks in the midst of 850 British and British-manned American tanks. Ritchie would be presented with the chance of winning the Desert War at a stroke, provided he concentrated his armour and wielded it with precision. British morale was high. Colonel (later Major General) Pip Roberts, whom we will meet later in this chapter, was commanding 3rd Royal Tank Regiment and recorded the prevailing enthusiasm:

> There was much to be done; a new tank [the Grant] to learn, HE [high explosive] shooting to master and new tactics to be evolved. But every one now felt that we had an answer to the anti-tank gun and wouldn't the Hun in his Mark IIIs and IVs, [German tanks] get a shock when the 75mm [carried by the Grants] came in . . . enthusiasm was terrific.[6]

The story of the two sorry months of June and July 1942 has none of the complex two-sidedness of *Crusader*. They flow in a cumulative progression of avoidable British disasters. No amount of tactical skill, courage and endurance at regimental level could make up for the failures of the British higher command. The ultimate success of the same troops only four months later at El Alamein under Montgomery underscores the inadequacy of the Auchinleck/Ritchie combination.

Rommel opened the Battle of Gazala during the night of 26–27 May with his long drive round Bir Hacheim. By dawn the massed columns of the DAK were scattering each of Messervy's widely dispersed motor brigades in turn, driving them eastwards towards Bir el Gubi, while the Italians masked the Free French positions and probed the minefields in the 10 mile gap between them and the 150th Brigade box. By midday Messervy's armoured brigade (the 4th) had been caught as it was deploying into its battle positions and had to withdraw on El Adem, having, however, inflicted considerable losses on their opponents, as, indeed, had the motor brigades. Messervy himself was captured when his tactical headquarters was overrun by a German reconnaissance unit. He managed to escape soon afterwards, but his division had been driven off the battlefield for the time being.

Elated by these initial successes, Rommel ordered Nehring to thrust on northwards with the DAK to reach the coast near Acroma by nightfall. Nehring obeyed but ran into Lumsden's and Gott's armoured and tank

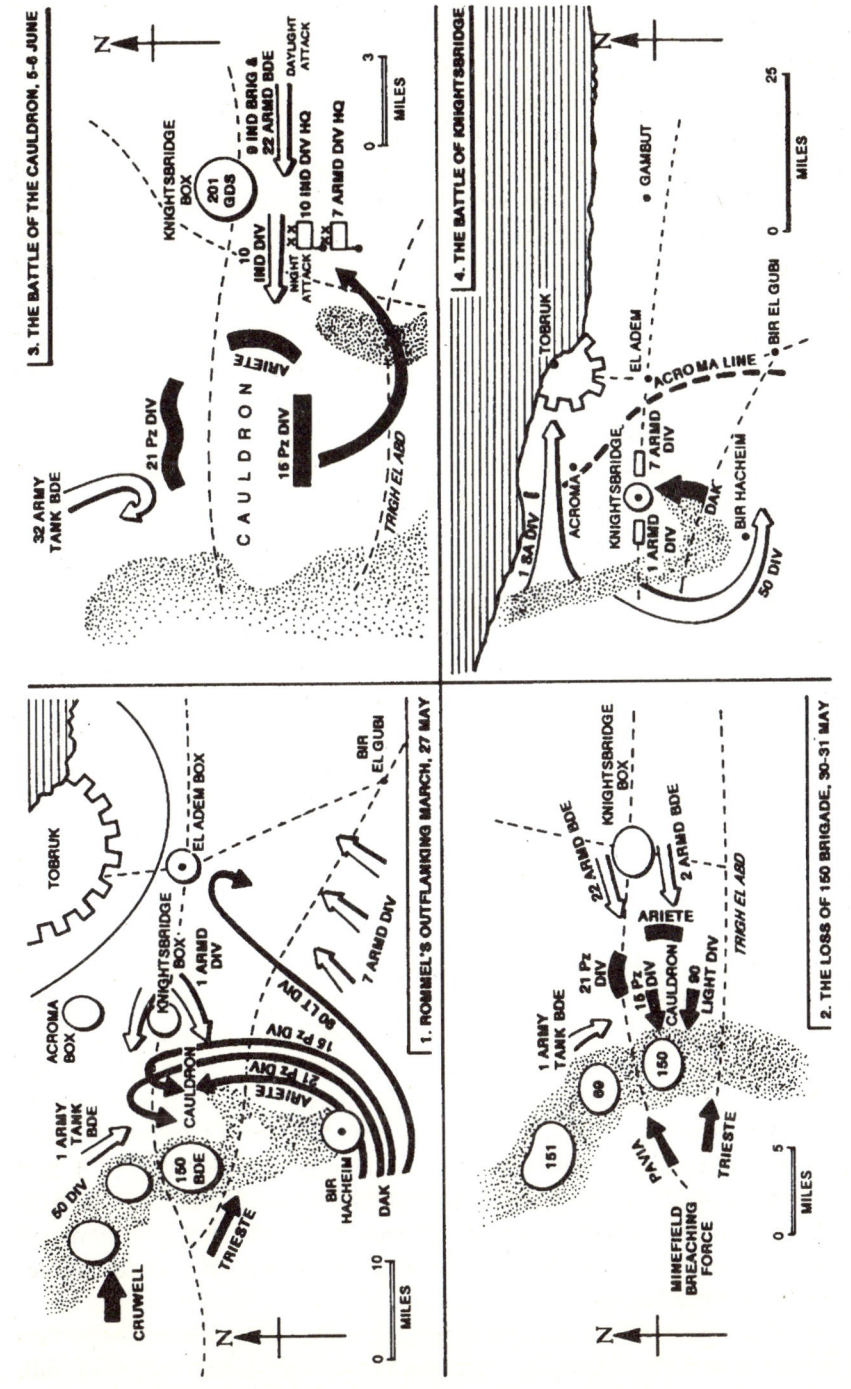

Map 13: The Four Phases of the Battle of Gazala: 26 May–21 June 1942

brigades, which were by then moving to oppose him. The British crews in the American Grant tanks were shooting well with their 75mm guns, and the desert south of Knightsbridge soon became a shambles. Rommel described the scene:

> The British armour, under heavy artillery cover, poured into the columns and panzer units of the Afrika Korps, which was visible for miles. Fire and black smoke welled up from lorries and tanks, and our attack came to a standstill. Again my divisions suffered extremely serious losses. Many of our columns broke into confusion and fled away to the south-west . . . [8]

That night Rommel confessed to his staff that he was worried but determined to strike northwards again next day, while at the same time establishing a firm base in what was to become known as the Cauldron just to the east of the 150th Brigade's box, which he did not, as yet, know existed. It was, in fact, blocking the Italians who were trying to clear the minefields on his proposed resupply routes along the Trigh el Abd and Trigh Capuzzo. His efforts to strike northwards were again defeated in two days' fierce fighting around Knightsbridge. By the evening of 29 May, Rommel was forced to give up his attempt to cut in behind Gott's 13th Corps. He turned all his energies to finding ways of running supplies to the hard pressed DAK, which 'hedgehogged' in the Cauldron, protected by its anti-tank guns and a few of the formidable 88mm AA guns.

* * *

Ritchie completely misread the battle during 30 May. He assumed that he had won the first phase of the battle, and that Rommel was trying to disengage. It was his turn, he concluded, to mount a counterstroke with Gott's 13th Corps, which would cut through the Italians in the northern sector while Norrie hammered the DAK to pieces in the Cauldron, primarily with artillery. Code-named *Limerick*, his plan envisaged advancing in triumph on Benghazi and Tripoli. He hoped to launch it next day, but Gott and Norrie persuaded him that they could not be ready until 1 June. In those 48 hours Rommel transformed the battle by storming the 150th Brigade box behind him, thereby opening up a supply route to the west.

How Ritchie's and Gott's staffs failed to realise the dire peril in which the isolated 150th Brigade stood until it was too late to intervene successfully has never been properly explained. Their attention seems to have been focused entirely on preparations for *Limerick*. 150th Brigade's three Territorial battalions and their supporting tanks threw back all Rommel's attacks on 30 and 31 May. Next day, Rommel, in some desperation, personally directed the assaults by 15th Panzer and 90th Light Divisions, which finally overran the stubborn Northumbrians. Their loss was inexcusable, and made all the worse by Ritchie's misplaced optimism. Part of his evening report to Auchinleck read:

> I am distressed over the loss of 150 Brigade after so gallant a fight, but still consider the situation favourable and getting better daily.[9]

The opposite was, in fact, happening, and Ritchie's corps commanders sensed this to be so. They became increasingly critical of his direction of the battle. They had always realised that he was Auchinleck's puppet, but as his instructions, based on GHQ Cairo's view of events at the front, became less and less realistic, they began to question their validity. Moreover, they themselves had different views on what should be done to win the battle. Gott favoured using Briggs's 5th Indian Division from 8th Army reserve for a modified version of *Limerick*, but Norrie believed, quite rightly, that the DAK must be emasculated first before any wide-ranging manoeuvres could be attempted. Ritchie accepted Norrie's view, and dropped *Limerick* in favour of a direct attack on Rommel's 'hedgehog' in the Cauldron, selecting its eastern face, held by the Italian Ariete Division, for his main attack. Realising that infantry must be used to break through the Axis anti-tank gun screen, he gave 5th Indian Division to Norrie for a night attack to clear a way for 7th Armoured Division to burst through when daylight came. Diversionary attacks would be mounted by Lumsden's 1st Armoured Division from the northern side of the Cauldron.

The battle of the Cauldron, which started after midnight on 5 June, was an unmitigated disaster. 5th Indian Division's night attack, supported by a heavy artillery barrage, reached all its objectives with suspicious ease. One hundred and fifty-six tanks of 22nd Armoured Brigade, supported by 9th Indian Brigade, advanced as soon as daylight came, and soon ran into a formidable anti-tank gun screen and heavy concentrations fired by the massed DAK artillery. The tanks were drawn into an armoured battle and had to leave the Indians to fend for themselves. It transpired later that intelligence of the Axis position had been grossly inaccurate. The night attack had fallen on a lightly held outpost line and empty desert: the main enemy anti-tank gun line was two miles further west.

Rommel mounted a vicious counter-attack that afternoon, in which he achieved complete surprise. Leading 15th Panzer Division personally through a recently cleared gap in the minefields on the southern side of the Cauldron, he overran both British divisions' headquarters and a number of Indian units held in reserve nearby. Control collapsed and three Indian battalions, a reconnaissance battalion and four gunner regiments were left stranded in the Cauldron. They fought on, defending themselves resolutely, hoping to be relieved. Sadly, the fog of war was so dense and confusion so great that help never reached them and they were eventually overrun. Lumsden's diversionary attacks on the northern face of the Cauldron were costly failures as well. 8th Army's total tank strength by the end of the day was down to 248: Rommel had 219 left. The starting figures had been 849 British to 560 Axis tanks – the writing was on the wall.

Rommel now smelt victory, and decided to clear the Free French from his rear before attempting once more to cut off Gott's 13th Corps from Tobruk. Koenig's Frenchmen, however, refused to be intimidated. On 8 June, they defeated all 90th Light Division's attacks, which were supported by over a hundred *Luftwaffe* bombers. Rommel then brought up 15th Panzer Division, which eventually gained a foothold in the French defences by dusk on 10 June. Ritchie authorised Koenig to abandon Bir Hacheim that night. All but 300 of his 3,000-strong force were successfully evacuated with the help of 7th Motor Brigade. Koenig had gained precious time for Ritchie to reorganise after the Cauldron disaster.

During the pause around the Cauldron, while Rommel was clearing his rear and bringing forward a recently arrived batch of replacement tanks, Gott worked hard to create a new defensive line running east–west on its northern side to stop Rommel if he tried to thrust his way north again. Norrie was reorganising due south of Tobruk, ready to attack his eastern flank if he did so. On 11 June, Rommel did thrust due north out of the Cauldron, and brought on the decisive battle for the Knightsbridge box, which stood between him and Gott's probable withdrawal route into or around Tobruk.

Knightsbridge was held by the 201st Guards Brigade and was soon supported on either flank by Lumsden's and Messervy's armoured brigades. Little went right for the British armour in the horrendous two-day tank battle which raged throughout 12 and 13 June. Their fortunes were not helped by Messervy getting himself captured and escaping again. Manoeuvred as a compact entity, the DAK gradually won the ascendancy, and the balance in surviving tank strengths swung decisively in Rommel's favour. Long before this happened, Ritchie should have ordered Gott to pull his corps back to the western outskirts of Tobruk to form a new front from the Acroma box to El Adem and thence to Bir el Gubi, called 'the Acroma Line', although it only existed as a line on commanders' maps. Again he misread the battle and decided not to do so because he felt sure that Rommel must have shot his bolt. By the end of the 13th, he had no option: 8th Army's tank strength was down to 50 Cruisers and 20 Valentines.

Gott's staff calculated that it was too late to pull back the whole of 13th Corps along the coast road in one night, so 50th Division was told to break out westwards through the Italian defences and make its way south round Bir Hacheim and thence back to Egypt, leaving the coast road free for the South Africans. Reporting his decision to Auchinleck, Ritchie triggered an exchange of signals between HQ 8th Army, GHQ Cairo and Whitehall, tangled with cross-purposes and half-truths, which was to lead to the unnecessary loss of 32,000 men in Tobruk.

* * *

After *Crusader* had ended Tobruk's first siege in December 1941, the Cs-in-C Middle East decided unanimously never to stand siege there again: the expense in terms of Naval and Air resources alone had been crippling. Auchinleck assumed that Ritchie only intended to fall back to the Acroma Line, still covering Tobruk, and had no intention of withdrawing any further, so there was no need, as yet, to decide whether to evacuate the port or not. Norrie and Gott, however, were quite clear in their own minds that there was no suitable line on which to halt their withdrawal short of the Egyptian frontier once the Gazala Line itself had been abandoned.

Churchill saw references in GHQ signals to the possible abandonment of Tobruk. Whether he was unaware of the Cs-in-C's policy of avoiding another siege or had forgotten about it, he now invested the port with high political and military significance, and insisted that it should be held at all costs. Auchinleck's consequential instruction to Ritchie, sent at midday on 14th June, read:

> ....Eighth Army must hold the line Acroma – El Adem and southwards and resist all attempts to pass it. Having reduced your front by evacuating Gazala and reorganised your forces, this should be feasible. If you feel you cannot accept responsibility of holding this position you must say so.[6]

Somehow Ritchie found himself unable to tell Auchinleck what was really happening, or to instruct his staff to conform to his C-in-C's instructions. He allowed it to appear to Cairo that he was doing his best to meet Auchinleck's wishes while agreeing with Gott and Norrie to moves more in keeping with their views on the need to withdraw to the frontier. One thing he could not do in view of Auchinleck's directive was to evacuate Tobruk while there was yet time to do so.

The evacuation of the Gazala line went far better than expected. Rommel's commanders and men were exhausted after Knightsbridge. The DAK restarted its northerly thrust towards the coast road late in the morning of 14 June with no great determination to push Gott's defensive screen aside. The hours of daylight slipped by all too slowly for the British units fighting to hold the coast road open for the South Africans, and all too quickly for the weary DAK, which was still well short of its objectives when darkness fell. Rommel demanded a continuation of the advance

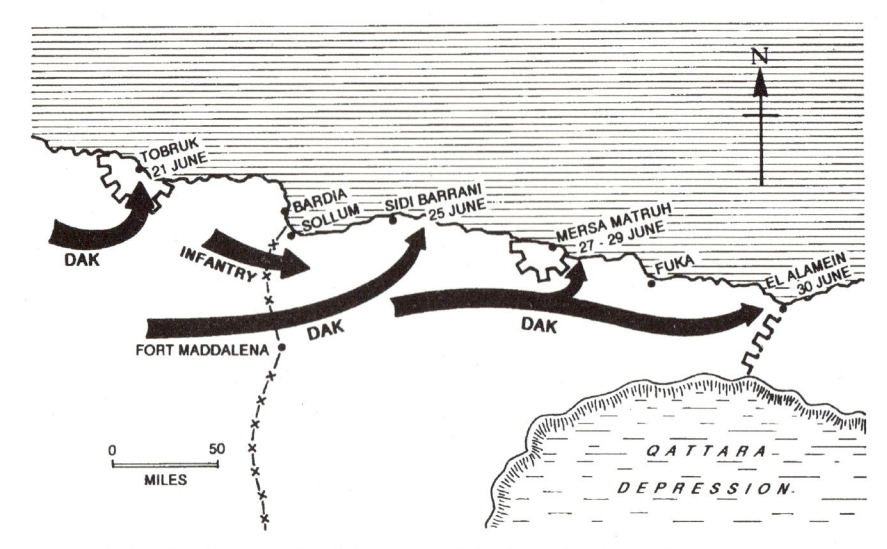

Map 14: Rommel's Advance to El Alamein: July–August 1942

through the night but to no avail. There were few German ears listening: the DAK had reached the end of its tether. Its men slept where darkness overtook them. 1st South African Division was away safely by dawn on 15 June, and 50th Division was equally successful in breaking through the Italians and escaping across the desert to the Egyptian frontier.

German lassitude was short-lived. As soon as Rommel realised that Gott had escaped, he turned the DAK eastwards in pursuit. Lip-service and no more was paid by Gott and Norrie to the defence of the Acroma Line. They made brief attempts to hold positions like the El Adem box, and the remains of the British armour fought several effective rearguard actions, but there was no real effort to establish a new line running south from Tobruk to prevent its second investment. On 18 June, Rommel swung 21st Panzer Division north and cut the coast road east of Tobruk. The port was back under siege just two days before the Luftwaffe's deadline for return to Russia.

Ritchie left Klopper's 2nd South African Division, 201st Guards, 11th Indian and 32nd Tank Brigades with three extra artillery regiments in Tobruk to hold it, as he thought, temporarily while 8th Army was reorganised for a counter-offensive. Klopper was no Morshead and his South Africans did not possess the resilience and determination of the Australians. Moreover Rommel and his commanders knew Tobruk better than they had done when they reached it in 1941. Using the plan elaborated for their assault on Tobruk, which was pre-empted by *Crusader*, Rommel smashed his way through Klopper's defences on 20 June in *blitzkrieg* style, supported by every aircraft that Kesselring could muster before the return to Russia began. Next day the fortress, which had defied him for so long, was in his hands, and he had an advanced base from which he could start his drive into Egypt. He deserved the field marshal's baton, which his grateful *Führer* bestowed upon him.

* * *

The fall of Tobruk, coming so soon after the loss of Singapore and Rangoon, shook British morale at home more than it did in the Western Desert, where spirits remained remarkably high. Churchill heard the news while conferring with Roosevelt in Washington. The American reaction was one of great generosity even though their Chiefs of Staff believed that the British should cut their losses in the Middle East and collaborate with them in preparing for an early cross-Channel invasion of Western Europe to help Russia and to win the war in the quickest and surest way. Roosevelt offered the tanks, aircraft, vehicles and supplies, which were to make Montgomery's victory at El Alamein a reality in four months' time. For instance, new Sherman tanks – the much improved successor of the Grant – already issued to units of the American Army, were withdrawn from them and dispatched immediately to Egypt in American shipping.

On the Axis side, an argument broke out between Rommel, who wanted authority to advance into Egypt and Kesselring, who was getting cold feet about going any further until his bombers had subdued Malta and ensured that Rommel's supply lines would not be cut by British naval and air action. Both the German and Italian naval and air staffs backed Kesselring, but they were no match for the newly created field marshal in Hitler's or Mussolini's eyes. Rommel appealed to both and won their authority to advance on Cairo. Mussolini was elated by the thought of avenging the loss of his Abyssinian Empire, but allowing Malta to survive was to lead to Rommel's eventual downfall.

The unexpectedly early fall of Tobruk dislocated Auchinleck's plans for reforming 8th Army on the Egyptian frontier. He accepted Ritchie's suggestion that he should copy the tactic used by Wavell against the Italians in 1940 of falling back to Mersa Matruh to give Rommel all the problems of supplying his Panzer Army, Afrika over another 120 miles of waterless desert. Moreover, this would give the RAF – now freed by the return of a large part of the *Luftwaffe* to Russia – greater opportunities to do real damage to the Axis columns as they thrust their way eastwards. As 8th Army fell back, the RAF would grow stronger like a coiled spring whereas those units of the *Luftwaffe* left to support Rommel would be increasingly overstretched.

Gott's 13th Corps covered 8th Army's withdrawal to Matruh, which started on 23 June. Auchinleck sent General Holm's 10th Corps headquarters from Syria to organise the Matruh defences, while Norrie's

30th Corps went right back to the potentially stronger El Alamein Line – stronger because there were only 40 miles of flattish desert between the coast and the marshy Qattara Depression protecting its southern flank. Gott handled his corps' withdrawal with great skill but the battle on the Mersa Matruh line, which started on 27 June, only lasted a couple of days because 8th Army was still too disorganised to make a determined stand, and because Auchinleck was persuaded by his staff and by Air Marshal Tedder that Ritchie had lost the confidence of his troops and should be replaced. It was the RAF rather than 8th Army, which was the British fighting force during the withdrawal. Brigadier Kippenberger, a New Zealander, watched the troops withdrawing from Matruh:

> Eighth Army poured back through us, not looking at all demoralised . . . but thoroughly mixed up and dis-organised. I did not see a single formed fighting unit, infantry, armour or artillery.[11]

* * *

Auchinleck now decided that he must himself take personal command of 8th Army if Egypt was to be saved. In London, Churchill was delighted, commenting that he should have done so far earlier; and in Egypt, there were disgraceful scenes of panic. The Fleet left Alexandria; a thin pall of smoke hung over the British Embassy and GHQ buildings in Cairo, rising from burning secret and politically sensitive papers; and many officers and officials, who should have known better, decided that they and their families should be elsewhere!

The stolidly dominating authority, which Auchinleck brought to 8th Army, drew order out of chaos and the El Alamein Line gradually congealed into a tenable defensive position. He issued no traditional 'Backs to the Wall' message because he was determined to keep 8th Army in being as a mobile fighting force. Instead, he sent out a laconic three liner:

> The enemy is stretched to the limit and thinks we are a broken army . . . He hopes to take Egypt by bluff. Show him where he gets off.[12]

Rommel was certainly overstretched, but determined to panic his opponents out of the El Alamein Line before they could settle down. He attacked in the northern sector of the front on 1 July with the few German and Italian mobile troops that he had managed to bring forward, but was repulsed by concentrations fired from the South African and British artillery of Norrie's 30th Corps. On 3 July, he accepted temporary defeat. His report to Kesselring read:

With present fighting strength and supply situation an attack on a large scale is not possible. It is hardly possible to supply the Army by night as the roads are almost completely denied by air activity.[13]

For the rest of July the struggle at El Alamein, often called the First Battle of El Alamein, developed into an evenly matched tug-of-war, in which the two teams grew in size as reinforcing units arrived on each end of the rope. In all, Auchinleck tried five heaves to Rommel's one, but at no time did the marker in the centre of the rope favour either side. Both sides settled down in acute discomfort, plagued by heat, flies and desert sores as they dug, wired and mined their front lines, creating defensive positions of great depth. There was no way round, and so the stalemate at the front gave way to naval and air battles to cut the supply routes across and through the Mediterranean, in which Malta played a decisive role.

Throughout July, Kesselring hammered Malta with his bombers, but failed to stop the *Pedestal* Convoy reaching and restocking the island. Only five out of 16 ships, which left Gibraltar on 11 August, survived, but they included the US tanker, *Ohio*, manned by a British crew, which arrived lashed between two destroyers to stop her sinking. The naval losses were severe: one aircraft carrier sunk, two badly damaged, and two cruisers sunk and two damaged. Nevertheless, Malta was saved, and Axis shipping losses rose steadily, Rommel complaining bitterly that he was barely receiving enough supplies to meet daily consumption let alone build up stocks for a final drive to the Suez Canal as the Axis strategic plan required.

At strategic level, great events were taking place on both sides. The American Chiefs of Staff, General George Marshall and Admiral Ernest King, had visited London in July to try to persuade their British allies to join them in a cross-Channel venture that autumn. They had not been successful, and had accepted instead the *Torch* plan for an Allied invasion of French North Africa to coincide with a major British offensive from Egypt to clear the Axis forces out of North Africa. But everything was dependent upon the Russians not collapsing under the weight of the German 1942 summer offensive, which had begun on 28 June. The German Armies were surging forward towards Stalingrad and the Caucasian oilfields. It was estimated that at their current rate of advance, they might well emerge through the Caucasus into the Middle East before winter. Rommel must be defeated and driven back from the Nile Delta before Auchinleck was forced to face north-east to meet the threat to the Persian and Iraqi oilfields.

The CIGS, General Brooke, decided that he must fly out to Cairo to review the situation personally. Churchill decided to go one better: he would fly out with Brooke and the two of them would fly on to Moscow to probe Stalin's intentions and Russia's prospects of survival. They arrived in Cairo on 4 August and after a whirlwind tour of units in the desert

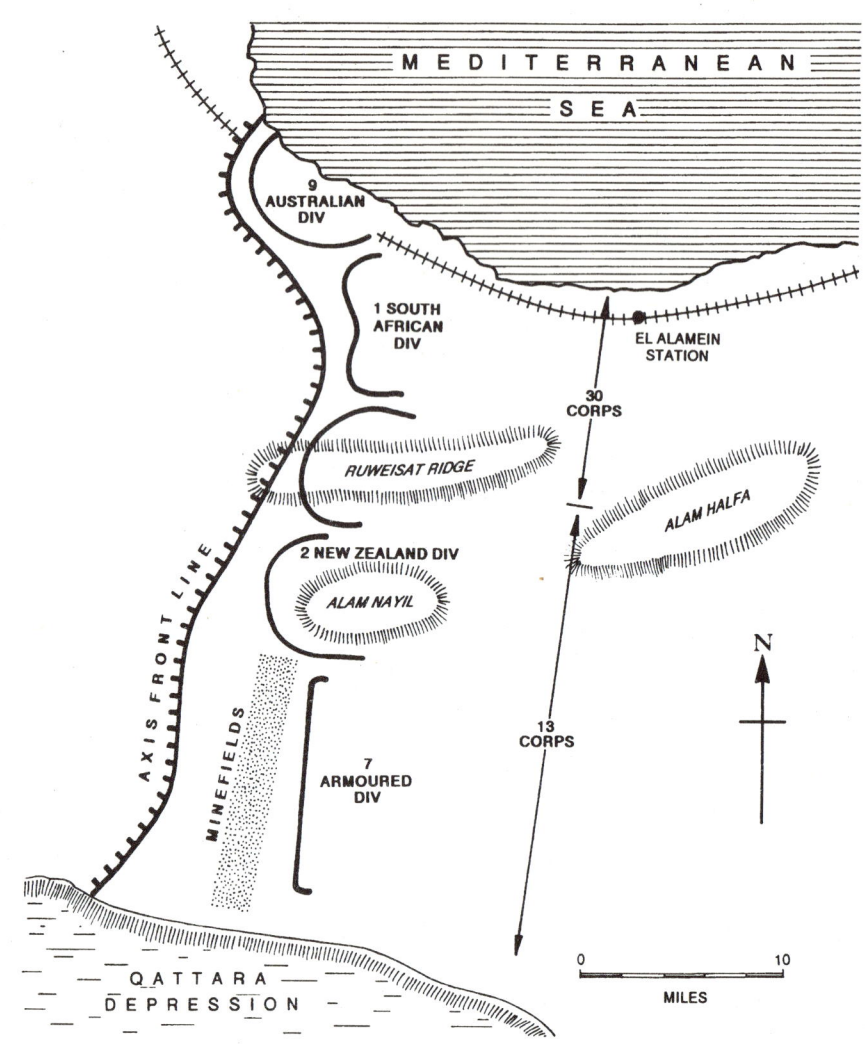

Map 15: The El Alamein Line at the end of August 1942

decided to make two fundamental changes: one personal and the other organisational. Auchinleck was to be relieved by Harold Alexander, who had come to Churchill's notice when he commanded the rearguard at Dunkirk and had recently conducted the withdrawal from Burma; and 8th Army would be taken over by Gott. Unfortunately, Gott was killed when the aircraft bringing him back to Cairo was shot down by German fighters. Bernard Montgomery was rushed out from England to take his place.

The organisational change was the splitting of the vast Middle East Command by hiving off Persia and Iraq as a new command, beamed on the problems of defeating any German advance through the Caucasus and developing overland supply routes across Persia into southern Russia. Auchinleck was offered the Persia and Iraq Command, but refused because he considered it an unworkable proposition. A few months later, he returned to his old post as C-in-C in Delhi when Wavell became Viceroy of India.

Montgomery's takeover of 8th Army and his famous battles of Alam Halfa and El Alamein have been recounted so often and will continue to be written about by revisionist historians for years to come so only a brief sketch of their highlights is needed here. In a remarkably short time, their new commander drew the 8th Army out of its mood of cynical disillusion and bewildered depression, and turned it into a battle-winning force that proved more than a match for Rommel's apparently invincible Panzer Army, Afrika.

There were six strands to his policy. First, he set about making himself and his tactical philosophy known to every officer and man, using astute, if ruthless, public relations methods. No one in the 8th Army at the time will ever forget his high, rasping voice and wickedly wounding asides about people whom he did not like. Second, he scrapped all plans for withdrawal from El Alamein, and instead reinforced the front with every unit that could be released from the rearward defences in the Nile Delta. In particular, he sent forward the newly arrived 44th Division to hold the vital Alam Halfa ridge in his left rear, overlooking the lower ground towards the Qattara Depression where Rommel might try to break through. Third, he decreed an end to the 'Jock' column and brigade group philosophy. Divisions were, in future, to be fought as divisions and not in 'penny packets'. Fourth, he insisted that it was to be the German tanks which ran onto anti-tank gun screens and not the British as had so often been the case in the past. There was to be no more 'loosing the armour' in cavalry style: British tanks would fight their battles in close co-operation with artillery and infantry. Fifth, 8th Army would always be operationally and logistically on balance, and deployed in such a way that it could not be upset by anything Rommel might do. And finally, there was to be no more 'belly-aching': orders were orders and not a basis for discussion. Commanders who belly-ached would go.

Like most new brooms, Montgomery brought out fresh men from England, whom he knew that he could trust. Brian Horrocks, a dynamic infantryman, arrived to take Gott's place in 13th Corps; Oliver Leese, a large and rather ponderous Guardsman, who was excellent at set-piece battering-ram operations, was brought out to take over 30th Corps; and Lumsden, from 1st Armoured Division, was tasked to turn 10th Corps into what Montgomery called his *'Corps de Chasse'*, comprising 1st and 10th Armoured Divisions, to rival the DAK. He retained Auchinleck's division of the front with 30th Corps holding the northern half and 13th Corps covering the less heavily defended southern sector.

Montgomery's effect on the 8th Army was electric, but it was his inner determination that there should be no more failure that mattered most. Risks were to be minimised. In his view, there were no short-cuts to victory. Like Wavell and Auchinleck before him, he was goaded by Churchill to act prematurely, but unlike them he refused to take the offensive until he was sure that everything had been done to command success. In stark contrast, Rommel was a man in a hurry. He planned to open his final offensive to throw the British out of Egypt at the end of August, provided he had enough fuel. He was promised seven tankers in the last week of August and four more in the first week of September. Four of his August ships were sunk. Nevertheless, he threw such caution as he had ever possessed to the winds and attacked during the night of 30–31 August, relying upon captured British fuel stocks to carry the Panzer Army, Afrika, through to the Suez Canal.

The only difference between Rommel's plans for the battles of Gazala and Alam Halfa was that instead of being able to motor round the desert flank, he had to force his way through the British minefields laid in the gap between the southern flank of their main position, held by Freyberg's New Zealanders, and the marshes of Qattara Depression before he could hook northwards to attack El Alamein Line from the rear. As at Gazala, his proposed route round the flank was covered by 7th Armoured Division; but unlike Gazala, it was Montgomery who planned a new 'Cauldron' for him below the Alam Halfa ridge. 44th Division was dug in on the ridge with its artillery concentrated and reinforced by 13th Corps guns, and Brigadier 'Pip' Robert's 22nd Armoured Brigade was deployed in hidden 'hull-down' positions across his most likely approach, waiting for him when he tried, as seemed most likely, to turn north to take Alam Halfa, which overlooked his route towards the British rear and Cairo. Once it was clear that he was, indeed, turning north, 23rd Armoured Brigade would be brought up to pre-planned positions to reinforce Roberts's brigade. If, on the other hand, he tried to bypass Alam Halfa and push on due east, he would be blocked frontally by 7th Armoured Division and the newly arrived 8th Armoured Brigade, and pounded from the flank by artillery massed behind Alam Halfa and by the RAF.

Rommel ran straight into the trap set for him. During the night of 30 August, he thrust his way through the southern minefields with the DAK, 90th Light Division and the Italian 20th Mobile Corps, suffering delays and losses inflicted by 7th Armoured Division as it fell back. Nehring, the DAK's Commander, was wounded and von Bismarck was killed in command of 21st Panzer Division. With his timings in hopeless disarray, Rommel was minded to give up and would have done so had it not been for Colonel Bayerlein, the DAK's Chief of Staff, who persuaded him to press on, but to shorten the distance that the DAK had to travel by turning north for Alam Halfa rather earlier than he had planned originally.

Defeating Hitler's Challenge 103

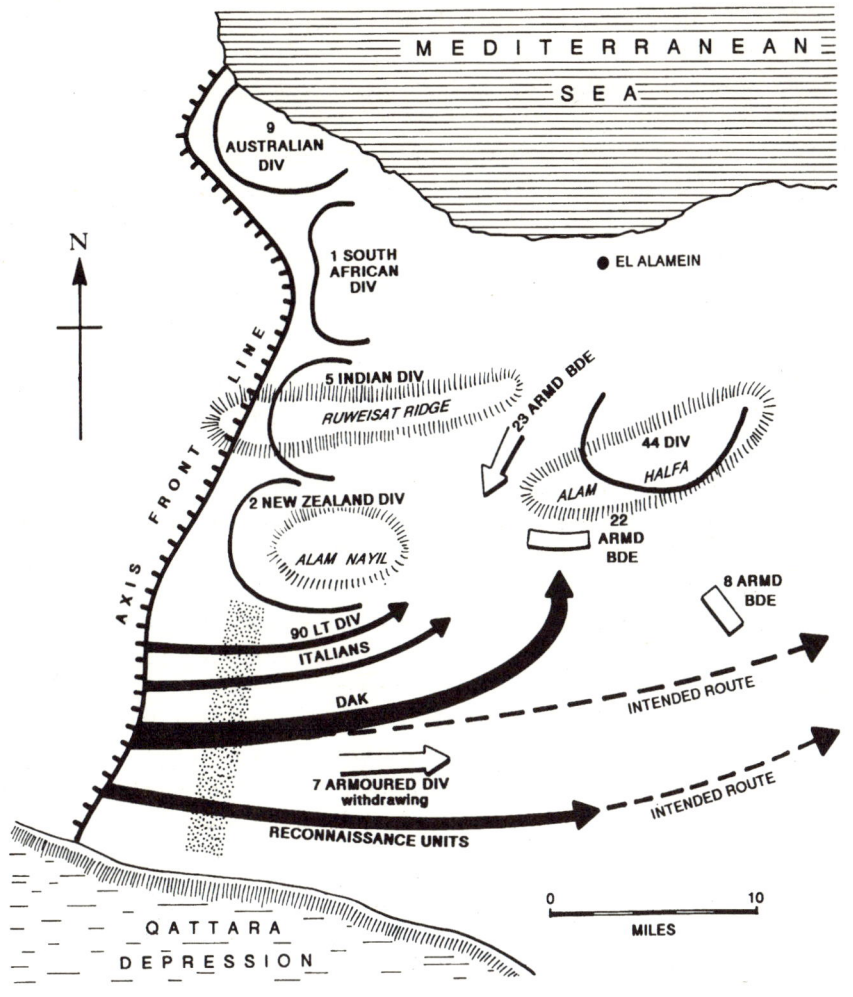

Map 16: The Battle of Alam Halfa: 30 August–3 September 1942

Dust storms on 31 August further delayed the DAK, but screened its columns from the RAF. There was only about an hour of daylight left when it ran into Pip Robert's anti-tank guns and tanks, which were waiting for him. Both sides hammered each other at close range in the failing light. This time it was the DAK which recoiled. Next day, Rommel found the whole of his striking force penned in the new 'Cauldron' between the Alam Halfa ridge, the Qattara Depression and the British minefields, but unlike Gazala he had the RAF as well as 8th Army's artillery and tanks to contend with and they were not prepared to pull any punches. After suffering three days of round-the-clock bombing and shelling, Rommel extricated his battered divisions through the minefields and set about preparing his defences to resist the inevitable British counter-offensive. Montgomery resisted the temptation to exploit success and made no real attempt to cut Rommel off as he withdrew: he was not yet ready for his own offensive and held steadfastly to his philosophy of refusing to take any risks.

* * *

Churchill wanted a September counter-offensive, but Montgomery refused to be hustled, guaranteeing, in his dogmatic way, complete success if he was allowed until the end of October to complete his preparations, including the absorption of the new American Sherman tanks, which Roosevelt had so generously supplied after the fall of Tobruk. Montgomery's plan was to deceive Rommel into thinking that he too was going to attack through the southern flank with Horrocks's 13th Corps, whereas, in fact, he intended to punch a hole in the Axis defences with Leese's 30th Corps in the centre of the front. Lumsden's *'Corps de Chasse'* would thrust through the breach and position its anti-tank guns and tanks on ground of its own choosing behind the Axis defences, on which he could defeat the DAK's inevitable counter-attacks. Once the DAK had been defeated, the Axis infantry divisions would be at Montgomery's mercy.

Montgomery envisaged a battle in three phases: a quick 'break-in'; a week's hard fought 'dog-fight' in which his infantry would 'crumble' the Axis defences behind the protection of Lumsden's armour while it broke the DAK's counter-attacks; and the 'break-out' when Axis resistance started to wane. The flavour of his plan comes through in the final paragraph of addresses which he gave in a whirlwind tour of units before the battle:

8. General Conduct of the Battle.
Methodical progress; destroy enemy part by part, slowly and surely.
Shoot tanks and shoot Germans.
He cannot last a long battle: we can.
We must therefore keep at it hard; no unit commander must release pressure; organise ahead for a 'dog-fight' of a week.
Whole affair about 10 days.
– Don't expect spectacular results too soon.[14]

At 9.40pm on 24 October, the rumble of over a thousand guns heralded the start of the decisive Battle of El Alamein. Rommel was away on sick leave in Germany, and his place had been taken temporarily by Panzer General Georg Stumme from the Russian front. Leese's 30th Corps with (from north to south) 9th Australian, 51st Highland, 2nd New Zealand and 1st South African Divisions set about clearing two wide mine-free corridors through the deep Axis defences, for Lumsden's

Defeating Hitler's Challenge

armour, while Horrocks's 13th Corps simulated a similar attack to hold the German reserves in the south. By dawn neither of Leese's corridors were completely clear, but Lumsden's armour passed through the infantry and tried without much success to fight its own way into the open. The Axis defences were deeper than expected and more heavily mined.

Attempts by the armour to force its way out of the corridors went on all the first day, and that night a depressed Lumsden recommended to Headquarters 8th Army that they should be stopped. Montgomery was woken up – a thing he objected to unless there was really good cause. It can be said that he won the battle that night by his firmness at the hastily called conference of Corps commanders held in his caravan at around midnight. Both Lumsden and Leese said that the battle had gone so wrong that it should be broken off to avoid further useless casualties.

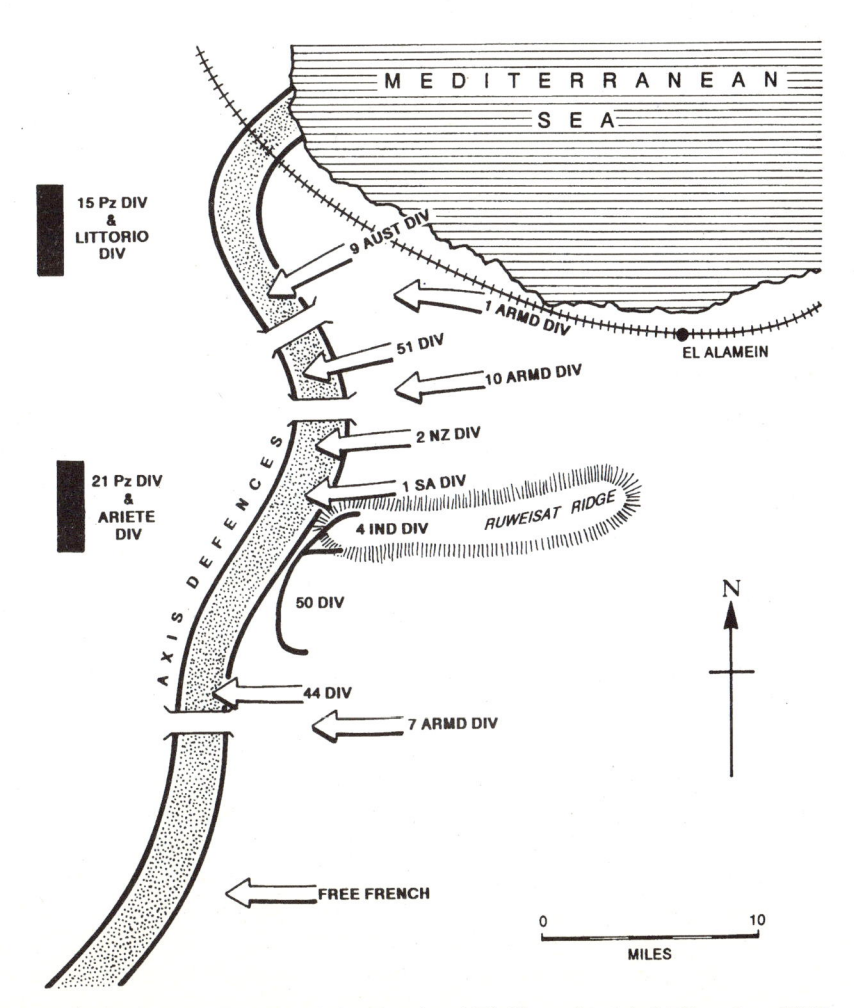

Map 17: The First Phases of the Battle of El Alamein: 24–31 October 1942

Their pleas fell on deliberately deaf ears. If his armoured commanders were not prepared to fight their way through, he would find others who were prepared to do so. This was the psychological, though not the actual turning point of the battle. Previous 8th Army Commanders would have flinched from giving such an order for fear of repeating the unreasoning obstinacy of the First World War generals. Montgomery did not hesitate. His subordinate commanders now knew where they stood, and the battle was fought on to the limits of German and Italian endurance.

Whether Montgomery liked it or not, the break-in phase was over, and the crumbling process of the dog-fight phase had begun on the second day of the battle. Stumme had been killed on reconnaissance during the first day and Rommel arrived back from Germany that evening. He took over the reins from von Thoma, Nehring's successor in command of the DAK, and began planning the concentration of his armour for a counter-attack, which after much delay, caused by the RAF preventing tank columns moving in daylight, was launched by 21st Panzer Division on 27 October against Kidney Ridge, held by the 7th Motor Brigade, covering the exit from the northern corridor. It was a typical *blitzkrieg* attack with every available dive-bomber supporting the assault, but there was to be no repeat of *Totensonntag*. 7th Motor Brigade stood its ground and inflicted crippling losses on the German tanks with their 6-pounder anti-tank guns. Colonel Victor Turner's 2nd Battalion of the Rifle Brigade, which was holding Kidney Ridge, fought its finest action of the war, for which he was rightly awarded the VC. Rommel could no longer snatch victory from defeat by the violence of his panzer attacks as he used to do. He ordered his Panzer Army to go over onto the defensive, hoping to impose a stalemate.

The crumbling process of the dog-fight phase had been going best in the northern sector where Morshead's Australians were gnawing away the Axis defences of the coast road and had repulsed counter-attacks by the 90th Light Division. By 29 October, Montgomery began to sense that the moment for launching the breakthrough phase was approaching, and so he started drawing divisions into reserve to form a striking force. Rommel, conversely, was becoming an increasingly worried man as the relentless attrition of the British artillery and air bombardment took its toll, and more of his fuel tankers were sunk at sea. As a precaution, he started reconnoitring a lay-back position at Fuka, although he realised he would have to abandon his immobile Italian infantry if he was forced to withdraw.

Rommel might well have imposed a stalemate against a less determined British commander. A number of apparently responsible people in Cairo and Whitehall were beginning to suggest that the 8th Army had shot its bolt. Even Churchill became restive as he noted the withdrawal of divisions from the front. He need not have worried: Montgomery was preparing *Supercharge*, his plan for breaking through and delivering Rommel his *coup de grâce*, which he launched just south of the Australian sector. Freyberg's

New Zealanders led the attack during the night of 1–2 November and by daylight Lumsden's armour was fighting its way through the last of the Axis positions to confront the remains of the DAK. Von Thomas' last counter-attacks were successfully repulsed and Leese's 30th Corps, led by the Highland Division, widened the breach south-westwards.

That night, von Thoma persuaded Rommel that he must save at least the German element of the Panzer Army by withdrawing to Fuka. The backward movement of logistic units started immediately and Rommel reported his intentions to OKW. Hitler, as was his wont, vetoed any withdrawal. Rommel hesitated and tried to obey, but even he could not stop the collapse of his Panzer Army. The Italians were beyond caring, and the Germans' power of endurance had reached its limit. At dawn on 4 November, Lumsden's armour pressed forward with snowballing success until, at around midday, the Axis defence snapped. Von Thoma was

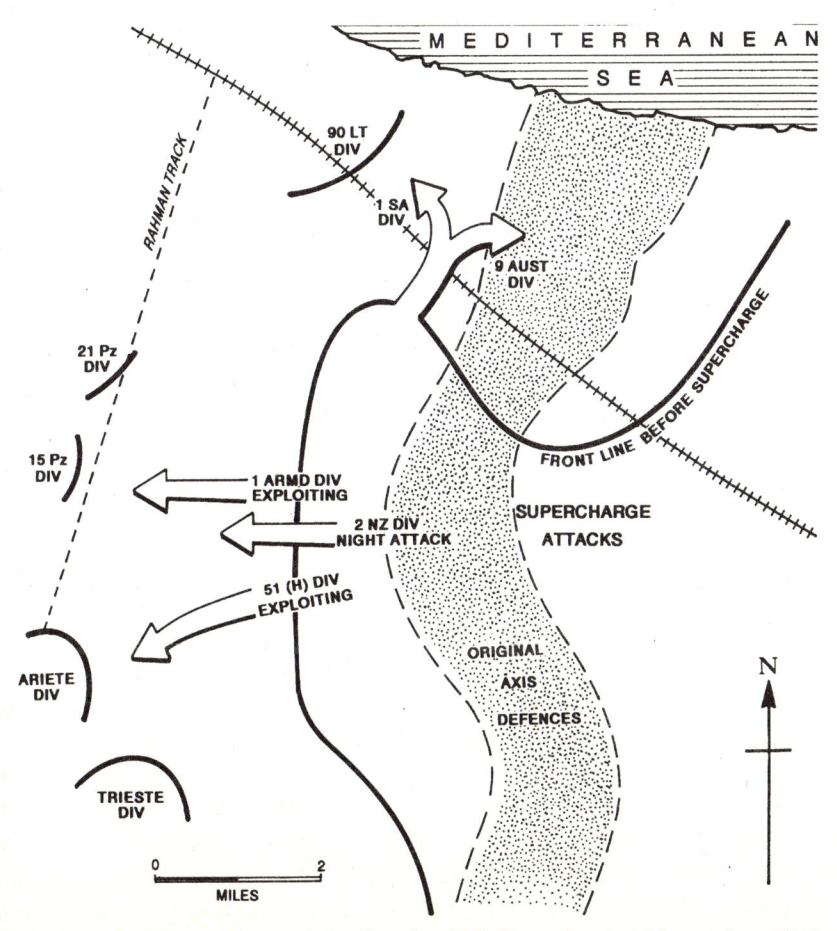

Map 18: The Final Phase of the Battle of El Alamein: 1–4 November 1942

captured fighting with the DAK's headquarters defence unit, trying to delay the British advance. Rommel knew by then he would have to abandon the Italian infantry if he was to save his mobile troops. As dusk was falling, he ordered a general withdrawal to Fuka.

* * *

We need not dwell on Montgomery's long pursuit of Rommel into Tunisia. Far away on the banks of the Volga, the Russian armies were building up for the decisive Battle of Stalingrad, which ended the German threat to the back-door to the Middle East. Napoleon, Kaiser Wilhelm II and now Hitler had all failed to open up the route to India via Persia and Afghanistan. Britain's vital interests in the Suez Canal and the oilfields in Persia and Iraq were secure once more.

However, a new threat from an entirely new competitor was just beginning to emerge in the Middle East. United States engineers had helped to improve the Red Sea ports for the arrival of Lend-Lease supplies for the British forces in Egypt, and had subsequently taken over the development of the supply routes through the Persian mountains into Southern Russia; and General Brereton's US Middle East Air Force had arrived in Egypt to reinforce the RAF's effort after the fall of Tobruk. American diplomats, civilian and military experts, and salesmen temporarily in uniform in the US Services, all began to acquire a taste for the Middle East, and to see post-war commercial opportunities in the area, which they had previously ignored, particularly the exploitation of its hidden oil resources. Unlike the French and Germans, who had tried to oust the British by military means, the Americans were to succeed by gradual political and commercial infiltration, which was unplanned and self-generating.

CHAPTER 4

THE UNEASY ANGLO-AMERICAN PARTNERSHIP
Palestine to Suez 1945–56

> *The benefits of partnership between Great Britain and the countries of the Middle East have never reached the ordinary people, and so our foreign policy has rested on too narrow a footing, mainly on the personalities of kings, princes and pashas. There is thus no vested interest among the people to remain with us . . .*
>
> Ernest Bevin, Attlee's Foreign Secretary.[1]

In 1918, United States' interest in the carve-up of the Ottoman Empire and establishment of the Middle East mandates had been brusquely cut short by a return to isolationism. In 1945, US forces straddled the globe and the American people had acquired a taste for world leadership. Isolationism still lay uncomfortably close beneath the surface of the American subconscious, and might have re-emerged had it not been for the rapid spread of the bushfire of international Communism, fanned by the Soviet Union and later by the People's Republic of China. Having experienced the costs and difficulties of maintaining the waning *Pax Britannica* during the inter-war years, Britain welcomed American leadership in the thankless task of restoring world stability for a second time in the 20th Century.

Two influences brought Britain and America together in their post-war partnership: the blatant Communist threat to both their interests, and the unwritten Anglo-American Special Relationship, which had been so strongly reinforced by close and successful wartime co-operation. But there were other trends, which tended to make for uneasiness in their partnership, particularly in the Middle East. There was the obvious rivalry caused by ambitious and none too scrupulous American corporations, seeking oil and other trading concessions in the Arab World, which had previously been the preserve of British and French companies. Friction inherent in the pursuit of national self-interest was exacerbated by sectarian lobbies in Congress, which could so easily override the needs of the Special Relationship. And perhaps strongest of all was the fundamental American dislike of British colonialism, from which they had freed themselves in the 18th Century, and were determined to bring to an end whenever and wherever possible in the 20th. Put another way, the unease in Anglo-American relations was caused by the national generation gap between the old imperial powers and the young, up-and-coming, anti-colonial United States.

Although Britain was already set on granting India independence as soon as agreement could be reached between Hindus and Moslems on an all-India constitution, she was not about to abandon her imperial role, nor her colonial attitudes of mind which so irked the Americans. She was intent upon continuing the process of converting Empire into Commonwealth, which had begun in the mid-19th Century with the grant of Dominion status to Canada. She was determined to do so at a prudent speed of her own choosing, which would allow each dependent territory to advance towards independence at its own pace. Even when independence had been granted, Britain would still have to retain the military capability to go to the aid of her fledglings, and so her lines of communication through the Middle East would still be vital to her.

When the British Chiefs of Staff began to formulate their post-war grand strategy, they concluded that its 'Three Pillars' were the defence of the British Isles within Western European defence; the defence of the sea lanes; and the domination of the Middle East, which they saw as the crossroads of Empire and Commonwealth, and the main source of cheap oil paid for in Sterling rather than Dollars. The first was, in due course, to be looked after by the formation of NATO; the second by close co-operation between the Royal and US Navies; and the third by the retention of a strategic reserve stationed in Egypt and Palestine to back Defence agreements negotiated or renegotiated with the Arab states in the region. While Indian independence might lessen the significance of the Suez Canal, the need to ship Persian and Iraqi oil by the shortest, and hence cheapest, route to Europe enhanced its strategic importance in the Chiefs' minds. In any case, so much capital had been sunk in the great complex of base installations in the Canal Zone, and so much blood and treasure had been expended upon the defence of the British position in the Middle East over almost two centuries of fighting, that there was no inclination amongst them to abandon the costly incubus of staying in the Middle East.

One man did question the validity of the Chiefs of Staff view. Clement Attlee, Britain's first post-war Prime Minister, who had served in Churchill's War Cabinet for most of the war and was well aware of the strategic arguments, did have his doubts, but Ernest Bevin, his Foreign Secretary, supported the Chiefs in their belief that Britain's position in the world still depended upon her strength in the Middle East. Until the

Commonwealth could stand on its own feet, the crossroads of Empire and Britain's oil supplies must be firmly held.

The American Chiefs of Staff had never been able to fathom why Britain had been so determined to stay in the Middle East. They gave the defence of Europe and the stabilisation of the Far East far higher priority than intervention in Arab affairs. They were, therefore, only too happy for the British to look after Western interests in the Middle East while they concentrated upon Europe and the Far East, so long as United States' trade in the region was secure and no American interests were endangered. Congress, however, was soon dissatisfied with British Middle East policy and friction began to mount.

★ ★ ★

Jewish immigration into Palestine was the initial cause of that friction, and led to the first post-war British military operations in the Middle East. The Arab Revolt of 1937–39 had been crushed by the time the Second World War broke out, and in default of international agreement on the way forward, Britain had imposed her own arbitrary solution set out in the 1939 Palestine White Paper, which gave the Jews a final immigration quota of 75,000 to be spread over five years. Thereafter, no new Jewish immigrants would be allowed to enter Palestine without Arab consent. President Roosevelt had questioned the British right to restrict Jewish immigration, and he had refused to support the British view that it would be illegal under their League of Nations Mandate to establish a Jewish state, as opposed to a Jewish home, in Palestine against the wishes of the Arabs. Indeed, Roosevelt assumed that the creation of a Jewish state was the prime purpose of the Mandate. The Second World War had broken out before the dispute could be taken any further.

The Jews made far better use of the war years to ready themselves for the struggle, which they were determined to wage to bring a sovereign Jewish state into existence. Planning was carried out by the Jewish Agency, which the British themselves had established to advise the Mandatory Government on local Jewish affairs. The Agency, headed by Ben-Gurion, who was later to become Israel's first Prime Minister, was determined to act politically as far as possible. It formulated three lines of policy: undermining the quota system through illegal immigration; obtaining military training by raising Jewish units to fight with the British Army against the Germans in Italy; and organising political support in the United States. The last was the most potent. Not only did American Jewry have the necessary financial resources, but they had political clout as well. No President, other than Woodrow Wilson, had reached the White House without winning New York, where the Jews held the political balance of power.

The only Jewish military force under the Agency's control in the early days of the Mandate was the locally recruited Hagana, which both the Turks and the British had allowed to exist for defence of Jewish settlements against Arab attack. During the war, the Jewish Agency raised clandestinely a force of regulars from men who had seen active service with the British and other European armies. Known as the Palmach, these full-time underground soldiers were concealed within the part-time Hagana. They were a disciplined force, and were equipped and trained to undertake offensive operations if and when the Agency decided it was time to strike militarily. There were also a number of breakaway groups formed by extreme Zionists, which did not accept Agency direction. Two of the most important were the Irgun Zvai Leumi, dedicated to establishing a Jewish state as soon as possible through terrorism, and the Stern Gang, whose aim was the same but whose *modus operandi* was political assassination.

Neither the Irgun nor the Stern Gang was prepared to wait for the Agency's political methods to work, and both chose misguided moments to strike. Just as news was breaking in February 1944 of the brutality of Hitler's 'final solution', which the Agency saw would help their political case for a Jewish state, the Irgun started its terrorist campaign by blowing up immigration and tax offices, thus alienating international support for the Jewish cause. Nine months later, just after Roosevelt returned to the White House, having sided with the Zionists during his election campaign, the Stern Gang obtusely assassinated Lord Moyne, British Resident Minister in Cairo and a close personal friend of Winston Churchill. Roosevelt saw no reason to change his pro-Jewish stance, but Churchill, who had been more pro-Jewish than the rest of his cabinet and the Chiefs of Staff, reversed his position. Minuting the Colonial Secretary and the Chiefs of Staff, he said:

> I do not think that we should take the responsibility upon ourselves of managing this very difficult place while the Americans sit back and criticise. Have you ever addressed yourselves to the idea that we should ask them to take it over? ... I am not aware of the slightest advantage which has accrued to Great Britain from this painful and thankless task.[2]

The Chiefs of Staff rejected Churchill's suggestion. Handing over to the United States would prejudice Anglo-Arab relations and place paramount British interests in the hands of another country. Moreover, they expected that the renegotiation of the Anglo-Egyptian Treaty, for which the Egyptian Government was pressing, would result in a British withdrawal from the Nile Delta and the Canal Zone, leaving Palestine as the next most suitable place for stationing the British strategic reserve for the Mediterranean and Middle East.

The end of the war in Europe brought increasing pressure for the resettlement of the victims of the Holocaust. In the Attlee Government's view, Palestine could not absorb all the Jews wanting to settle there, even if the Arabs would agree to accept them, which was most unlikely. The war had been fought to rid Europe of Hitler's anti-Jewish tyranny: now that tyranny had been broken, the Jews should be resettled in their old homes. Many had, indeed, gone home, and only about 50,000 were waiting in the displaced persons camps for resettlement. Unfortunately, two regrettable leaks of British policy documents occurred in the autumn of 1945, showing the growing divergence between London and Washington over Palestine. The Jewish Agency became aware that the British Government intended to maintain the 1939 White Paper policy; and that Attlee had turned down a request from President Truman for the immediate issue of 100,000 immigration permits. A wave of fury swept through the Jewish communities, bringing moderates and extremists together in a determination to establish the state of Israel by all available means.

The Agency decided to adopt a two handed strategy: the ageing Chaim Weizmann, who had negotiated the original Balfour Declaration in 1917, was to head a political offensive to engage American support; and Ben-Gurion would mount military operations aimed at unnerving the Mandate Government. The actions of the Hagana, Palmach, Irgun and Stern Gang were to be co-ordinated by a special committee called 'X Command'. American Zionist organisations, like the Sonnenborn Institute, would provide clandestine financial and logistic support.

The Agency's military plan was also two handed: to concentrate on headline-catching acts of sabotage, timed to coincide with specific political events; and to swamp the British immigration controls with illegal landings from armed ships. To achieve the latter, Jewish agents in Europe worked untiringly to persuade as many Jews as possible to opt for resettlement in Palestine, and members of the Hagana were sent to buy, man and arm the immigrant ships for the new Exodus from southern European ports.

The British security forces in Palestine in the autumn of 1945 consisted of the 5,000 strong Palestine Police Force, the Arab Transjordan Frontier Force and the Bedouin Arab Legion. In addition, the 1st Division was resting and retraining after the campaign in Italy in camps in the northern half of Palestine; and the 6th Airborne Division was arriving to constitute the Middle East Strategic Reserve in the southern half of the country. Both these divisions were available to support the Police, but their primary task was to be ready for general war with a hostile power: they were not equipped or trained for internal security operations. The independent 7th Infantry Brigade garrisoned Jerusalem.

Throughout the painful birth of Israel, the British sought to reconcile the irreconcilable without going to war with the Jewish people or alienating the Arabs. There were five spasms of birth contractions, each coinciding with a specific political initiative. The first spasm started on 31 October 1945 with 154 simultaneous sabotage attacks on the railways, on immigration control posts and vessels, and on the Haifa oil refinery, which was only slightly damaged. This Jewish effort, about which the Jewish Agency disclaimed all knowledge, was designed to impress an Anglo-American Committee set up to examine how many European Jews actually wanted to settle in Palestine, and how many the country could reasonably absorb. Quite fortuitously, Ernest Bevin increased the severity of the first contraction spasm by making an over-forthright speech in the House of Commons, showing scant sympathy for the Jews by suggesting that they were not the only people without a home and they should stop trying to jump the post-war resettlement queues. Spontaneous anti-British rioting broke out in Jerusalem and Tel Aviv on 14 November. The police dealt quite easily with the Jerusalem trouble, but had to call for army help in Tel Aviv. The well-disciplined 3rd Parachute Brigade took five days to quieten the city at a cost of six Jews killed and 60 injured. The Jewish community, many of whom were well versed in evading the Gestapo, never again resorted to rioting as long as the mandate lasted.

The Anglo-American Committee did not report until 1 May 1946. In the meantime, X Committee had kept up the pressure with three more waves of sabotage. Just before the Anglo-American Committee reported, Committee X lost control of the Stern Gang, which murdered seven unarmed British soldiers in cold blood. It was only with the greatest difficulty that British army discipline was maintained and no unauthorised retaliation occurred. The Anglo-American Committee's report, however, only met the Jews half way. It accepted the validity of Truman's request for 100,000 entry permits, but came down against the formation of a Jewish state. Bevin refused to allow the 100,000 permits to be issued until another group of British and American officials had examined the practicability of the proposal. In his view the aggressive attitude of the Jews was poisoning Anglo-American relations and would continue to do so unless the Americans shared some of the responsibility for putting theory into practice on the ground. He warned James Byrn, the US Secretary of State, that the British Government was contemplating giving up the Mandate.

Bevin's refusal to grant the 100,000 permits straightaway triggered the second spasm of contractions. The Hagana launched another wave of attacks on communications, but it was the Irgun that caught the headlines by kidnapping five British officers from the Tel Aviv officers' club on 16 June. This was not difficult to do because British servicemen were unarmed when not on duty. The Agency, as usual, claimed innocence, but were in for a nasty surprise. General Sir Alan Cunningham, whom we last met when he had to give up the command of the 8th Army in the Western Desert during *Crusader*, was the High Commissioner. He had been authorised to plan the arrest of the Jewish leadership in an operation code-named *Agatha*, if the Attlee Government received clear evidence of the Agency's involvement in the terrorism. That evidence was, by this time, available because the Agency's communication codes had been broken by British Intelligence. The kidnap of the five officers was the last straw: Cunningham was authorised to act.

Agatha was launched on 28 June. It had been well planned and caught the Agency completely by surprise, despite 17,000 troops being involved, including the 3rd Division, which had recently arrived from Germany. Only two important members of the Agency escaped: Ben-Gurion, who was abroad, and Moshe Sneh, who eluded capture. The Hagana ceased operations and hopes ran high that a more moderate Jewish leadership would emerge. This did not happen: instead the extremists' grip on the community tightened. There had been too little intelligence on their organisations for many of Irgun and Stern Gang members to be caught in the net.

The extremists' response to *Agatha* was to blow up the King David Hotel, outside Jerusalem, which housed General Headquarters, on 22 July. Although heavily guarded, it was still in use as an hotel. Irgun managed to place seven milk churns packed with explosive in the café on the ground floor. They mismanaged the warning, and 91 people (41 Arabs, 28 Britons, 17 Jews and five others) died when the whole of one wing collapsed.

The counter-response by the British was Operation *Shark*, mounted in Tel Aviv on 30 July by 6th Airborne Division, using its own three parachute brigades and an infantry brigade from 1st Division. It constituted a cordon and very thorough search operation over four days in which over 100,000 people were screened, 800 arrested and quantities of arms unearthed. Irgun's leader, Menachem Begin, a future Israeli Prime Minister, escaped detection cooped up in a hideaway in his house, without food and water, while troops camped in his garden!

Meanwhile, hopes of Anglo-American accord were fading fast. There was little difficulty in agreeing the constitutional outlines of a cantonised Palestine with a number of Arab and Jewish provinces and with Jerusalem governed as a neutral state by the Mandatory power. No agreement, however, could be reached on immigration quotas. The US Chiefs of Staff advised President Truman not to commit American troops; and they also warned him of America's growing dependence on Middle Eastern oil, and hence of the need for Arab co-operation. But Truman was faced with placating the Jewish lobby before the New York elections in October, and only listened to the first half of this military advice. He demanded the immediate issue of the 100,000 permits without offering the military resources that would be needed to deal with the consequences. Attlee stalled: he refused to issue the permits until the constitutional proposals had been put to a conference of Arab and Jewish leaders, which Bevin was assembling in London.

The Jews declined to attend Bevin's conference unless their leaders, arrested during *Agatha*, were released. However, they were showing signs of less rigidity in their approach, so Bevin authorised the release as a goodwill gesture. Irgun, however, construed it as a sign of weakness and set in hand another wave of sabotage in November, whilst the Hagana started to develop their attempts to flood the immigration control with illegal landings. Their agents had managed to persuade over 250,000 European Jews to enter the Allies' resettlement camps and demand permits for Palestine. They had also purchased, fitted out and armed a fleet of dilapidated immigrant ships, using money provided by American Jewry. Into these ships they crammed thousands of would-be immigrants, whom they had secretly assembled at French and Italian Mediterranean ports. Most of the ships were intercepted by the Royal Navy and their 'passengers' were interned in Cyprus.

Faced with continuing violence, despite the release of the Jewish leaders, Cunningham was authorised to clear the decks for military action. Families were sent home; administrative staffs were withdrawn into heavily protected areas; and three divisional sectors were established with 6th Airborne in the north, 1st Division in the centre and the 3rd in the south. The Army was well balanced to act decisively if the protracted London Conference failed.

* * *

The winter of 1946/7 was particularly depressing for the British people, faced, as they were by severe weather, food rationing, shortages of everything and a seemingly never-ending series of military operations to establish post-war stability in places they knew little about and cared about even less. Trying to reconcile Arab and Jew in Palestine seemed a particularly futile exercise. Why not let them fight it out without the British Army acting as referee? Churchill, as Leader of the Opposition in Parliament, articulated this popular mood of disillusion and demanded the return of the Mandate to the United Nations as the League of Nations successor.

On 18 February, Bevin's London Conference did collapse in failure, and Attlee's Government following Churchill's advice, submitted the Palestine problem to the United Nations, although not actually surrendering the mandate. The usual UN diplomatic minuet was danced; a special commission was set up to establish the facts; and the Irgun and the Hagana redoubled their efforts to make the British position untenable.

The appointment of a UN Special Commission in Palestine triggered the fourth spasm in the re-birth of Israel. The Irgun decided to impress the Commission with the Jewish resolve to win the whole of Palestine as the future Jewish state, and the British Army struck back. On 1 March, the Irgun managed to blow up the Jerusalem Officers' Club, killing 13 people and injuring another 16. Next day, Martial Law was imposed on

Jerusalem and Tel Aviv; trade came to a halt; and the Jewish community faced economic ruin. If the local commanders had appreciated that the damage being done to trade had come near to breaking Jewish resolve, they would not have lifted Martial Law just over a fortnight later. They only saw the other side of the coin: that enforced unemployment was providing the Irgun with recruits.

The Irgun redoubled their efforts. They blew up part of the Haifa Oil refinery, which burned for three weeks, and on 4 May succeeded in breaching the wall of Acre prison with explosives. Forty-one Jews and 214 Arabs escaped. Of the Jews, 13 were recaptured, including three Irgun members under sentence of death for murder. At sea, the Royal Navy fought and won a running battle with the *President Warfield*, a Great Lakes steamer, renamed the *Exodus* by the Hagana, who had bought her and fitted her with anti-boarding devices and a defended bridge below decks. She was carrying 4,500 refugees. After a prolonged struggle in which the Royal Navy could not use its weapons against the crowded ship, she was successfully boarded and taken into Haifa, whence her passengers were sent back to Europe in British ships.

The UN Commission arrived in mid-June and stayed for six weeks, but it was not their machinations that led to the fifth and last spasm of contractions which resulted in the birth of Israel. The Irgun seized two British sergeants and held them hostage for the three Irgun men sentenced to death for their part in the Acre prison escape. There was no reprieve and they were hanged in Acre. In retaliation, the two sergeants were strangled by the Irgun and their bodies were strung up in a forest. The officer who cut them down was badly injured and one body was blown to pieces when a mine planted below the bodies exploded. A wave of revulsion swept through Britain with anti-Jewish demonstrations in London and all the larger cities, particularly those hit by the post-war economic depression. The chances of Britain carrying on with the Mandate died with those two sergeants.

***

The Special Commissions report, which was debated in September in New York, recommended: the ending of the British Mandate; the partition of Palestine into separate Jewish and Arab states; the continuation of the British administration for two years, after which the new states would be given their independence; and the immediate issue of 150,000 entry permits for Jews. Britain would have none of it, considering it an impracticable solution; and the Chiefs of Staff advised that the friendship of the Arabs was more important than hanging on to military camps in which to house strategic reserves. The British representative abstained when the vote was taken, making it clear during the debate that Britain would play no part in implementing partition, but would need nine months to wind up her administration and evacuate her troops and vast accumulation of military equipment and stores. The Russians surprisingly supported the Zionists in favouring partition; and the Americans used blatant economic blackmail to persuade the smaller member states to vote with them for partition as well. The date for ending the Mandate was set for 15 May 1948 with 1 August for completion of the British evacuation.

The final vote was taken on 29 November 1947. Next day, the first Arab–Israeli war broke out. The British troops held the two sides apart only to the extent necessary to ensure their own orderly withdrawal. Until the end of March 1948, the Arabs held the initiative, but, through their lack of preparation, disunity and military incompetence, they failed to abort the live rebirth of Israel. From April onwards, the Jews fought back and exposed the Arab feet of clay. The last British troops, weapons and stores left Haifa on 30 June.

The saddest outcome of the ending of the Palestine Mandate was the temporary damage it did to the Anglo-American Special Relationship. The power of ethnic and other congressional lobbies to sway American foreign policy in a decisive way had been fully demonstrated. It was soon to be the influence of America's deep-seated anti-colonialism that was to cause further friction, and, in the end, lead to Britain handing over Western leadership in the Middle East to the United States, which had done so much to bring the unloved and unwanted state of Israel into existence within the Arab world.

* * *

The Anglo-American disunity over Palestine was relatively short-lived. Both countries were drawn together again by the rising communist threat. The Americans had their hands full with the problems of Europe and the Far East, where Mao Tse Tung's victories led to the proclamation of the People's Republic of China in October 1949; the Korean war started in June 1950; and these events were seen in the West as a prelude to a Soviet military offensive in Europe, which would be launched when sufficient Anglo-American forces had been drawn towards China. Washington was only too anxious for London to continue playing the leading role in the Middle East.

Successive American administrations tried to adopt a neutralist stance in Middle Eastern affairs, acting as 'honest brokers' in disputes that arose between the British and French on the one hand and the growing spirit of Arab nationalism and Moslem unity on the other. But American neutralism was not to last indefinitely: the oil and Zionist lobbies in Congress were to force growing US political involvement in the region. Fortunately for the Western Allies, Islam and Communism were like oil and water, which limited the Soviet Union's ideological attraction in the Arab world although, to Arab nationalists, Moscow was a potential source of political and military support.

In London, the Cabinet was split on Middle East policy. Clement Attlee, the Prime Minister, and Hugh Dalton, his Chancellor, who naturally wanted to cut overseas expenditure, were ranged against Ernest Bevin, the Foreign Secretary and the Chiefs of Staff. In Attlee's view, it was pointless to pretend that Britain could defend the region in a general war with the Soviet Union, nor did she need to do so. Oil supplies were reasonably secure in that the Persian and Iraqi economies had become so dependent on selling oil on world markets that cutting off supplies for political purposes was far less likely than it had been in the past. Indeed, the presence of British forces in the Persian Gulf was perhaps a counter-productive source of local irritation. And as far as the Suez Canal was concerned, with India and Pakistan independent, there seemed little further point in expending vast sums on its defence when the Cape Route could always be used in emergency anyway.

Bevin and the Chiefs of Staff disagreed: to them, the Middle East remained as strategically important to Britain as a world power as ever it had been, and she had no intention of abdicating that status. But Bevin, a lifelong and down-to-earth Socialist, was acutely aware that Britain's power in the Middle East rested on too narrow a political base. As he pointed out in the quote at the head of this chapter, it had depended on a partnership of mutual benefit with kings, princes and pashas, in which their increasingly articulate subjects had no vested interest. He wanted to replace all the existing treaties with regional defence pacts, creating more broadly based international partnerships, which met the aspirations of the local peoples.

Before Bevin died in 1951, he had come close to success in negotiating just such an agreement with Egypt, but King Farouk's ambition to become King of the Sudan, to which Britain had already promised independence, prevented final agreement with its consequential departure of British troops. As a gesture of goodwill, however, they had been withdrawn during the negotiations from Cairo and Alexandria into the Canal Zone, and there they stayed in uncomfortable makeshift camps, waiting for a political settlement.

No such settlement was to be reached with King Farouk. Within the Egyptian Army, a clandestine 'Free Officers' movement, led by Colonel Gamal Abdel Nasser, had been plotting in a desultory fashion since the end of the war to free Egypt of British tutelage. Their plotting was given fresh impetus by the disgust felt within the Egyptian Army by the disunity of the Arab League and its own pathetic performance in southern Palestine during the first Arab–Israeli war in 1949. They attributed the latter, not to the British, but to King Farouk's corrupt regime. They began to see the overthrow of Farouk as the first step on their road to freeing Egypt.

The opportunity to depose Farouk came in an unexpected way. The Persian Government of Dr Mossadeq, copying the Attlee Government's nationalisation of British railways and coal, succeeded in nationalising the Anglo-Persian Oil Company in May 1951. Farouk decided that if the Persians could tweak the British Lion's tail, so could he. He abrogated the 1936 Anglo-Egyptian Treaty in August and laid economic siege to the British troops in the Canal Zone, making their life as uncomfortable as possible and triggering the series of events that led to his own downfall.

There were only two British brigades in the Canal Zone when Farouk started his programme of aggravation. These were quickly reinforced by two more together with pioneer units from Cyprus and Mauritius to replace Egyptian labour, which had been coerced into leaving British employment. General Sir George Erskine, the GOC British Troops Egypt, was not prepared to tolerate attacks on British targets by Egyptian snipers and terrorists, which Intelligence sources revealed were being directed by the Egyptian police. In January 1952, he took reprisals by bulldozing flat villages from which sniper fire came, and he ordered the disarmament of the Egyptian police in the Canal Zone. On Farouk's instructions, the police fought back and tanks had to be used against one of their barracks. In that action, five British soldiers were killed and nine wounded, but the police lost around 50 dead and double that number wounded.

The popular reaction in Cairo, which was no longer dominated by a British Garrison, was one of horror. The city mob, swollen by unemployed from the Canal Zone, rampaged through the streets, looting in the wake of organised gangs, which set fire to British commercial buildings and institutions. Revered establishments like the Turf Club and Shepheard's Hotel were burnt down, and a great pall of smoke darkened the city and gave 26 January its name, 'Black Saturday.'

Anthony Eden, then Foreign Secretary, authorised Erskine to march on Cairo if British lives were in danger. No call, however, came from the British Embassy because residential areas were not attacked. It was the Egyptian Army that quelled the rioting. Farouk, like Nero, fiddled while Cairo burned, celebrating the birth of a son. Out of the embers of Cairo came Colonel Nasser's determination to rid Egypt of Farouk without further delay. Five months later, his 'Free Officers' staged the coup, which ousted the King, much to the delight of all Egypt and the bewilderment of the British and American diplomats, who were uncertain whether the change should be welcomed or not. Nor were they certain who was the real power behind the Revolutionary Command Council, set up under the affable General Neguib.

* * *

The Egyptian nationalist mantle of Arabi Pasha (1882) and Saad Zaghlul Pasha (1919) had fallen on Nasser's massive shoulders although he remained in the background. He had the dynamic drive and singleness of purpose of Arabi, and the subtle intelligence of Zaghlul – a formidable combination. He made no secret of his triple aim: to get rid of British imperialism; to end Egyptian feudalism; and to lead the Arab League in the destruction of Israel. London and Washington saw no insurmountable difficulty in accommodating his ambitions. The door to the departure of British troops was wide open and only needed the finalisation of the Anglo-Egyptian treaty, which depended upon the willingness of the Command Council to accept Sudanese self-determination and agree to the alignment of Egypt with the West against Soviet penetration of the Middle East. Ending feudalism was an internal matter, and could but be applauded by the Western Powers. Both the British and American Governments were prepared to offer generous aid to help the Egyptians solve their pressing problems of an exploding birthrate and the miserably low standard of living of the fellahin, with which British administrators had been grappling for nigh on a century. As far as Israel was concerned, there was the Tri-Partite Declaration of 1950 in which the US, Britain and France agreed to control the supply of arms to Israel and her Arab neighbours, aiming to stop further Arab–Israeli conflict.

Nasser swept the Sudanese problem out of the way by persuading the Command Council that getting rid of the British was more important than winning sovereignty over the Sudan. In April 1953, the Revolutionary Command Council gave him the task of re-opening Anglo-Egyptian treaty negotiations with Churchill, who had been returned to power for the last time and was more wedded to the maintenance of the British position in the Middle East than Attlee had ever been.

Two new stumbling blocks emerged when the negotiations reopened. The first was Churchill's insistence that the maintenance staffs, left to look after the Canal Zone base installations after the British troops had been withdrawn, should be uniformed, citing the precedent of US troops serving in the United Kingdom. Nasser, however, demanded that they should be in civilian clothes, pointing out, with some justification, that Britain did not have to prove her independence. And the second was the conditions on which the base could be reactivated in time of war. Nasser was prepared to accept attacks on other Arab states as justifiable triggers, but not on Turkey or Iran, which Britain and the US wanted to incorporate in a Middle East security zone – the future Baghdad Pact – to extend NATO's flank from the Bosphorus to the Himalayas. The Revolutionary Command Council was determined to adopt a neutralist stance in the Cold War: Israel and not the USSR was Egypt's enemy. Negotiations were broken off in October 1953, and the Egyptians reimposed their blockade of the Canal Zone.

British and US Middle Eastern policies were in theory, convergent. Both aimed at preventing Soviet penetration of the region; saw partnership with the existing Arab regimes as the best way of doing so; and appreciated that Israel must not be allowed to upset that partnership. In practice, their policies diverged because they backed opposite sides in the local political struggle between Baghdad and Cairo for dominance of the Arab world. The British tended to support the Hashemite Kingdoms of Iraq and Transjordan, which they had helped to create: oil interests led the Americans to back Saudi Arabia and hence the Saudi's allies, the Egyptians. In terms of personalities, the British looked to the Anglophile Nuri es-Said, Prime Minister of Iraq, to underpin Middle Eastern security, while successive American Ambassadors in Cairo covertly advised the Anglophobe Nasser on how to deal with the British! Jefferson Caffrey (1949–53), an Irish American, and Henry Byroade (1953–56) served American interests well, but both were at heart anti-colonial and hence anti-British. They were confidants of Nasser, and were heartily disliked and distrusted by their British diplomatic colleagues in Cairo.

The crucial Anglo-American difference in Cairo was over the best way to secure the safety and continued operation of the Suez Canal. The Americans did not support the British view that they could not leave Egypt without adequate safeguards being built into the Anglo-Egyptian Treaty for the defence of the Suez Canal. They believed that only a British withdrawal without strings would bring Egypt whole-heartedly into the Western camp. They thought that they had enough economic levers to influence Egyptian policy once the irritant of the British military presence was removed. The British Government did not agree and was to be proved right by events. Nevertheless, they did agree under intense American pressure to resume treaty negotiations again with Nasser in July 1954.

By this time the British Chiefs of Staff had come to the conclusion that large sprawling logistic bases were hostages to fortune in the nuclear era, and that the Canal Zone installations were becoming obsolescent and too expensive to update. The soundest policy would be to maintain them only for as long as it took to provide smaller alternative bases elsewhere: perhaps in Cyprus and Aden, either side of the isthmus of Suez. Civilian contractors could be used to maintain the installations in the meantime, thus meeting the Egyptian objection to uniformed British soldiers remaining on Egyptian soil. This change of policy brought negotiations to a successful conclusion. All British troops would be withdrawn within 20 months; civilian contractors would maintain the base for seven years; an attack on Turkey would be added to the 'reactivation trigger' list; the RAF would be accorded over-flying and landing rights in Egypt; and Egypt reaffirmed the 1888 Constantinople Convention, guaranteeing freedom of passage through the Canal to the ships of all nations in peacetime. Israeli ships were, however, still barred on the grounds that Israel was at war with the Arab League.

* * *

The new Anglo-Egyptian Treaty was signed on 19 October 1954 and Anthony Eden had replaced Churchill as Prime Minister in 1955. The last British troops, the 2nd Grenadier Guards, sailed away from Port Said on 13 June 1956, just 74 years since their forbears had taken part in the battle of Tel-el-Kebir, which brought Egypt 'temporarily' under British protection in 1882. Dispersed and smaller British military bases were set up or expanded in Cyprus, Kenya, Aden and the Persian Gulf to replace the large Canal Zone complex.

London and Washington had every reason to think that their combined diplomacy had dealt Nasser a very favourable hand, which should satisfy him. Egypt was free of British troops and he had promises of substantial American and British economic aid. But they failed to take full account of the wild card in his hand – hatred of Israel – or of the tuition in how he might play it, which he had received from Afro-Asian leaders such as Nehru, Chou En-Lai and Sukharno at the Bandung Conference of non-aligned states in April 1955. He came away from Bandung convinced that small states could play the superpowers off against each other to secure maximum help from each with minimum commitment to either. He was to prove himself an apt pupil in the art of the neutralist double-cross and blackmail.

No sooner was the ink dry on the Anglo-Egyptian Treaty than Nasser was on the search for arms to deal with Israel. Chou En Lai had advised him at Bandung to forget his Moslem antipathy to Communism and to seek the arms, which the West refused to provide under the Tri-Partite Declaration, from behind the Iron Curtain. The Russians were not slow to pick up the scent: they offered Eastern Bloc arms to Egypt in May 1955. By September, Nasser was able to announce a barter agreement with Czechoslovakia to supply all the arms Egypt needed in exchange for cotton. There were no political or financial strings attached as there would have been with any Western deal.

The Western Allies were tempted to cut off economic aid, but the neutralist double-cross came into play. To have done so would have risked driving Egypt into the arms of Moscow. It was thought wiser to counter Soviet influence with increased economic aid, and, in particular, by financing the jewel in the Egyptian development plan, the Aswan dam, which would add a third to Egypt's cultivable land.

Unlike the stringless Czech arms deal, the World Bank insisted on a number of unexceptional financial conditions to secure its loan for the Aswan dam. Nasser, remembering the Anglo-French exploitation of

Khedive Ismail's bankruptcy in 1875, saw any terms as an affront to Egyptian dignity. The US Congress were equally affronted by Nasser's recent recognition of Communist China as well as his dealing with the Eastern Bloc; and the American cotton growers and the Zionist lobby started pressing for cancellation of the promised loan. Nasser, fearing that the double-cross was not working too well, sent his Ambassador post-haste to Washington to clinch the deal, strings and all. At a meeting in the State Department on 19 July 1956, the Egyptian Ambassador foolishly blurted out that the Soviet Government had agreed to finance the dam if the West refused. This was more than John Foster Dulles, the American Secretary of State, could stand, and he withdrew the offer there and then. Nasser countered a week later by nationalising the Suez Canal Company to provide the financial resources he needed to carry forward his development of the Egyptian economy without Western aid, and to rid his country of the indignity of foreign control of its greatest asset.

The tragedy of the Suez crisis was that it was handled on the Western side by three sick and politically hobbled men, whose judgement was to some extent impaired. Eisenhower was recovering from an operation for ileitis; he was running for re-election as President on the ticket of 'A man of peace'; and he was a blinkered devotee of the United Nations as the hope of the world. Dulles, his mentor, was suffering from cancer, which had to be operated on 3 November at the height of the coming crisis and he too was inhibited by Presidential election considerations. Furthermore, he was not only another devotee of the United Nations but was also strongly influenced by the anti-imperialism of Nehru's non-aligned group of newly independent states. To both the American leaders, the Suez Canal was little more than a pawn in the all-pervasive game of East–West Confrontation, whereas, to their British colleagues, it had been strategically vital for two centuries and still remained largely so in their minds.

On the British side, Eden was suffering from a repetition of an abdominal complaint, which had laid him low in 1953 and was to do so again soon after the Suez crisis was over. He was hobbled by his past rather than the future. In the 1930s, he had resigned as British Foreign Secretary over the failure of the League of Nations to take effective action to stop Mussolini's conquest of Abyssinia, and had served in Churchill's government throughout the Second World War, grappling with the consequences of Hitler's and Mussolini's ambitions. To him, Nasser was another emergent dictator with equally unbridled ambitions, and he saw Nasser's surprise unilateral nationalisation of the Canal as the equivalent of Hitler's march into the Rhineland. In his view, Nasser had to be stopped before he could do untold damage to Western interests in the Middle East. Thus, while Eden and his Foreign Secretary, Selwyn Lloyd, strove to avoid another Munich, Eisenhower and his Secretary of State, John Foster

Dulles, played Chamberlain to the Egyptian dictator. Nestling in the pack of future events, ready to upset all their plans, there still lay the wild card of Israel.

When Eden's Cabinet met on 27 July, the day after Nasser's surprise nationalisation announcement, with the Chiefs of Staff present, there was general agreement that a new Munich crisis must not be allowed to develop. The policy agreed was well expressed in Eden's first letter to Eisenhower about the crisis:

> We ought in the first instance to bring the maximum political pressure to bear on Egypt. For this, apart from our own action, we should invoke the support of all the interested powers. My colleagues and I are convinced that we must be ready, in the last resort, to use force to bring Nasser to his senses. For our part we are prepared to do so. I have this morning instructed our Chiefs of Staff to prepare a military plan accordingly.[3]

This letter also reflected the mood of the British electorate at that time. Hugh Gaitskell, the Labour leader of the opposition in the House of Commons, gave Eden his support, saying:

> It is all very familiar. It is exactly the same that we encountered from Hitler and Mussolini before the war . . . I believe we were right to react sharply to his move.[4]

The French were equally incensed and so, it seemed, were the Americans. By 1 August a conference of 22 Maritime powers, including the USSR and the Eastern Bloc countries, met in London to concert world action. A five-point negotiating position was agreed by the three Western Foreign Secretaries – Selwyn Lloyd for Britain, Pineau for France and Dulles for the United States: domination of the Canal by a single power was intolerable without international control; the 1888 Convention should be the basis for negotiation; force should be used in the last resort; world opinion should be mobilised in favour of international operation of the Canal; and a two-thirds majority should be sought amongst the 22 powers for action.

There was, indeed, little divergence of view between Britain, France and the United States at this early stage. The difference lay hidden in the length of negotiating time fuse that each envisaged as reasonable before resorting to the use of force. Britain and France measured the time in weeks rather than months, and intended to use preparations for military action as part of their negotiating strategy. The Americans, with no vital interests at stake and a Presidential election in full swing, saw no reason to hurry, or to use force themselves.

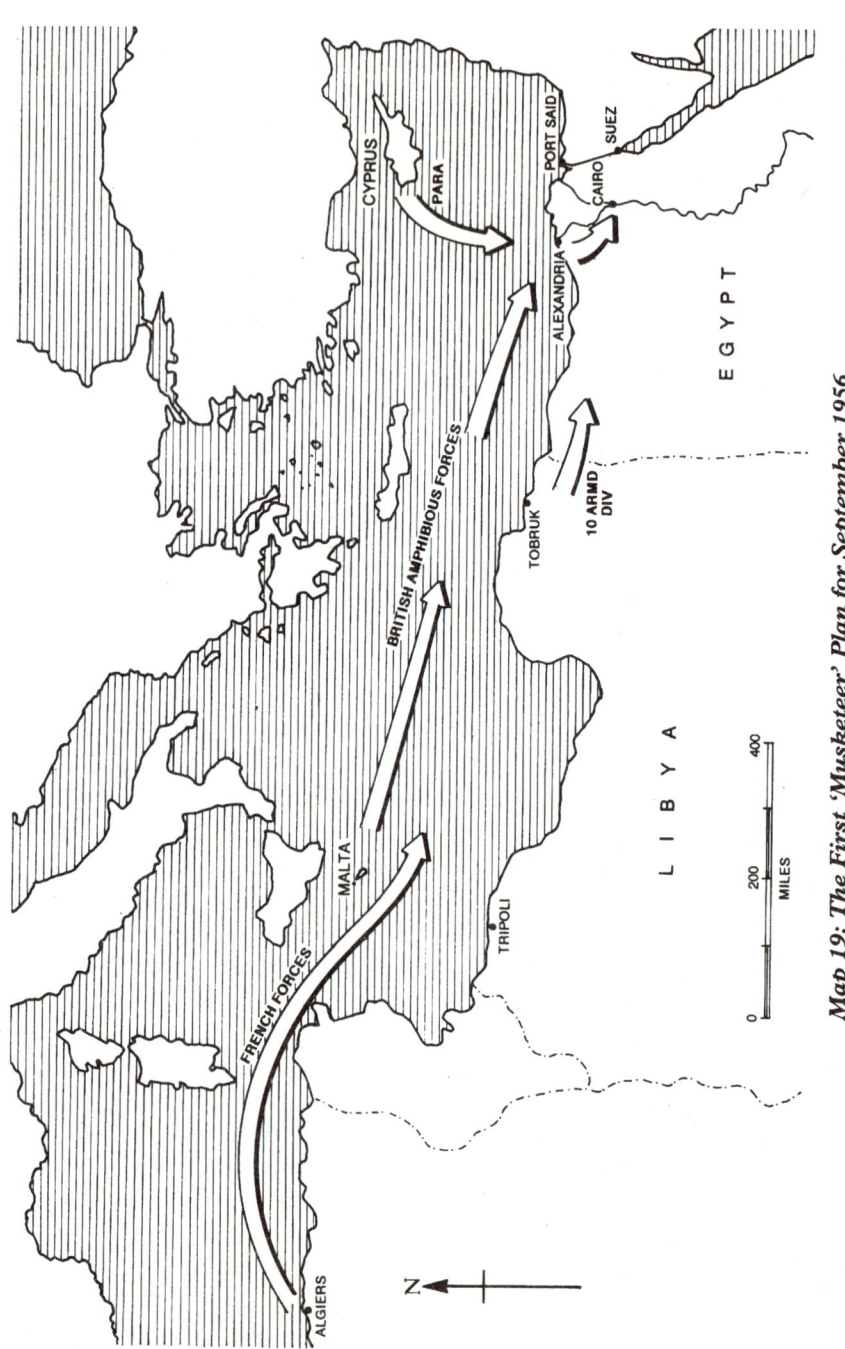

Map 19: The First 'Musketeer' Plan for September 1956

The Uneasy Anglo-American Partnership

The first military contingency plan put to Eden's Cabinet envisaged a force of 80,000 troops (45,000 British and 34,000 French). The plan itself was dictated by the facts of geography and the limited availability of assault shipping and parachute aircraft, most of which had been scrapped since their heyday of the Normandy landings in 1944 and the Rhine Crossing in 1945. There were two obvious points of entry into Egypt from the Mediterranean as there had been in Wolseley's day[5]: Alexandria and Port Said. Alexandria was a deepwater port, requiring a minimum of assault shipping because the quays could be used for landing the main force from ocean-going ships after the port had been seized by parachute and commando landings. Port Said was a lighter port at which few deep draught ships could be brought alongside jetties. Moreover, the hinterland behind Port Said was impeded with canals and inundations and it would be a more difficult breakout towards Cairo than across the desert from Alexandria. As Eden's political objective was to topple Nasser rather than to seize the Canal in the first instance, Alexandria was chosen as the point of entry.

Once Alexandria had been chosen, the plan hinged upon the availability and position of assembly ports. Cyprus was nearest, but it had no deepwater port or secure anchorage, and could only be used as an air and parachute base. Malta was the best assembly area for amphibious forces, but it was several days' sailing from Alexandria. Algiers, the French assembly port for their 7th Division, was even further away, and the main British force, the Strategic Reserve's 3rd Division with its tank and logistic support, was back in England and needed 14 days to reach Alexandria. But there was also the skeletal 10th Armoured Division garrisoning Tobruk port and El Adem airfield, which could advance along Rommel's old desert route to threaten Alexandria from landward.

The *Musketeer* Plan was elegant in its simplicity. Anglo-French aircraft would start the destruction of the Egyptian Air Force two days before British and French parachute troops and commando forces from Cyprus and Malta, and 10th Armoured Division from Tobruk, seized the port of Alexandria, through which the main forces from England and Algiers would be landed. The build-up ashore would take about a week, and then the advance on Cairo would begin, with there being every probability of the decisive battle, like Napoleon's Pyramids and Wolseley's Tel-el-Kebir, being fought not far from the Egyptian capital.

The Chiefs of Staff warned the Cabinet that preparations would take six weeks, and that 20,000 reservists would have to be called up. Mid-September was the earliest time for military action, but the weather would begin to deteriorate by mid-October so the window of opportunity would be very narrow, and it would need considerable diplomatic finesse to bring about conditions for the use of force at exactly the right time from the military point of view. The ideal timings would be:

2 September: Decision to mount *Musketeer*.
3 September: British transports leave English ports.
11 September: French transports leave Algiers.
15 September: Air action begins.
17 September: Airborne and amphibious landings at Alexandria.
24 September   Build-up ashore completed.
Early October: Decisive battle near Cairo.

★ ★ ★

Dulles led the diplomatic minuet, which brought 18 of the 22 Maritime states to agree on six principles on which a replacement of the 1888 Convention should be negotiated with Nasser for international control of the Canal without reversing Nasser's nationalisation of the Canal Company. They were respect for Egypt's sovereignty; freedom of passage for ships of all nations in peacetime; isolation of the Canal from the internal politics of any country; equitable tolls for its use; a fair division of revenue between the Egyptian treasury and the Canal's future development; and the settlement of disputes by international arbitration.

Regrettably, when it came to sending a delegation to Cairo to put these ideas for an equitable solution to Nasser, Dulles declined to lead it and began to distance the United States from the Maritime powers. World reaction to the crisis had shown that the non-aligned Afro-Asian states led by Nehru, and the Eastern Bloc countries, were forming up behind Nasser and were doing their utmost to change the international complexion of the dispute into an anti-colonial crusade. Dulles did not wish to be on the wrong side of world opinion. Worse still, he talked about imposing sanctions and did nothing to introduce them; he would not instruct US shipowners to pay their Canal dues to the Canal Company as the other 18 states had done; and he did not stop American nationals replacing British and French Canal pilots when they were withdrawn as part of the international pressure being applied to Egypt.

In the end, Australia's Prime Minister, Sir Robert Menzies, undertook the leadership of the international delegation which did not leave for Cairo until 3 September, the day on which the *Musketeer* force should have sailed from England. Instead it stayed riding at anchor with only maintenance crews embarked to look after the tanks, guns and vehicles already loaded.

The pause while Menzies was in Cairo gave time for second thoughts all round. The Cabinet had to decide what should be done if the Menzies mission failed. An appeal would clearly have to be made to the Security Council before force could be used, despite Dulles's objections to such a course because of the probability of a Soviet veto. All this would take time and the summer weeks were slipping by all too fast. Moreover, the early support given by Gaitskell, the Labour Party and the trades unions at the start of the crisis for tough action was also evaporating as more and more of the 'chattering classes' in the press and media expressed anxiety about the possible use of force against the trend of Commonwealth and world opinion.

There were politico-military reasons for disquiet as well. Was Alexandria the right target? If the aim was still to topple Nasser, well and good; but Nasser would have to make some aggressive move or fail to keep the Canal traffic flowing before war could be justified. Thanks to the advice of the American Embassy in Cairo, Nasser had not put a foot wrong and showed no sign of doing so. The London Conference had narrowed down the issues to finding a way of establishing an international Canal authority acceptable to Egypt. If a *casus belli* were to emerge, it was likely to be linked directly with the Canal. The political attractions of Port Said rather than Alexandria as the point of entry had been growing more compelling as the weeks went by.

There were doubts also about the plan itself: was it necessary to mount a Normandy-style landing at all? Could not Egypt be brought to accept the internationalisation of the Canal in some way that did not risk high civilian and military casualties? The Air Staff thought that there was: primarily by air action with the *Musketeer* force following up as a temporary occupation force while a settlement was hammered out. The airborne and amphibious assault forces would be retained in readiness at Cyprus and Malta in case air action did not prove decisive. A new plan, *Musketeer (Revised)*, for a ten-day 'aero-political' campaign to break Egypt's resistance was born.

The new concept of operations had obvious political attractions: civilian casualties could be minimised by careful selection of targets; the timing and weight of the attacks could be orchestrated to respond to political needs; and Port Said could be used because speed of the land force build-up would no longer be crucial. There was one military advantage as well: the assault convoys need not be sailed within range of Egyptian Ilyushin bombers (probably manned by Eastern Bloc volunteers) until air superiority had been won. But there were several military disadvantages: landing at Port Said would be slow; and a landing force, if it were needed, could be bottled up amongst the Port Said irrigation canals and inundations, especially if Egypt's Czech tanks and guns were manned by East European 'volunteers'. But the greatest disadvantage of all was not squarely faced by the Chiefs of Staff, although the Naval and Army staffs did have grave doubts about the new plan. The RAF's bombing capacity had neither the weight nor accuracy in those pre-high tech days to destroy the Egyptian will to resist quickly enough before world political opprobrium forced a cease fire. The Foreign Office was, nevertheless, convinced that the first bomb falling on Egypt would be decisive in returning Nasser to the negotiating table, and so the Chiefs acquiesced in this premature attempt to use virtually unsupported air power.

* * *

Unknown to anyone but the French, the Israeli wild card was about to be played. Although not enamoured of the 'aero-psychological' plan, the French high command favoured the switch to Port Said for its own clandestine reasons. French supplies of arms to Israel had brought the French and Israeli General Staffs into close liaison. The possibility of an Israeli autumn offensive against Egypt had been evident in Paris for some time. Nasser's constant harping on the theme of the coming destruction of Israel; the build-up of Czech-supplied arms to Egypt; the intensification of Arab guerrilla raids into Israel; the Egyptian refusal to allow Israeli ships through the Suez Canal; and the siting of Egyptian guns on the tip of the Sinai peninsula at Sharm el Sheikh to close the Gulf of Aqaba, all added

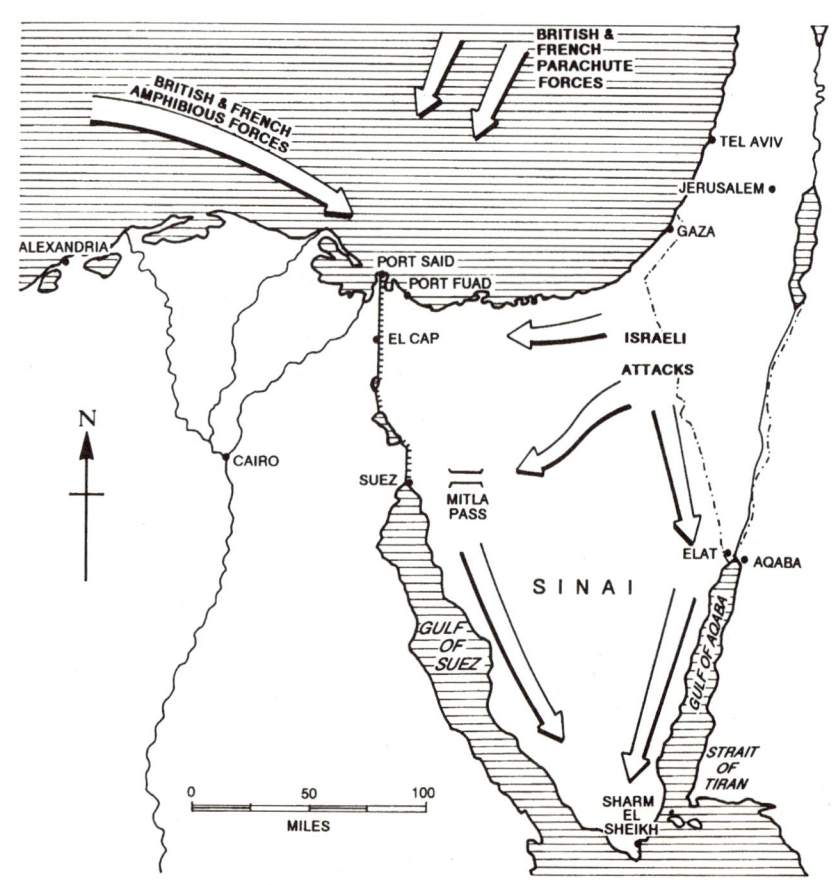

Map 20: The Anglo-French and Israeli Attacks on Egypt in November 1956

up to a threat that Israel could not ignore. The launch of *Musketeer* would provide the ideal opportunity for an Israeli pre-emptive strike against Egypt. The French General Staff appreciated that the greatest help that France could give Israel was air and naval support, which could best be provided during landings at Port Said rather than Alexandria.

Secret Franco-Israeli military planning started in September while Menzies was in Cairo. The Israelis planned to launch their three available divisions in succession against Nasser's Sinai garrison of one Egyptian and one Palestinian division, assuming that the Anglo-French force, landing at Port Said, would neutralise Nasser's main reserves in the Canal Zone. Three axes of advance would be used. The initial advance, designed to throw the Egyptians off balance, would be a wide turning movement in the south, aimed at the Mitla Pass only 40 miles from Suez. The main assaults would be along the central routes, used by Kress von Kressenstein in the First World War, and along the coast. Subsequently the Gaza strip would be occupied and the guns at Sharm el Sheikh destroyed. The French and Israeli governments were quite prepared to go it alone if the British pulled back at the last moment. British co-operation, however, would be a welcome bonus: benevolent neutrality was all that the plotters needed. The greatest service Britain could render the Franco-Israeli cause was to keep the United States neutral as well.

★ ★ ★

The Menzies mission failed because it did not have the whole-hearted backing of the Eisenhower administration, and Nasser knew that he had Soviet and Afro-Asian support. In desperation, the British and French Governments, in spite of United States' opposition, did finally submit their case for the internationalisation of the Canal to the Security Council early in October. A consensus was articulated in a two-part resolution. In the first, the 18 users' six principles were restated and passed unanimously on 13 October. The second set out Menzies' management proposals and was vetoed by the Soviet Union and Yugoslavia. Eden now feared that he would be forced by the United States Government and British public opinion into another Munich to end the crisis, leaving Nasser, like Hitler, stronger and more ambitious than ever. Cairo rather than Baghdad would become the capital of the Arab world with the Anglophobe Nasser as its undisputed leader. The French, however, had fewer inhibitions about world opinion as far as their national interests were concerned: they were determined that Nasser was to be toppled in collaboration with Israel whatever the Anglo-Americans might do.

After the rebuff in New York, Eden was in honour bound to concert future plans with the French Prime Minister, Guy Mollet, while the UN Secretary General, Dag Hammarskjöld sought other ways of resolving the crisis. Eden, accompanied by Selwyn Lloyd, flew to Paris on 16 October and conferred with Mollet and Pineau, his Foreign minister with no staff present. How much collusion there was will not be revealed until either the British or French government opens its files on the affair to public scrutiny. However, the degree of co-operation with Israel fades into insignificance against three glaring errors of political judgement made by Eden and his closest ministerial colleagues. They did not keep Eisenhower or Dulles informed, nor indeed did they make any attempt to carry them along with their plan. They chose a *casus belli*, which lacked national and international credibility. And, in the event, they stopped short of their objective of toppling Nasser, as the Americans were to do 25 years later with Saddam Hussein.

On 17 October a diplomatic and military blackout descended in Whitehall and Paris. Washington was totally excluded as were all but the most senior officers in Whitehall. The final positioning of British and French air, airborne and amphibious forces assigned to *Musketeer (Revised)* at Malta and Cyprus was completed, and on 20 October the follow-up from England and Algiers set sail. Three days later, the world's attention was distracted by the Soviet invasion of Hungary, and Nasser announced the formation of an Arab joint military command embracing Egypt, Syria and Jordan, tasked with the destruction of Israel. On 26 October Israel mobilised, and on 29 October invaded Sinai.

Collusion with Israel seemed confirmed by the speed with which Eden and Mollet issued ultimatums to Egypt and Israel to cease fire, withdraw to 10 miles either side of the Canal, and accept the temporary reoccupation of the Canal Zone by British and French forces. An answer was required within twelve hours. To highlight Anglo-French determination the British amphibious force was sailed from Malta: the French force, from Algiers, was already at sea. The combined amphibious forces could not be off Port Said before 6 November.

The Israelis accepted the ultimatum: they had nothing to lose by doing so as their troops were still some distance from the Canal. The Egyptians with Soviet backing did not. At 4.15pm on 31 October, British Valiant and Canberra bombers took off from Cyprus to start the neutralisation of the Egyptian Air Force and the 'aero-psychological' campaign. If Nasser did not return to the negotiating table by 5 November, the Anglo-French parachute and amphibious forces would start the reoccupation of the Canal Zone. The timings envisaged were: Port Said 6 November; Ismailia 11 November; Suez 12 November. The five-day gap between Port Said and Ismailia covered the expected slowness of the discharge rate of the troop and store ships at Port Said.

Under normal circumstances, six days of increasing military pressure should have allowed time for decisive diplomatic action, but circumstances were not normal. The high-handed Anglo-French action smacked too much of 19th-Century gunboat diplomacy. It united most of the world and at least half of the British electorate against Eden's Government. At least tacit American support was needed for success and was expected by Eden, but outright hostility took its place.

Eden's and Mollet's cabinets gravely misjudged the effect of their actions upon Eisenhower and Dulles. Harold Macmillan, Eden's Chancellor of the Exchequer, had been a close colleague of Eisenhower's when he was his British political adviser at Algiers during the campaigns in French North Africa, Sicily and Italy in 1943. He had also got to know Dulles well as Eden's Foreign Secretary in 1955. In his memoirs, Macmillan takes full responsibility for the Cabinet's underestimate of the wave of resentment that surged through the minds of the two American leaders and their closest advisers when they heard of their allies' unilateral action. Macmillan had advised the Cabinet that the Americans would probably protest vigorously in public, but in private would be relieved that decisive action was being taken without involving the United States.

The Eisenhower/Dulles reaction was as emotionally illogical as it was unexpected. They had consistently opposed an approach to the United Nations and had refused to enforce the lightest of economic sanctions against Egypt like withholding Canal tolls and discouraging US nationals from replacing British and French Canal pilots. And yet, when British, French and Israeli patience ran out, they rushed to the Security Council and joined Soviet Russia in impeaching their allies and imposing the most vicious economic sanctions that they could devise: refusal to allow Britain to withdraw funds from the IMF to support Sterling; deliberate selling of pounds by the Federal Reserve Bank; and a refusal to make up lost Middle East oil with American supplies at a reasonable price. It seemed as if the United States was trying to complete some unfinished business left over from the Great American Rebellion of 1776 by humiliating their erstwhile enemy and ally of those far-off days.

★ ★ ★

The Egyptian Air Force was destroyed in the estimated 48 hours, its surviving aircraft being flown out of range to Luxor and Saudi airfields. Cairo Radio was put off the air, but such was the world outcry against the bombing that oil targets, the destruction of which would have made life in Cairo very uncomfortable, were deleted from the target list. Nevertheless, the reverse was not the case: the Syrians blew up the British oil pipelines from Iraq to the Mediterranean coast, but left the American Aramco Tap Line intact. At the same time, the Egyptians started scuttling block-ships in the Canal. As the aircraft carriers of the amphibious force came within range, their planes started attacks on military targets in the Canal Zone.

There was no diplomatic breakthrough by the evening of 4 November.

Next morning, the 3rd Parachute Battalion dropped on and took Gamal airfield a few miles west of Port Said, and the French paratroopers took Port Fuad on the eastern side of the Canal's entrance (Port Said is on the western side). Next day, the Royal Marine Commandos started to land by helicopter and landing-craft on the Port Said seashore, and tank-landing ships started putting tanks ashore. On neither day was opposition negligible, but it was swept aside and all regular resistance had ceased in Port Said and Port Fuad by the evening of 6 November as planned. The unloading of the main force could begin.

In London, the success of the landings was overshadowed by the threats of dire consequences emanating from both Moscow and Washington. Bulganin sent letters to Eden, Mollet and Ben-Gurion, threatening to intervene with 'volunteers' and, if need be, atomic weapons. This *démarche* worried Washington more than London, where it was seen as a cynical attempt to divide the NATO allies and to consolidate the Soviet penetration of the Middle East, turning Egypt into a Russian satellite. Eisenhower, who was about to be re-elected President on his 'Man of Peace' ticket, phoned Eden during the morning of 6 November and gave him a brutally phrased ultimatum: cease-fire by midnight or forfeit Anglo-American friendship and solidarity. Hoping that compliance would lead to a more constructive and realistic policy, Eden accepted the ultimatum in good faith and ordered a cease-fire for midnight 6–7 November without waiting for Ismailia and Suez to be occupied, thus completing the reoccupation of the Canal Zone, which was well within his grasp, given another 12 hours. His hopes were not to be realised.

General Sir Hugh Stockwell, who was commanding the landings, received his orders for a midnight cease-fire at 5pm. A dynamic, forceful character, he must have been sorely tempted to ignore the order as Nelson did at the battle of Copenhagen in 1801, putting his telescope to his blind eye, but modern communications made that impossible for him. Collecting as many tanks and vehicles of the 6th Royal Tank Regiment as were ashore by that time, he sent them off with the 2nd Parachute Battalion down the west bank of the Canal towards Ismailia with orders to halt and go onto the defensive at whatever point they reached by midnight. There was no opposition. They just managed to reach El Cap, 23 miles from Port Said, by midnight and halted there. They could have been in Suez, another 78 miles south, by dawn. The reoccupation could then have been completed in slower time without breaching the ceasefire as troops came ashore from the follow-up convoys at Port Said.

During the six days of *Musketeer*, the Israelis had cleared Sinai, Sharm el Sheikh and the Gaza Strip, but the Americans held all the cards and their policy did not soften in the wake of the cease-fire. By not occupying the whole length of the canal, British and French naval clearance teams could not remove the 17 sunken ships from the Canal, and without their removal the flow of oil from the Persian Gulf could not be restored and the steep US increase in the Western hemisphere oil price represented the imposition of oil sanctions in all but name. A United Nations Emergency Force started to arrive in the Canal Zone on 19 November to enable the British and French troops to withdraw. They were all away by Christmas 1956, but the Israelis, made of sterner stuff and with more to lose held out until 8 March before withdrawing from Sinai. The Canal was reopened to oil tankers on 25 March.

Nasser had survived thanks to the two superpowers ganging up to put the old colonial powers in their place. His power, influence and ambition to lead the Arab and Moslem worlds was immeasurably enhanced. The Americans seemed to have come a step nearer to fashioning the world after their own image with the United Nations under their leadership becoming the final arbiter of world affairs. But in reality they had saddled themselves with the political problems of the Middle East. If Nasser had been toppled, Israel might have reached a *modus vivendi* with her Arab neighbours. Instead she was forced to retain her wild card status to America's detriment for the rest of the century.

CHAPTER 5

AMERICA TAKES OVER
The Israeli Wild Card 1957–78

> *Whenever a new president arrives in the Oval Office, the system changes because he brings with him a new set of advisers and associates, a conception of his own interest, and a new attitude towards the proper policy roles of the bureaucracy, Congress, and interest groups. Each President sets the rules and helps determine the victors in the war for Washington that is waged between the Arabs, the Israelis, and their respective American supporters.*
>
> Steven Spiegel in The Other Arab–Israeli Conflict.[1]

The Suez crisis did three things: it transferred the mantle of Western leadership in the Middle East, which Britain had worn for over a century and a half, to the United States; it determined the British to accelerate their premeditated withdrawal from empire; and it gave Nasser the temporary leadership of the Arab world. It did surprisingly little real damage to Anglo-American relations. There were guilty consciences on both sides of the Atlantic: Eden had acted out of desperation with Dulles's devious diplomacy, without consulting Eisenhower; and Eisenhower had pulled the rug out from under Sterling in a fit of 'holier than thou' pique. The whole affair, although irritating at the time, was a relatively minor aberration within the larger context of the Cold War in which Britain was America's closest ally. They could not fall out for long without doing irreparable damage to the Western Alliance, and gratuitously presenting the Soviets with lucrative political and military opportunities in the Middle East.

Before the Suez Canal was cleared of sunken Egyptian block-ships and re-opened to shipping in March 1957, fence-mending between London and Washington was well under way. The process was helped by the personal friendship of Eisenhower and Harold Macmillan, who had taken over as Prime Minister from the ailing Eden in January. Like Churchill, Macmillan had an American mother and was attuned to the processes of American thought and prejudices. And the British Chiefs of Staff had all served with their American colleagues in the Second World war and still kept in close touch with each other bilaterally and through NATO. Rapport was re-established at the Bermuda Conference between

Eisenhower and Macmillan in March 1957 when 'interdependence' became the name of the game. Powerful though the United States had become, both men recognised that even the Americans could not go it alone against the combined hostility of Russian and Chinese Communism. Britain would provide active political and military support when and wherever she was in a position to do so – with one unspoken exception. She would distance herself from Israel: her oil supplies depended upon Arab friendship.

Picking up the mantle, which the British were only too happy to bequeath to their American cousins, was no easy task. The Americans were the first to admit that they lacked the British depth of experience in the region, and they hamstrung themselves with their determination not to be seen as the new imperialists. They chose to depend on political pressure, backed by economic aid and arms deals rather than gunboats and bayonets.

But their greatest problem lay in their own policy-making system in Washington, which has an inherent inconsistency about it. The President as Chief Executive has to heed the advice not only of his party in Congress, the bureaucracies of the great departments of state and his own appointed staff in the White House, but also the aggressively presented demands of vote-catching Congressional lobbies, representing ethnic, commercial, industrial and other interests, and, of course, the pressures created by the press and media. The eventual outcome of any foreign policy debate depends upon the personal background, thinking and whims of each President, and upon the decision-making process that he establishes in the White House. All are different. For instance, Truman lacked a formal decision-making process, and so he was influenced more by outside lobbyists than by the officials of the State and Defence Departments. While official Washington was pro-Arab, Truman was swayed in favour of the Jews by Congressional pressure, the powerful Zionist lobby and his own biblical readings. Eisenhower, on the other hand, as a former Supreme Allied Commander, had a highly structured decision-making system, which filtered out extraneous advice and gave the bureaucracy, and hence the Arabs, the advantage.

The canker at the heart of American Middle East policy during the latter half of the 20th Century was Israel. Official Washington argued that United States' and Western interests depended more upon Arab friendship than Israeli survival. The US Joint Chiefs of Staff were particularly anxious that American support for Israel should never so alienate the Arabs as to drive them into the Soviet Bloc, as Dulles's handling of Nasser had shown was all too likely. Nevertheless, Congress, the American electorate and the powerful Jewish organisations took the opposite view. While acknowledging increasing Western dependence on Arab oil, they were determined that Israel should not only survive, but should become a prosperous, civilised

Western bridgehead in a potentially hostile Arab world. Furthermore, all Presidents of the United States, apart from Eisenhower, were strongly influenced by the Jewish vote in domestic politics. As Harry Truman is reported to have remarked, he had numerous Jewish constituents and very few Arabs.

★ ★ ★

For Britain, Suez was a blessing in disguise. Plans were already being drawn up to end National Service and to revert to Britain's traditional volunteer all regular armed forces. Indeed, while one half of the War Office staff was calling out reservists to flesh out the *Musketeer* force for the Suez operation, the other half was planning the rundown to a much smaller regular army. To make the manpower books balance, there had to be root and branch pruning of overseas commitments. It was tacitly agreed between London and Washington that the United States should take the lead in Egypt and the Levant while Britain continued to support the Gulf States and provide the Western naval presence in the Indian Ocean and the Persian Gulf.

Macmillan charged two men with the task of doing the pruning. Churchill's son-in-law, Duncan Sandys, was appointed Minister of Defence to do the military side of the exercise, while Iain McLeod was made Colonial Secretary to do the commitment slicing. Sandys offered two military solutions: dependence on nuclear weapons would allow Britain's forces in Europe to be drastically reduced; and dependence upon centrally held air-transported and amphibious forces would allow overseas garrisons to be cut back and in some cases eliminated altogether. McLeod argued that the tide of post-war nationalism within Britain's dependent territories was running too strongly to be resisted by military means. The alternative was to speed up their progress to independence. Macmillan accepted his thesis and made the policy of Britain's accelerated withdrawal from empire public in his famous 'Wind of Change' speech in Cape Town in 1960.

In the Middle East, Aden was the only British colony as such, but Britain was the protecting power with longstanding treaty obligations to the Gulf and South Arabian sheikhdoms. With the Suez Canal in the area of American influence, Britain's main strategic concern became the free and uninterrupted flow of cheap oil from Iraq and Iran through the Gulf to Europe. British oilmen and the leaders of commercial firms trading in the Gulf believed that it was time to revert to the 18th-Century practice of working with the Gulf sheikhdoms on the basis of mutual benefit without the backing of British gunboats and bayonets, which only served to exacerbate Arab nationalism at traders' expense. They appreciated that any precipitate withdrawal of the British military presence would create instability and open the door to Soviet infiltration. Plans were, therefore, drawn up to encourage the Sheikhs to raise and equip their own local defence forces with the help of British training teams so that British forces could be gradually phased out. Contingency plans were also laid for intervention by Britain's recently formed air-mobile strategic reserves, which were being stationed in the United Kingdom, Kenya and Singapore.

Aden's original *raison d'être*, when Britain annexed it in 1839, was as a coaling station on the route to India. It was a hot, barren and uncomfortable hell-hole of a place to garrison. The War Office had resisted turning it into a major base after the withdrawal from the Suez Canal Zone in 1955, and, under McLeod's Colonial Office plans, Aden was to be groomed for early independence as the capital of a new South Arabian Federation, embracing the Eastern and Western Aden Protectorates in its hinterland. It was soon found, however, that both Singapore and Kenya were too far away from the Gulf for rapid intervention operations. The limitations of aircraft range and payload in the 1960s forced Aden into the role of an advanced operating base to enable Britain to meet her military obligations in the Gulf. Despite the best of intentions, Aden grew into a sizeable base with a plethora of new barracks and married quarters to make living conditions just about tolerable for long-service regular troops and their families.

★ ★ ★

In the 1960s and 1970s it was Egypt and the Levant rather than the Persian Gulf which dominated Middle Eastern affairs. Despite opposing Britain and France in toppling Nasser in 1956, the Eisenhower administration had few illusions about Nasser's ambitions to become the leader of the Arab world, but they saw little harm in this. What worried them was not his Arab nationalism, but his close ties with the Soviet Union, which had provided him with the cash for the Aswan Dam and equipment for his armed forces. As soon as the Israelis had withdrawn from the Canal and Sharm el Sheikh in March 1957, Eisenhower flexed America's military muscles by persuading Congress to accept the Eisenhower Doctrine whereby US forces would be used to support any Middle East state that asked for help to thwart an armed take-over by another state controlled by international communism. Eisenhower described his doctrine as:

> The US resolve to block the Soviet Union's march to the Mediterranean, to the Suez Canal and the pipelines; and to the underground lake of oil which fuels the homes and factories of Western Europe.[2]

Laudable though his doctrine may have been in the Cold War scenario, it was aimed at the wrong target. Communism had little appeal in the Moslem world, but the Arab states had learnt from Nasser how to blackmail both superpowers into providing arms and economic aid. It was Arab nationalism, as peddled by Nasser in Cairo, which was the real and immediate threat to Western interests.

It was not long before the Eisenhower Doctrine was put to the test, but not by a communist threat. In February 1958, Nasser announced the creation of the United Arab Republic, comprising Egypt, Syria and later the Yemen, the aim of which was to accomplish the destruction of Israel with Eastern Bloc support. Although all Arab states were dedicated to this aim, the Hashemite monarchies of Iraq and Jordan, and the Christian Maronite-governed Lebanon were not prepared to accept Nasser's leadership. In consequence, he placed them on his political 'hit list'. Nasser-style 'Free Officers' cells were established in the Iraqi and Jordanian armies with revolutionary intent. At the beginning of July 1958, Brigadier Kassim marched into Baghdad with his brigade. He overthrew the monarchy, brutally assassinated the Royal family and the pro-British Prime Minister, Nuri al-Said, and set up a military dictatorship favourable to Moscow although not as friendly to Egypt as Nasser might have hoped: Kassim was his own man with more Communist than Nasserite supporters.

Anglo-American intelligence agencies warned that similar coups were being hatched in Lebanon and Jordan. Neither Eisenhower nor Macmillan hesitated when requests for military support were received from both threatened governments. US Marines landed at Beirut from the US 6th Fleet on 15 July; and the British 16th Parachute Brigade was flown from Cyprus into Amman with air support two days later after an initial, but short-lived, refusal by the Israeli Government to sanction the over-flying of its territory. The British troops in Jordan were supplied from Aden via the port of Aqaba. Both operations were successful in preempting the Nasser inspired coups. Macmillan commented caustically in his memoirs on the marked change in American attitudes since Suez:

Not merely in words but deeds, a recantation – an act of penitence – unparalleled in history.[3]

Eisenhower's use of the US Marines in Beirut was in true imperialist style, but it was the last time that American troops were to be deployed in the Middle East before the trauma of Vietnam temporarily undermined American military confidence. However, the United States did at last join the Baghdad Pact, extending NATO's flank from Turkey through Iran to Pakistan. Dulles, although the original instigator of the pact, had backed off when he found it was bitterly opposed by Egypt and the Afro-Asian bloc, leaving Britain to bring it into being. Kassim's coup in Baghdad forced the move of the Pact's headquarters to Ankara where it was renamed the Central Treaty Organisation (CENTO) in the following year.

Despite American and British military intervention in the Lebanon and Jordan, Nasser's influence continued to spread throughout the Moslem world. The raucous propaganda of the 'Voice of the Arabs', broadcast from Cairo Radio, blared out in every *souk* from Morocco to Pakistan and beyond. Egyptian agents were active all over the Middle East, creating Nasserite fifth columns in all the conservative Arab states. At the Sultan of Oman's request, British troops were sent from Aden and Kenya in the summer of 1958 to help crush a Nasser-inspired rebellion, which broke out in central Oman. The Sultan's writ was soon re-established throughout his domains except in the mountain fastnesses of the formidable Djebel Akhdar. In January 1959, Lieutenant Colonel Tony Deane-Drummond's 22nd SAS Regiment was returning to England from jungle operations against the Chinese Communist terrorists in Malaya and was diverted to Aden to deal with the Djebel Akhdar. In a short but brilliantly conducted campaign, in which Captain Peter de la Billière, the future British commander in *Desert Storm*, led a troop, the mountain was scaled and the rebels driven into exile. It was the first time that the Djebel Akhdar had been stormed by foreign troops since the Persians took it in the Tenth Century!

* * *

The Sandys' policy of depending upon air-transported and amphibious forces rather than garrisons was again put to the test in June 1961 when the British protectorate of Kuwait was replaced by the Anglo-Kuwaiti Defence Agreement. Brigadier Kassim immediately laid claim to Kuwait, as Saddam Hussein was to do in 1990. Kassim, with some historic justification, argued that Kuwait had been part of the former Ottoman province of Basra and hence was Iraqi territory. British intelligence gave a warning of his movement of tanks southwards by rail from Baghdad to the Kuwaiti border, and on 28 June Macmillan authorised the assembly of an intervention force at Bahrain and Aden, and the dispatch of an amphibious force to the Gulf, which was to lie 'over the horizon' off Kuwait ready to react to the Ruler's request for help under the Anglo-Kuwaiti Defence Agreement.

Fortuitously, the new commando-carrier *Bulwark* was just finishing hot weather trials in the Indian Ocean with 42nd Royal Marine Commando embarked. She was sailed to the Gulf to join three frigates and the Amphibious Squadron carrying tanks, which were already there. At Aden the 3rd Carabiniers were ready to fly north to man tanks stockpiled in Kuwait under the Defence Agreement; and the 11th Hussars with armoured cars and 45th RM Commando were alerted to follow them. In Kenya there was Brigadier Derek Horsford's 24th Infantry Brigade of the Strategic Reserve, and in Cyprus the 16th Parachute

Brigade was also available if needed. Air support was to be provided by two fighter squadrons of Hunters and four Shackleton bombers from Aden, and by a Canberra squadron flown out from Germany.

On 30 June, the Ruler did request British military assistance to deter or pre-empt an Iraqi invasion. Early next day *Bulwark* landed 42nd RM Commando by helicopter on Kuwait's airport; the Hunters were flown in; and the tanks of the Amphibious Squadron were unloaded in the port. By evening the first battalion and the headquarters of 24th Brigade were being flown in from Kenya; 45th RM Commando and two companies of Coldstream Guards were arriving from Aden and Bahrain; and the tanks of the Carabiniers were moving up to support the Kuwaiti army deployed in defensive positions on the Mutla ridge north of the city. There had been a slight delay in flying the Canberras from Germany while diplomatic action was taken to persuade Turkey and the Sudan to allow over-flying, which they had refused initially.

By the end of the first week, Brigadier Horsford, who was appointed force commander, had the equivalent of five battalions with artillery, tank and air support ready to meet the Iraqi invasion. Kassim backed down, but the whole affair was a useful exercise in strategic mobility and deterrence. The operation had not been faultless because the necessary air transport and amphibious shipping were not as yet available and improvisation had been the order of the day. Nevertheless, it was a far cry from the ponderous Normandy-style amphibious deployment during the Suez crisis.

By this time Nasser was beginning to overreach himself. His United Arab Republic had broken up during 1961 when the Syrians refused to tolerate the centralising activities of Nasser's bureaucracy in Cairo. Then the old Imam Ahmed of the Yemen died in September 1962 and was succeeded by his son, al Badr. He was immediately overthrown in an Egyptian-inspired republican revolution led by General Sallal. Unfortunately for Nasser and Sallal, al Badr had not been killed as first reported, and managed, with Saudi support, to raise the mountain tribes in a royalist counter-revolution, leading to a long and bloody civil war. Nasser intervened on Sallal's side with 20,000 of his best troops. The Americans, despite strong British misgivings, overprecipitately recognised Sallal's regime on the grounds that it could hardly be worse than the autocratic regime of the old Imam. Before doing so, they were given categoric assurances by Nasser that he would withdraw his troops from the Yemen. He did just the opposite, reinforcing Sallal and creating a Vietnam for himself in an unwinnable five-year civil war. At its peak, 70,000 Egyptian troops – half the Egyptian Army – were sucked into the fighting. The drain on Nasser's resources did much to diminish his chances of destroying Israel and of making himself master of the Arab world.

★ ★ ★

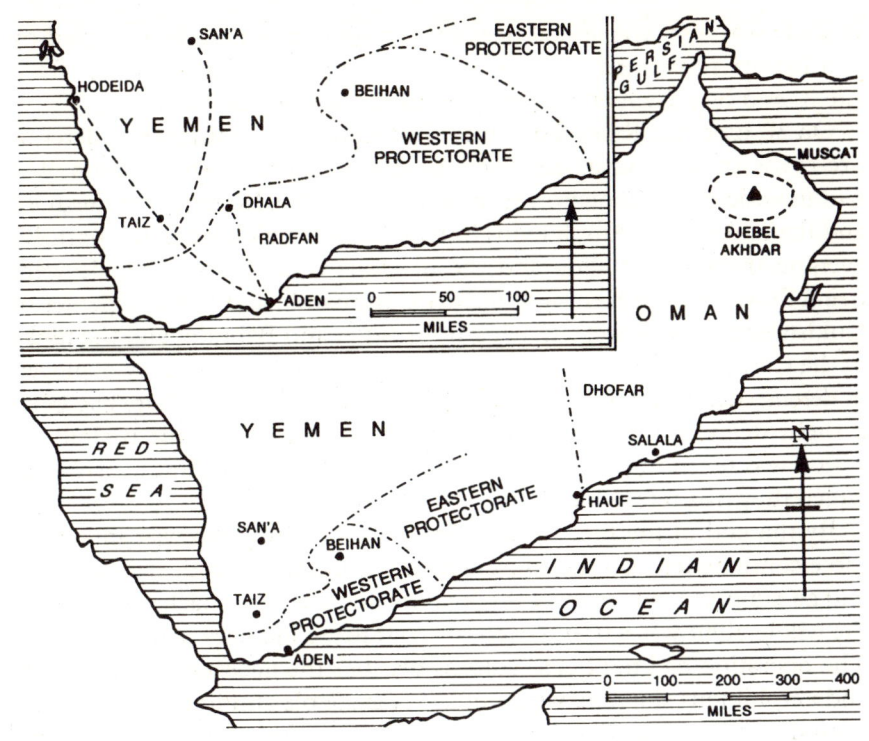

Map 21: The Aden Protectorate

Sallal's revolution in the Yemen had a direct and immediate effect on Aden. The local opponents of British rule in Aden – largely the Aden Trades Union Council, whose membership was dominated by Yemenis working in the large BP oil refinery – jumped on the revolutionary bandwagon and started demanding union with the Yemen rather than membership of the British-sponsored South Arabian Federation, which Aden eventually joined in January 1963. Cairo was not slow to use the Yemen as a base from which to try to drive the British out of what the Arab nationalists called 'Occupied South Yemen'. A National Liberation Front (NLF) was formed to pursue a terrorist campaign in Aden, which was to be supported by strikes and rioting organised by the Aden Trades Unions Council and its political wing, the Peoples Socialist Party (PSP). The first terrorist bomb of the earliest NLF campaign was lobbed at the Governor, Sir Kennedy Trevaskis, as he was boarding an aircraft with several Federal Government ministers to fly back to London in December 1963 for a constitutional conference. The Governor was unhurt but there were two killed, including the Governor's Assistant, who shielded him from the blast, and 52 injured. A state of emergency was declared and 280 Yemeni undesirables were deported and 57 Adeni subversives detained.

Nasser's agents were also active amongst the tribes in the mountainous Radfan, 60 miles north of Aden. They had little difficulty in persuading the tribal leaders that the British were on their way out and no longer had the power to stop them reverting to their favourite way of making a living – robbing caravans on the Dhalah road, running north from Aden to the Yemen. The tribes soon found that the British could still bite. In January 1964, Brigadier James Lunt, the commander of South Arabia's Federal Regular Army (FRA) – an amalgam of the old Aden Protectorate Levies and the Tribal Guards – led a highly successful punitive operation in the Radfan. When his force was eventually withdrawn, Cairo Radio, and its satellites in the Yemen, blared out totally fabricated stories of the great victories won by 'the wolves of the Radfan' in their struggle for 'the liberation of Occupied South Yemen'.

Attacks on the Dhala road started again in April and triggered the series of operations by British and Federal troops known as the Radfan Campaign. So stretched was the British Army at that time, with operations in progress in Cyprus, East Africa and Borneo, that calls had to be made on NATO for the release of units for the Radfan. NATO made no difficulties because it was US policy to encourage Britain to continue her role East of Suez. While reinforcements were awaited, an *ad hoc* force from the Aden garrison was assembled under Brigadier Louis Hargroves, consisting of 45th RM Commando, 3rd Parachute Battalion, 1st East Anglians and two FRA battalions with artillery, armoured car and air support. In fighting reminiscent of the North West Frontier of India with temperatures around 120 degrees, and with helicopters to help picketing the heights, a useful foothold was gained within the Radfan fastnesses from which pacification operations could be launched as soon as reinforcements from Europe could arrive. This success was not achieved without loss, and the tribesmen's reputation for brutality was soon confirmed when the international press carried pictures of the heads of two SAS soldiers, killed in action, on public display in the nearby Yemeni town of Taiz.

Brigadier 'Monkey' Blacker (later General Sir Cecil) arrived with his HQ 39th Brigade from Northern Ireland in May, together with the King's Own Scottish Borderers and the Royal Scots. Using the five available British and two FRA battalions, Blacker forced the submission of most of the dissidents by the end of October. In the final battle, the 3rd Parachute Battalion roped themselves down into the Wadi Dhubsan canyon, surprised and defeated the main dissident force. During the action, the Scout helicopter carrying the CO, Lieutenant Colonel Farrar-Hockley (later General Sir Anthony), was forced down by hostile rifle fire. The pilot managed to land just near enough to the forward troops for them to rescue Farrar-Hockley and the crew. As tribal opposition faded away, Blacker instituted an energetic 'hearts and minds' campaign, which did much to bring about the final pacification of the region when the tribes made their formal submission to the Federal Government in March 1965.

In an attempt to defuse the Aden situation, Duncan Sandys, who was now Colonial Secretary, announced that South Arabia would be granted its independence not later than 1968. Aden would continue to be a British military base under a Defence Treaty to be negotiated with the Federal Government. Sandys expected his announcement to generate an atmosphere of co-operation in the run-up to independence. It did nothing of the sort: it heralded a vicious internal struggle between the various factions in Aden to inherit the British mantle. Political groups vied with each other in demonstrating their virility by their attacks on the British.

When Harold Wilson won the October 1964 General Election, he tasked Denis Healey, as Defence Secretary, to carry out a ruthless Defence Review to help the ailing British economy by reducing military expenditure. The recent fighting in the Radfan, and the opening of a major NLF terrorist campaign in Aden in November 1964, strengthened the school of thought in Whitehall, which believed that the presence of British troops in Arab lands endangered rather than protected British interests, and that it was perverse to keep a military base in a place where the local inhabitants were hostile. Moreover, the Labour Party had a deep-seated suspicion of the unelected sheikhs who together comprised the Federal Government of South Arabia. The writing was on the wall for the Aden base.

Denis Healey's first Defence Review, published in February 1965, laid down three principles for handling overseas commitments: Britain would not, in future, undertake military operations without allies; nor accept military obligations unless the host nation would provide base facilities; and would not maintain a base in an independent country against its wishes. The case against the Aden base was so strong that Wilson announced that it would be abandoned within two years. There would be a modest increase in the British military presence within the Persian Gulf, principally at Bahrain, Sharjah and Masira island, off the Muscat-Oman coast, where British forces were still welcome. Singapore would continue to be the main British base East of Suez for as long as its government agreed 'acceptable terms'; and negotiations were to be started for an alternative base in Australia – negotiations which withered on the vine as Britain's financial position worsened.

There were few tears shed over the decision to abandon the barren rocks of Aden, but there was general agreement in London that everything possible should be done to give the young South Arabian Federal Government a reasonable start as an independent state. The effort was totally unavailing: the sheikhs in the Protectorates started to reinsure with the Yemen or Saudi Arabia, and the Adenis intensified their local struggle for power to the point of civil war. As ever, the British soldiers rose to the occasion as they tried to keep the powderkeg from exploding. They were mostly young national servicemen in their late teens or early twenties, who accepted the discomfort of the heat and squalor of the Arab back streets, the dangers of ambush and sniping, and the frustration of applying the principle of the use of minimum force against an unseen enemy, who played to no such rules. Loyalty to the reputations of their regiments played a greater part in their minds than any sense of political purpose in their being in Aden.

By the beginning of 1967, the two main contenders to form the future government of Aden were the NLF and a grouping of left-wing factions calling themselves the Front for the Liberation of Occupied South Yemen (FLOSY). British troops could do little more than hold the ring while these two fought each other for local supremacy. Then the Arab defeat by Israel in the Six Day War in June brought Aden to boiling point. Cairo Radio started blaring out totally unfounded accusations that the Israeli victory was all due to American and British help. Nasser's 'big lie' caused mutinies in the Federal Army and Aden Police. On 20 June, Federal soldiers ambushed a 3-ton truck carrying Royal Corps of Transport men back from rifle practice on a range near the airfield, killing eight and wounding another eight; and several civilian cars were shot up and the occupants killed.

The Federal Army mutiny was quickly crushed at the cost of another British soldier's life and 13 more wounded, but not quickly enough to stop the wildest rumours of British intervention reaching the armed police barracks in the Crater – the old city of Aden. Thinking that they would be attacked next, the police manned the walls with riflemen and machine-guns. By mischance, two British landrovers containing two officers and seven men from the Royal Northumberland Fusiliers and the Argyll and Sutherland Highlanders, who were carrying out a battalion relief, came in sight of the barracks and were raked with automatic fire. Only one man survived and the vehicles were set on fire. Another officer and three men were killed trying to reach the scene. All British troops were temporarily withdrawn from the Crater while plans were made to restore the situation.

In the evening of 3 July, just a fortnight after the ambushes, the Argylls, led by their CO, Lieutenant Colonel Colin Mitchell, the controversial 'Mad Mitch', and supported by the Queens Dragoon Guards in armoured cars, reoccupied the Crater in a well planned operation. Under the critical eyes of the world media, the Argylls advanced to the stirring skirl of their pipes and with the red and white hackles of the Fusiliers flying from the aerials of the armoured cars. There was no organised resistance and by dawn next day the Union Flag was flying once more over the Crater.

The Governor was unfortunately less successful in restoring confidence amongst the ministers of the Federal Government, which virtually collapsed. The decision was taken in London to bring forward the timings for the withdrawal from Aden, and to complete the evacuation by the end of November.

The NLF won the civil war and were recognised by the British Government on 3 November as their successors in Aden. A large naval task force assembled in the bay, including two carriers and an assault ship in case the evacuation turned into a fighting withdrawal. No attempt was made to impede it and the last helicopter carrying the CO of 42nd RM Commando, Lieutenant Colonel Dai Morgan, flew off to the fleet at 3pm on 29 November. No one regretted leaving. The only pity was the waste of the large sums of money recently spent on new barracks and married quarters, which could have been better used elsewhere if a decision to leave had been taken earlier.

★ ★ ★

Whilst these events were taking place in Southern Arabia, American diplomatic efforts in the Middle East had been directed towards finding a lasting solution to the Arab–Israeli conflict. Every American President since Truman had tried, on entering the Oval Office, to find a new way of using America's power and influence in an even-handed way to bring the two sides together in a sensible compromise, which would benefit them both and safeguard Western interests in the Arab world. Kennedy inherited an Arab–Israeli legacy of bitterness from Eisenhower in 1961. The Jewish lobby in Washington and Israeli Government in Tel Aviv judged American economic aid and arms supplies to be inadequate for ensuring Israel's survival; and the radical Arab states – Egypt, Syria, Iraq and the Yemen – were openly hostile and depending upon Soviet backing to accomplish the destruction of Israel. Kennedy's youthful enthusiasm for 'progressive forces' led him to seek Nasser's friendship, but he was rebuffed. During his short Presidency, however, the affairs of the Middle East were forced onto 'the back burner' in Washington by the superpower confrontation over the Cuban missile crisis, and by the growing conflict in Vietnam. Fortunately, the British deterrent intervention in Kuwait had secured Middle Eastern oil supplies from immediate danger.

Kennedy's assassination in November 1963 brought no significant change in American Middle East policy, which can be summed up as the aim to help Israel to survive and prosper without alienating the Arabs. During Johnson's first term, Vietnam dominated his foreign policy, while in the Middle East the Arabs tried to get their act together for a renewed assault on Israel. Their efforts were hampered by a growing dissatisfaction in Damascus and Baghdad with Cairo's domination of Arab affairs. The Arab socialist Ba'ath (Renaissance) Party began to challenge Nasser's leadership as lacking in anti-Zionist zeal.

The Ba'ath had been formed in Syria in 1949 and ten years later was established in Iraq as well, becoming the Pan-Arab focus for the northern

Arabs of the Fertile Crescent. Extreme in its nationalist fervour, it was contemptuous of Egyptian efforts against Israel. In Iraq, Brigadier Kassim's military regime was seen to be standing in the way of the Ba'ath's march to power so plans were laid to eliminate him. The first attempt was in October 1959, when a Ba'athist hit squad, which included the young Saddam Hussein – described as a powerfully built and imposing man with a reputation as a murderer and thug – tried to assassinate Kassim as he drove through a narrow Baghdad street. The ambush was botched: Kassim was wounded in the shoulder and survived, and Saddam was hit in the leg and escaped. The second attempt in February 1963 was initially more successful. It was a better planned coup, which brought the Ba'ath to power in Baghdad and cost Kassim his life. Soon afterwards, the Ba'ath seized power in Damascus as well, and created a shaky union between Syria and Iraq, both states agreeing to adopt the same flag but on little else. The union collapsed in November when a military counter-coup ousted the Ba'ath regime in Baghdad.

Dissatisfaction with Nasser's failure to mount a more aggressive campaign against Israel was also rife amongst the Palestinians, who had formed the Palestine Liberation Organisation (PLO) to fight for the restoration of an Arab Palestine. They built up what amounted to a conventional army, recruited from the Palestinian refugees in Jordan and the Lebanon. The most effective of the early anti-Israeli organisations, however, was Yasser Arafat's El Fatah. By 1965, Arafat was launching damaging raids into Israel with Syrian and Jordanian support. Not to be outdone, Nasser increased the efforts of his own Egyptian-trained terrorists, the Fedayeen, in raiding southern Israel. Continually goaded by his Ba'athist rivals and the Palestinians to mount a full-scale attack on Israel, Nasser decided that he must act in some headline-catching way, short of all-out war, to defuse criticism while half his army was still locked in the Yemen.

Nasser's first step came on 16 May 1967 when he demanded the withdrawal of the United Nations peace-keepers from the Gaza Strip and Sinai. U Thant, the UN Secretary General, acquiesced without consulting the Security Council. Nasser's troops immediately occupied the UN positions in Gaza and, more importantly, at Sharm el Sheikh, enabling him to control shipping through the Strait of Tiran (*See Map 20 on page 130*). Setting aside the agreements reached when Israel had withdrawn from Sinai in 1957, and in breach of international law, he reimposed the blockade of Israel's southern port of Elat by closing the Strait to Israeli shipping, despite it being deemed to be an international waterway. Israel, seeing her survival threatened, mobilised her defence forces. President Johnson could no longer ignore events in the Middle East.

★ ★ ★

Washington's handling of the Straits crisis was, if anything, more confused and confusing than in the Suez affair ten years earlier. The British Government, which, in 1967, had more warships East of Suez than the Americans, suggested the formation of an international maritime force to challenge Nasser's closure of the Strait of Tiran. Cynics dubbed the proposed international naval force 'Wilson's Red Sea Regatta', and Johnson insisted that it should operate under United Nations auspices to avoid the United States being directly involved in British gunboat diplomacy! The Jewish lobby vociferously demanded determined action to snuff out Nasser's challenge, and was generally supported by Congress, and by the American electorate and media. Four factions, however, emerged within the Johnson Administration, each pressing for different solutions. The State Department favoured Wilson's plan; its own Near East Bureau wanted diplomatic action only, seeking to reduce the risks of alienating more Arab states than absolutely necessary; the Pentagon, with Vietnam on its hands, objected to any action that might lead to US military involvement in the Middle East; and in the White House, Johnson's predilection for caution was mixed with a strong sense of obligation to Israel. For several vital weeks, US policy-making was stalemated.

The US Administration's uncertainty was unfortunately reflected in a plethora of conflicting statements by its leading personalities, and gave the Israeli Government no confidence that the US would act. As with the British and French during the Suez crisis, they could not keep their forces mobilised indefinitely without doing untold damage to their economy while the Americans argued out a policy in Washington, trying to reach a consensus on how to act. Pre-emptive action to disrupt Arab plans for an offensive seemed the only course open to Israel.

The US Joint Chiefs of Staff in Washington were adamant that there was no hard Intelligence evidence of an Arab offensive in preparation, and that, in any case, the Israelis could easily defeat any Arab attack with the American equipment already supplied to them. The Israelis were far less sanguine about Nasser's intentions and their own abilities. On 30 May, Nasser cleared away any doubts in Israeli minds by signing a mutual defence pact with Syria, Iraq and Jordan; and by announcing on 3 June the formation of a joint military command to direct all Arab forces facing Israel. Next day, the joint command began moving some 250,000 Egyptian, Jordanian, Iraqi and Syrian troops and 2,000 tanks towards the Israeli borders. The blockade of the Strait of Tiran had become irrelevant: the survival of Israel was at stake.

Like the British and French in 1956, Israeli patience with American consensus building ran out. Soon after dawn on 5 June, the Israeli Air Force launched a devastatingly efficient pre-emptive attack on all Arab airfields within striking distance and quickly won air supremacy. Stripped of air cover, the Egyptian troops in Sinai collapsed. Within three days the

Israeli tanks were back on the banks of the Suez Canal and at Sharm el Sheikh, having defeated seven Egyptian divisions, most of whose Russian equipment fell into Israeli hands. On the same day, the Israelis took the Moslem eastern half of Jerusalem and advanced to the west bank of the Jordan. Two days later they had switched their forces rapidly northwards and had seized the Golan Heights from Syria and were approaching Damascus when the Arab high command accepted a cease-fire on 11 June. The Six Day war had cost Israel as few as 800 casualties. To save Arab face, Nasser propagated his 'Big Lie', accusing Britain and the United States of giving decisive help to Israel, which caused so much trouble in Aden. Kuwait and Iraq reacted by imposing an embargo on oil exports, but, as America was not yet a net oil importer, their action proved futile at that time although it provided a dangerous precedent for future Arab action.

The Israeli forces dug in on the banks of the Suez Canal and on the Syrian side of the Golan Heights as feverish diplomatic efforts were made in the UN to persuade the Israelis to withdraw from the Arab territory, which they had taken. The Canal remained firmly closed, and the increased costs of shipping oil round the Cape contributed to the British economic crisis and the devaluation of Sterling in November 1967. Denis Healey reopened his Defence Review, and, much to President Johnson's alarm, Harold Wilson announced the acceleration of the British withdrawal from East of Suez. Instead of disengaging by the mid-1970s, as originally intended, British forces would depart by the end of 1971, leaving just three years in which to find alternative ways of ensuring the safety of Western interests in the Persian Gulf.

The obvious country to inherit the British role in the Gulf was the Shah's Iran. It seemed stable, anti-communist and Western orientated; it had large reserves of trainable manpower; and it had surplus oil revenues with which to buy modern weapon systems from the West. Saudi Arabia was another possibility. It was also stable and had surplus oil wealth, but it lacked the manpower needed for sizeable armed forces. The Iranians had always wanted to be masters of the Gulf and so it did not take much British and American encouragement for the Shah to seize the opportunity with both hands. He bought vast quantities of advanced weapon systems from the West; set up training schools for military technicians; and started to build an Iranian defence-industrial base at break-neck speed.

Although Britain was to withdraw from the Gulf militarily, she had no intention of reducing her political and commercial presence there. Embassy diplomatic and commercial staffs were gradually increased in Saudi Arabia and the smaller Gulf states. Military advisory staffs and training teams were also augmented to help raise local defence forces. Moreover, with Americans tarred in Arab eyes as supporters of Israel, the British ambassadors could and, at times, did play useful parts in protecting Western interests, especially in Cairo where the American diplomatic staffs were being treated as hostile to the Arab cause. For instance, in the United Nations, the British Ambassador, Lord Caradon, succeeded in winning agreement to Resolution 242, whereby the Israelis were directed to give up their territorial gains in exchange for the Arabs ending their state of belligerency with Israel. It seemed a diplomatic triumph at the time, but regrettably it led nowhere. The Israelis would not withdraw without definitive peace treaties, which their Arab neighbours refused to negotiate unless the Palestinian refugees were allowed back into Israel, a demand, which the Israelis saw as placing a Trojan horse within their boundaries.

★ ★ ★

By 1969, when Richard Nixon became President of the United States, the Arabs, despairing of the United Nations, and United States, efforts to enforce an Israeli withdrawal, had begun a war of attrition, hoping to break the Israeli will through the economic strain of continuous mobilisation. The Egyptians adopted a policy of shelling and raiding the Israeli defences on the Suez Canal; and the PLO, now led by Yasser Arafat, together with the other Arab terrorist organisations, started an orgy of attacks not only across the Israeli frontiers but also against Western targets. Hijacking of Western civilian aircraft and ships kept Palestinian grievances in the forefront of international news coverage.

Like Eisenhower, Nixon had a foreign policy and national security tsar, Henry Kissinger, who played a similar role to that of Foster Dulles, but with deeper perception of Middle Eastern realities and greater consistency of purpose. He had a clear policy for the region: resist Soviet infiltration, weaken the radical Arab states, encourage the conservative ones, and ensure the survival of Israel. During Nixon's first term he was National Security Adviser and crossed swords frequently with the Secretary of State, William Rogers, whose nebulous Arab–Israeli peace plans he deemed impracticable. He preferred to use pragmatic power broking and a step by step approach in secret negotiations. Nixon disposed of Rogers during his second term, and Kissinger took over as Secretary of State whilst remaining National Security Advisor. With Nixon distracted by Watergate, Kissinger became dictator of American Middle East policy.

Like all other American Presidents, Nixon tried to be even-handed between Jew and Arab, especially in the supply of arms to Israel and to the conservative Arab monarchies – Jordan and Saudi Arabia. He tried to persuade Moscow to damp down the growing arms race, but received no worthwhile response. Instead, Nasser was invited to Moscow in January 1970 and returned to Cairo with promises of a significant supply of the latest Soviet anti-aircraft and anti-tank missile systems together with advisers to train the Egyptians to use them and technicians to install and maintain them. In response, the United States reluctantly started to rearm

Israel to offset the Soviet flow of arms to the radical states – Egypt, Syria and Iraq. A new Arab–Israeli flare-up was clearly in the making, but Nasser was destined to play no part in it. He died in September that year, and was succeeded by one of the last of his former colleagues in the 'Free Officers' movement, Anwar Sadat.

Sadat tried to improve Egypt's relations with the United States, convinced that William Rogers could bring effective pressure to bear on Israel to withdraw from the occupied territories, if he, Sadat, showed a genuine willingness to compromise. Rogers needed no convincing, but was thwarted by the powerful Zionist lobby in Washington and by Israeli supporters in Congress, who forced the acceleration of arms supplies to Israel, despite the opposition of departmental officials and some of the White House advisors, including Kissinger. In desperation, Sadat turned back to Moscow and started to plan the expulsion of the Israelis by force with Russian help. In May 1971, he signed a new treaty of friendship and cooperation with the Soviet Union, and visited Moscow personally in October. Thereafter, he carried through one of the most remarkable pieces of political and military deception in highly secret planning for the destruction of Israel. The keys to his plan were the defeat of the Israeli air force, using the latest Soviet Surface to Air missiles (SAMs) to cover his army; the destruction of the Israeli armoured forces with advanced Soviet anti-tank missiles, which had not been used, as yet, in any war; and the economic strangulation of the West through a Saudi and Iraqi imposed oil embargo.

The idea of using oil as a blackmailing weapon had been developing in Arab minds for some time. It had not been effective in the Six Day War because it was over too quickly and the US was not yet a nett importer of oil. By the early 1970s, however, both American and Western European economies had become crucially dependent on Middle East oil. At first, only Libya's Colonel Gaddafi and subsequently OPEC had used this trend to force up oil prices. In 1973, Sadat succeeded in persuading King Feisal of Saudi Arabia to play a more active part in the destruction of Israel by using the oil weapon as his contribution to the Arab effort.

Quite how the Americans and Israelis failed to appreciate what was being planned by Sadat is hard to understand. Large numbers of Soviet advisers were training the Egyptian, Syrian and Iraqi armies; SAM sites, together with their radars and fire control systems, were being constructed just west of the Suez Canal; special water-crossing and bridging exercises were being carried out on replicas of the Canal; experiments were being made with water canon to ramp down the steep Canal banks; and large shipments of Soviet ammunition were arriving in Egypt and Syria. And yet an hour after the Egyptians had started crossing the Canal and the Syrians were attacking on the Golan Heights in the early hours of 6 October 1973 at the start of the Yom Kippur war, the National Security Council's Intelligence Committee concluded:

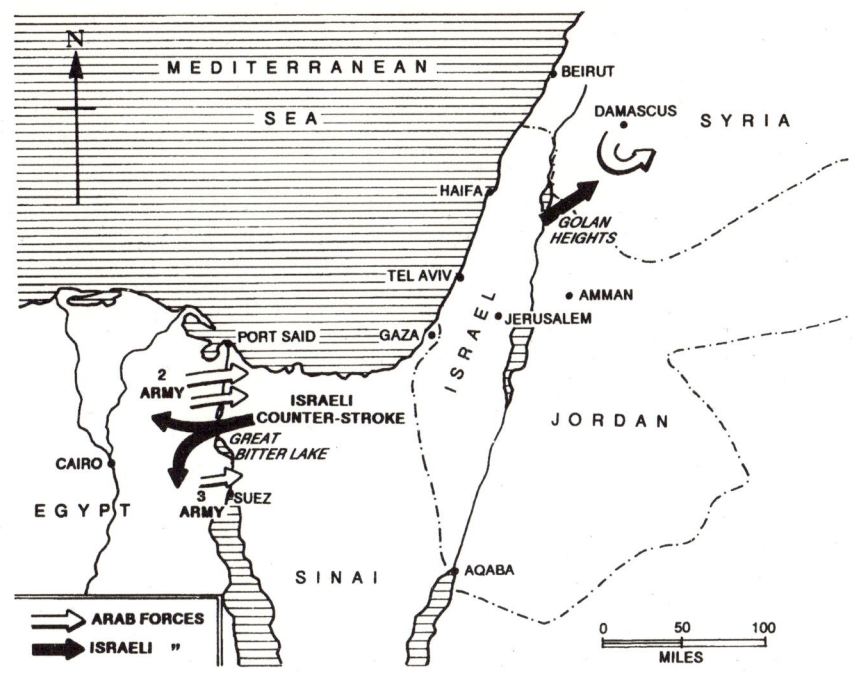

Map 22: The Yom Kippur War: October 1973

We can find no hard evidence of a major Egyptian–Syrian offensive across the Canal and in the Golan Heights area.[4]

There seem to have been several reasons for this lapse: the Israelis had cried wolf so often when trying to build up their case for more American equipment; the Egyptians were credited with knowing that they could not beat the Israelis in battle and so were unlikely to start a war they could not win just to restore their self-respect; clever diplomatic deception on Sadat's part, including the publicly announced expulsion of all Russian advisers in July, confirmed the unlikelihood of a combined Arab offensive; and at the recent superpower summit between Nixon and Brezhnev, the Russians had promised, as a measure of East–West *détente*, to warn the Americans of potential threats of aggression by Moscow's satellites, which included Egypt, Syria and Iraq. No warning came from Moscow, although the Kremlin was aware of Sadat's intentions two or three days before he attacked.

Sadat had chosen his moment well. The Israeli Defence Forces were not mobilised and their defensive line on the Canal was at minimum manning levels; the religious observance of Yom Kippur (the Day of Atonement) reduced Israeli alertness although it speeded mobilisation because all the reservists were at home; and diplomatic negotiations were about to start in New York for a renewal of Arab–Israeli peace talks. The

Egyptian diplomats had been deliberately kept in the dark and were taken aback when the news of the Arab offensive reached them.

The Syrians attacked the two Israeli brigades holding the Golan Heights with five divisions, and the Egyptians crossed the Canal on a wide front with another five and dug in on the east bank while their armour was ferried across. On both fronts the Israeli airmen suffered unexpectedly high loses from the Soviet SAMs, and when the Israeli tanks counter-attacked, they too suffered severely from the Soviet anti-tank missiles. However, as soon as the Egyptian and Syrian armour advanced beyond the SAM cover, the Israeli airmen were once more masters of the battle-field. Concentrating on the Golan front first, the Israelis drove the Syrians off with the loss of over 800 tanks for the loss of some 200 of their own. They then switched their armour to Sinai, but hesitated to commit it until they were sure that the United States would make good their equipment losses.

Whilst the first week's fighting was in progress, Kissinger was playing a devious game. The Israelis screamed for weapon replacements and missile supplies from the United States, which Congress was willing to sanction at once. Kissinger, nevertheless, felt that a sweeping Israeli counter-stroke, leading to a decisive victory, would make any solution of the Arab–Israeli dispute, on which US–Arab relations, and hence Western oil supplies, depended, all the more difficult. He managed to stall the start of the US airlift of the latest weapons to Israel, while he tried to engineer an immediate cease-fire through the good offices of the British Embassy in Cairo. Sadat foolishly rebuffed the British approach whilst the battle seemed to be going well for the Egyptians, and thus cut the ground from under Kissinger's feet. A massive Soviet airlift had already begun to Egypt and Syria, leaving him no option but to allow the United States airlift, which was to exceed the 1948 Berlin airlift in tonnage carried, to go ahead on 12 October. The Saudis responded immediately by imposing their oil embargo.

The start of the American airlift emboldened the Israeli Government to 'go for broke'. Their armoured forces in Sinai, reinforced from the Golan, crashed through the Egyptian Second Army, crossed the Canal just north of the Great Bitter Lake, and had all but surrounded the Egyptian Third Army west of the Canal when a cease-fire, negotiated by Kissinger in Moscow, was accepted by both sides on 22 October. Foolishly, the Egyptians broke it within a few days with an artillery bombardment of Israeli positions. Israel reacted by completing the encirclement of the Egyptian Third Army. For a few days it looked as if the Kremlin might intervene. United States forces went briefly onto nuclear alert on 24 October. When the crisis of the threatened US–Soviet military confrontation had faded, Kissinger set about his self-imposed task of bringing about a Middle East peace settlement through step by step diplomacy while Nixon grappled with his Watergate accusers. Although the fighting was over, the Saudis decided to maintain their oil embargo as a part of the Arabs' negotiating position to compel the United States to force an Israeli withdrawal from the occupied territories.

Kissinger carried out no less than eleven diplomatic shuttles between Washington and the Middle Eastern capitals during 1974 and 1975, each time achieving a modest step forward. To the Arabs he offered the chance of regaining what they had lost by war, and to the Israelis he proffered more secure frontiers and the return of their prisoners of war – an obsession within their small, closely knit community. In January and May 1974 he reached disengagement accords on the Sinai and Golan fronts respectively, and the Saudis lifted the oil embargo. Nixon resigned over Watergate in August 1974 but Gerald Ford kept Kissinger on as foreign policy tsar. A year later, Kissinger had coaxed the Israelis back from the western half of Sinai in exchange for an assured supply of American arms, including Lance and Hawk missiles; and Sadat had reopened the Canal for international shipping. Although Kissinger had made real progress by the end of his last shuttle in August 1975, the Israelis had not won definitive peace treaties with their Arab neighbours, nor had the Arabs turned the Israelis out of eastern Sinai, the Gaza Strip, the Jordan West Bank or the Golan. Middle Eastern peace was still a long way off.

Important though Kissinger's efforts in defusing a further Arab–Israeli military conflict had been, it was the Saudi oil embargo that had the most far-reaching effects. The hike of the oil price from $3 per barrel in 1973 to $20 in 1975 induced an unprecedented transfer of wealth from Western countries to the Arab oil-producing states. Some of this wealth was drawn back by Western arms dealers and building contractors, but the bulk of it led to undreamed of economic development in the region. Less happily, it provided the financial resources needed by the whole spectrum of terrorist organisations, ranging from El Fatah to the IRA.

* * *

British troops had intervened in Northern Ireland in August 1969, but they were also drawn into a less well-known counter-terrorist campaign in the Middle East. Ever since the SAS's successful storming of the Djebel Akhdar in central Oman British officers and NCOs had been serving in the Sultan's armed forces to ensure the continued stability of the Oman, which dominates the Strait of Hormuz, the gateway to the Persian Gulf, and hence is an attractive strategic target for the Kremlin. The despotic and medieval rule of the old Sultan, Said bin Taimur, made it fertile ground for subversion and communist take-over by nationalist proxy. After Aden had been evacuated in 1967, Arab nationalist gangs, equipped with Russian and Chinese weapons started to infiltrate Dhofar, the southern province of the Oman, from Hauf in the former Eastern Aden

Protectorate (*See Map 21 on page 143*). They styled themselves the Dhofar Liberation Front, and by 1970 had 'liberated' almost the whole of the province, having won the loyalty of its tribes. The Sultan's writ only ran in the coastal plain around his summer capital and airfield at Salala.

In July that year, the Sultan's Sandhurst-trained son, Qaboos, overthrew his father in a bloodless coup, and put in hand a vigorous political and economic development programme to drag the Oman into the 20th Century. This was made practicable by the large oil revenues that had started to flow into his government's coffers, and by the British Government's willingness to provide British civilian advisers and military officers to steer the Sultanate forward at a sensible, practicable pace, and to win back the Dhofar through a combination of political, economic and military action.

The young Sultan's Sandhurst training led him to use the British colonial policy of raising standards of living and education with one hand while fighting the rebel tribesmen to regain Dhofar with the other. Officers and NCOs, seconded from the British Army and RAF, played leading roles in the latter. They were not just advisers in the American style: they held the key command posts within Omani regiments and supporting units, taking all the risks and more with their men in the time-honoured traditions of the old Indian Army and British colonial forces. The campaign was not easily won and involved hard, patient work to trap the illusive rebel bands in the vastness of djebel country. Brigadier John Akehurst, who commanded in Dhofar during the crucial battle-winning period from early 1974 until final victory in the autumn of 1975, gave six reasons for the young Sultan's success: his political and economic reforms; regaining the confidence of the people of Dhofar; joint civil and military planning and control of executive action; cutting the rebel's supply lines; the use of air power, particularly helicopters; and winning the Intelligence battle. A unique feature of the campaign was the part played by the squadron of the Special Air Service that was maintained on the djebel throughout. Fresh from their brilliant 'hearts and minds' successes in Borneo during Confrontation with the Indonesians, the SAS quickly realised that if they could persuade the Muslim rebels in Dhofar that the communist-inspired agitators who were behind the rebellion were, in effect, the enemies of Islam, it might be possible to 'turn' some at least of them, provided that they could be wooed by the imaginative and very positive measures being taken by the Sultan (on SAS advice) to improve the lot of the Dhofari people. Wells were being sunk (by British Royal Engineers), schools established, roads built and improved veterinary support provided for the Dhofari flocks. It worked like a charm and very soon, small bands of former rebels, under SAS leadership, and known as *firqats*, were operating on the djebel. Others were acting as 'home guards' for the djebel villages. It was a masterstroke and a perfect example of enlightened British counter-insurgency technique. Thirty-five British officers and NCOs lost their lives and many more were wounded in helping to ensure that the Oman did not slip into the Eastern bloc by default.

★ ★ ★

No one was more conscious than Kissinger that his task of bringing about an Arab–Israeli peace settlement was only half completed when Jimmy Carter won the 1976 presidential election and he had to retire from the State Department and National Security Council. Egypt's Sadat was equally conscious of his own failure to force the Israelis out of Eastern Sinai and the Arab West Bank territories, and to improve the lot of the Palestinians. He had had enough of American negotiators, who could never bring enough leverage to bear on the Israeli Government to make constructive compromises, due to the powerful influence of its Jewish supporters in Washington. He decided to cut out the American middlemen and attempt to deal with Israel direct. Much to the world's surprise, he invited himself to Jerusalem and was allowed to address the Knesset in November 1977. It was a bold step, which led to him being ostracised by most of the Arab world. Menachem Begin, the Israeli Prime Minister and former terrorist leader during the British mandate of Palestine, paid a return visit to Egypt in December, meeting Sadat at Ismailia, but the two men found themselves just too far apart to reach a compromise peace agreement. They were too much the prisoners of their own people's preconceptions, which only time could moderate.

The Carter Administration in Washington may have felt frustrated about being bypassed, but Cyrus Vance, the new Secretary of State, was a conciliator by nature and ready to offer his good offices to help the direct negotiations to make progress. As soon as the Ismailia meeting broke up, Carter, on Vance's advice, stepped in to keep the two men talking by inviting them to Camp David for discussions on neutral ground, free from the glare of publicity. Carter himself offered to mediate personally and did so with remarkable success. There were two Camp David sessions in 1978: a preliminary meeting in January, and substantive negotiations in September. Framework documents were agreed by which Israel would evacuate the rest of Sinai in exchange for Egyptian recognition of the State of Israel. Subsequent drafting of the actual treaty ran into the sands of differing interpretations of the framework agreements. In desperation, Carter flew personally to Cairo and Jerusalem in March 1979 to break the impasse. With some deft political footwork, he just succeeded in doing so. The Egyptian–Israeli peace treaty of 1979 was signed at the White House on 26 March, ending the state of war between Egypt and Israel, with Israel withdrawing from Sinai, but retaining the Gaza Strip, the West Bank and East Jerusalem. As far as the rest of the Arab world was concerned, the

Palestinians had been cheated: the Arab–Israeli war would go on without Egypt.

Sadly, Sadat was to pay for his efforts to bring peace to the Middle East with his own life. He was to be assassinated on 6 October 1981, while attending a military parade, marking the 8th Anniversary of the Yom Kippur War. One of the troop carriers in the march-past halted in front of the reviewing stand. Soldiers jumped out and Sadat stood up to take their salute. Instead of saluting they gunned him down in a hail of automatic fire as a traitor to the Arab cause.

But this is anticipating events. While Sadat, Begin and Carter had been negotiating at Camp David, the Lebanon had collapsed in civil war, which stemmed from ethnic, religious and economic causes. The new factor, which triggered loss of stability in this once happy and prosperous part of ancient Syria, was the arrival and political activity of large numbers of disillusioned Palestinians, who gradually upset the delicate balance of power between the Christian Maronite minority, who had ruled the country with success since the French left after the Second World War, and the disunited Moslem factions, who felt compelled by the growing size of the Moslem majority to challenge Maronite rule. The PLO established themselves firmly in southern Lebanon and in camps around Moslem West Beirut. With Syrian help and encouragement, they began harassing the northern Israeli settlements with raids, artillery and mortar fire.

The signing of the Egyptian/Israeli peace treaty shifted Israeli attention from their Egyptian to Lebanese borders. The World's attention, however, swung towards the extraordinary events taking place in the autumn of 1978 in Tehran, where the Shah's rule was tottering towards collapse under pressure from the Moslem fundamentalists, led by the exiled Ayatollah Khomeini, who abhorred the Shah's Westernisation of Iran. The Iranian revolution was to bring Britain and America closer together in Middle East policy and military action than at any time since Suez.

CHAPTER 6

PARTNERSHIP IN THE GULF
The Iranian Revolution and Desert Storm 1979–91

> *In purely practical terms, there is no doubt that British, American and French forces could have reached Baghdad ... But in pressing on to the Iraqi capital we would have moved outside the remit of the United Nations authority, within which we had worked so far... [We] would have been presented as foreign invaders of Iraq and we would have undermined the prestige which we had earned around the world for helping the Arabs resolve a major threat to the Middle East. The whole of Desert Storm would have been seen purely as an operation to further Western interests in the Middle East.*
>
> *General Sir Peter de La Billière.*[1]

The Islamic fundamentalist revolution in Iran opened a Pandora's box of rabid Moslem and Arab nationalist fanaticism, which was to bring British and American forces back into the close co-operation, reminiscent of the Second World War. Britain's traditional view of the strategic importance of the Suez Canal and Persian Gulf oil had changed. On the one hand, interest in the Canal had waned, because it had been closed so often in the years since the Suez crisis of 1956 that ways and means had been found of mitigating the effects of its closure on the British economy. On the other hand, British oil and trading interests in the Persian Gulf had in no way diminished: only the means of protecting them had altered. The 1980s were to show that defending those interests by diplomatic means alone, as the Wilson Government intended when it withdrew British forces from the Gulf in 1971, was no more practicable in the Middle East than it ever had been since Nelson arrived off Aboukir Bay in 1798.

Few in the West had recognised how brittle the Shah of Iran's regime had become by the late 1970s through his alienation of the Shia fundamentalist mullahs, who saw his Westernisation of Iran as a violation of the precepts of Islam. They vehemently opposed his enfranchisement of women, secular education, land reform and, above all, what they saw as the 'Coca Cola colonisation by the Great Satan' – the United States. Unlike Turkey or Egypt, which had large and well-developed administrative classes, the Shah had had to depend on a very limited pool of able, educated men and his own relatives to carry forward his 'White Revolution', which he had begun in 1962. They made enormous profits, and the disparity between their wealth and that of the average Iranian family grew to revolutionary proportions, which the Ayatollah Khomeini exploited ruthlessly from his exile in Iraq and latterly in Paris.

The Shah's troubles started with mullah-inspired strikes in the oilfields during the summer of 1978. They soon spread to other industries in the autumn, and many of the wealthier families left Iran, fearing the worst. The Americans brought pressure to bear on the ailing Shah, who was suffering the early stages of cancer, to widen his Government. By the time he did so, it was too late to deflect the growing tide of fervent discontent. On 6 January, he left Iran ostensibly for medical treatment, but he was destined never to return. The Islamic fundamentalist upsurge, which followed his departure, outstripped the French Revolution in its speed and brutality. The large well-trained Iranian Army, which had more British Chieftain tanks than the British Army of the Rhine, and the Iranian Air Force, equipped with the best American combat aircraft and helicopters that money could buy, went over to the Ayatollah Khomeini's side. On 11 January, the Imperial Guard was forced to surrender; the Ayatollah was triumphant; and Iran ceased to be the West's guardian of the Gulf. It had all happened so quickly and the Islamic revolution was so complete that there was little Washington or London could have done about it.

1979 was an eventful year. In March, President Carter, as already recorded, brought about the signing of the Egyptian–Israeli peace treaty, and Margaret Thatcher became Britain's first female Prime Minister, giving British foreign policy a cutting edge. In July, Saddam Hussein took over the leadership of the Ba'ath government of Iraq, becoming Iraq's president and chairman of its Revolutionary Command Council. In October, the Shah was allowed to enter the United States for medical treatment. The Ayatollah responded by demanding his extradition to Iran to stand trial. When this was refused by Washington, Shia fundamentalist students seized the US Embassy in Tehran and took the 63 American nationals on the staff hostage. And in December, the strategic balance of power in the Middle East was further upset by the Russian invasion of Afghanistan. It did not take much imagination to perceive a renewed Soviet threat to the Gulf's oil from Afghanistan via Iran, which was showing every sign of breaking up as its ethnic minorities sought greater autonomy in the wake of the Islamic revolution.

President Carter's reaction to events in Afghanistan and Iran was, like other presidents before him, to enunciate a doctrine – the Carter Doctrine. In an address to Congress in January 1980, he declared that any attempt by outside forces to gain control of the Gulf would be deemed an attack on US vital interests. In other words, 'Moscow keep out or risk nuclear war'. Surprisingly, the large Soviet forces deployed found Afghan resistance no easier to master than the British had done in the 19th Century, and they became mired in an Afghan 'Vietnam' of their own making. It was, however, Saddam Hussein and not the Russians, who set

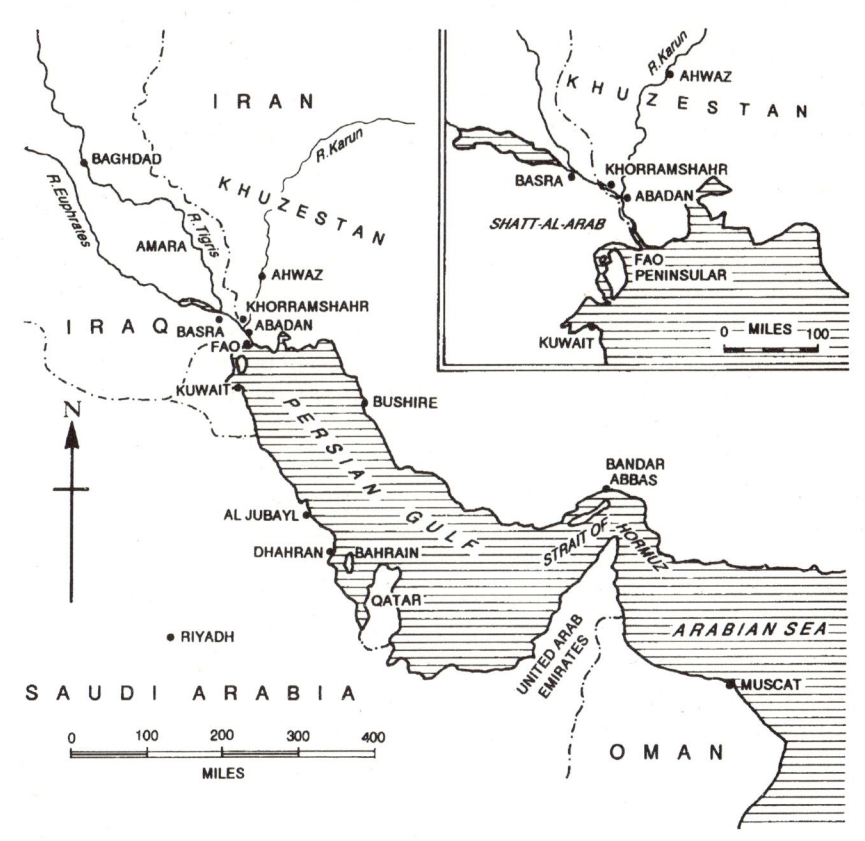

Map 23: The Persian Gulf in the 1980s

the Gulf aflame, but not in a way which immediately triggered the Carter Doctrine. Saddam decided that the time was ripe for Baghdad to oust Cairo from the leadership of the Arab world in the struggle against Israel. He saw himself assuming Nasser's role, which Sadat had so tarnished in Ba'athist eyes. He knew that he needed more oil revenues if he was to give the Iraqi people both 'guns *and* butter'. The 'guns' he had in mind were long-range nuclear and chemical weapons with which to destroy Israel. Assuming that the Iranians were in such internal chaos as to be unable to defend themselves, he decided to filch their main oil-producing province of Khuzestan (Arabistan to the Iraqis), embracing Ahwaz, Khorramshahr and Abadan in south-west Iran. In doing so, he would also be able to seize control of the whole of the Shatt el Arab water-way, Iraq's only exit into the Gulf. He began planning an offensive, which he believed, with some justification, the Americans would support as a means of checking the spread of the Ayatollah's malign Islamic fundamentalism in the Gulf.

Saddam invaded Iran with a blitzkrieg-style attack on 22 September 1980. At first all seemed to be going well for him, but he had overestimated the disorganisation of the Iranian armed forces, and underestimated the fanaticism engendered in their ranks by the fundamentalist mullahs. He took only one major town, Khorramshahr, to which he restored its old Arab name of Mohammerah as it had been known to British soldiers and sailors in the 19th Century. The Iranians took time to mount their counter-offensive. When they were ready, they gradually forced the Iraqis back in fighting reminiscent of the First World War, and had recovered most of their lost territory by mid-1982. Judging Saddam's Ba'ath nationalism to be preferable to the Ayatollah's Islamic fundamentalism, Washington and London blinked at the clandestine sale of arms to Iraq, and sent warships into the Gulf to protect the tanker traffic from interference by either side. The British 'Armilla Patrol' of two frigates started its contribution to the safety of Gulf shipping in October 1980. By March 1987, the risks to shipping had risen so steeply that it was reinforced by a third frigate. A fourth was to be added during the Gulf War of 1990–91.

One state did not blink. The Israelis appreciated that Saddam's nuclear ambitions threatened their security. Israeli aircraft attacked and destroyed his French-built nuclear weapons plant in June 1981. His more widely dispersed chemical and biological weapon development programmes continued unscathed.

★ ★ ★

When Ronald Reagan became President of the United States in February 1981, he had an immediate diplomatic success in winning the release of the US Embassy hostages held in Tehran. Carter's botched attempt to rescue them in April 1980 had made them the symbol of Iran's determination to resist superpower pressure, but the Iranian Government needed spares for its large holdings of American aircraft and British tanks, the existing contracts for which would not be honoured unless the hostages were released. The change of administration in Washington gave the Iranians the opportunity to make a conciliatory gesture by doing so.

In the wake of Jimmy Carter's Camp David success, it was with some relief that Ronald Reagan turned away from the Arab–Israeli conflict, which had plagued all American Presidents since Truman's day, to grapple with the growing threat to Gulf oil supplies. In this, he had the full support of Margaret Thatcher, who was equally concerned about events in the Gulf. But both leaders, however, soon found that the two Middle Eastern conflicts were closely interrelated and could not be dealt with separately.

The first direct linkage became evident as Washington and Whitehall sought a new local guardian for the Gulf. Saudi Arabia was the most obvious and willing candidate, having much to fear from the Ayatollah's and Saddam's ambitions. While Britain looked to the strengthening of the smaller Gulf states with whom she had always had close and friendly ties, the US Congress was asked to approve the sale of advanced combat aircraft and other equipment to the Saudis, including five Airborne Early Warning Aircraft (AWACS) for operations over the Gulf. The Jewish lobby in Congress became alarmed by this increase in Arab armament, which could just as easily be used against Israel as over the Gulf. The President's advisers were, as usual, split between the pro-Israeli and pro-Arab schools. Al Haig, the Secretary of State, backed Israel: Caspar Weinberger, the Secretary for Defence, was as staunchly pro-Arab as Margaret Thatcher. After a long and tortuous debate, Congress approved the AWACS sale in April 1981, but only just.

The second linkage occurred after the Israeli forces invaded the Lebanon in June the following year to put an end to PLO harassment of northern Israeli settlements. They trapped Yasser Arafat's men in Moslem West Beirut, and then horrified the world by enabling the Maronite Phalangist forces to commit the atrocious massacres in the Palestinian refugee camps of Shatila and Sabra. Reagan supported the United Nations' decision to intervene, and ordered the US 6th Fleet to land 800 Marines to form a UN force with small French, Italian and later British contingents, which was to cover the evacuation of the trapped PLO fighting men by sea from Beirut, and also to help to end the Lebanese civil war. This was all too much for the Ayatollah's fundamentalists in Tehran, who believed that it was their sacred duty to go to the aid of their Shia brethren and to drive all Western forces out of Lebanon. They dispatched parties of fundamentalist ideologues via Syria to inspire, organise and train young Shia fanatics in terrorism and kidnapping, which was to be directed against the West in general and the United States in particular.

The Iranian-inspired Hezbollah (Party of God) and other extremist groups were remarkably successful in hamstringing UN and US peace-keeping efforts. The US Embassy in Beirut was the first to be blown up by a suicide bomber driving his explosive-filled truck at the building in April 1983, killing 63 people. Six months later a similar attack on a building within the US Marine compound, housing 350 Marines, killed 245 of them. Another truck bomber killed 59 French paratroopers in a billet in West Beirut. The US Marine disaster was avoidable. There had been plenty of Intelligence warnings, but the precautions to foil such an attack had been woefully inadequate. Hezbollah was intent on creating another 'Vietnam' for the Americans, but Reagan wisely pulled the Marines back to their ships and thereafter used the 16-inch guns of the battleship *New Jersey* and carrier-borne aircraft to influence events ashore. All American,

French, British and Italian troops were out of Beirut by the end of February 1984. They had been powerless to stop the spate of kidnapping of Western nationals – academics from the American University, journalists, and peace-makers like Terry Waite.

By the summer of 1982, the Iranians decided that they were strong enough to invade Iraq and made Basra their primary objective. The similarity with the First World War became even more striking. Saddam's troops had been unable to defeat the Iranians defending Khuzestan: the Iranians, in their turn, were equally unsuccessful when attacking the Iraqis, despite the gross numerical superiority that they enjoyed. The defence had the upper hand, which led to a horrendous war of attrition, in which the Iranian use of human wave tactics resulted in grotesque casualty lists. In their two offensives in 1982, the Iranians lost over 30,000 men to the Iraqis' 9,000. The Iranian casualties were highest amongst the young fanatics of the Republican Guard, who leapt forward with prayers on their lips, plastic 'keys to heaven' dangling around their necks and certainty of enjoying Allah's everlasting kingdom gripping their minds. Five further Iranian offensives in 1983 brought even heavier casualties and temporary exhaustion. Both sides then decided to turn the struggle into an economic war by attacking each other's oil exports.

From February 1984 onwards the 'tanker war', which drew increasing numbers of Western warships into the Gulf to protect shipping, was interspersed with renewed Iranian offensives to take Basra. At sea, the Iraqis tried to destroy the Iranian oil terminals by air attacks, which were poorly executed, and by imposing exclusion zones to stop tankers reaching them but with only partial success. The Iranians retaliated by attempting to close the Strait of Hormuz to tankers destined for Kuwaiti and Saudi terminals, using gunboats and random mining of Gulf waters. The Armilla Patrol was reinforced with British mine-hunters, of types which the Americans did not possess, to deal with the mining. All the European navies, and even Soviet warships in the Gulf, co-operated with the powerful United States fleet in protecting commercial shipping. Incidents like the accidental Iraqi air-launched missile attack on the USS *Stark*, the mining of the American flagged Kuwaiti supertanker *Bridgeton*, and the constant but random Iranian gunboat attacks on tankers of all nations, kept the naval conflict illuminated in headlines of the world press. The oil continued to flow to the West, albeit at new peak prices.

In the battles on land, Iranian numerical superiority and fanaticism were offset by the flow of aircraft and weapons to the Iraqi forces, bought in the world arms market with large financial loans provided by those Arab states with most to fear from an Iranian victory. These were principally Saddam's closest neighbours, Kuwait, Saudi Arabia and the smaller Gulf states, who were eventually to regret their largesse. There is also some evidence that the United States provided the Iraqis with satellite intelligence of Iranian concentrations, and that the Iraqis used chemical weapons from March 1984 onwards, whenever the Iranians were on a point of breakthrough.

In February 1986, the Iranians massed a million men in the Basra area, which they proclaimed would win the war. Feinting towards Amara on the Tigris, their main point of attack was, in fact, the Fao peninsular south-east of Basra on the southern side of the Shatt el Arab. They succeeded in crossing the Shatt and seizing Fao, which gave them access to either Basra or Kuwait. They had fought their way into the southern outskirts of the former before Saddam could bring back his troops from Amara. Then the tide of battle, helped by the use of chemical shells, turned in Saddam's favour as his reinforcements arrived. The Iranians never entered Basra and suffered devastating losses trying to hold onto the Fao area, which Saddam turned into a killing ground.

It was during this period that the Irangate scandal of the US arms for hostages, taken by Hezbollah in the Lebanon, broke in Washington. Compared with the quantities of Western arms sold to Iraq throughout the war, the loads of anti-aircraft and anti-tank missiles clandestinely sold to Tehran by Admiral Poindexter and Colonel North were not war-winners. Nevertheless, it was to be another eighteen months before Saddam felt strong enough to drive the Iranians off the Fao peninsular and out of Iraqi territory. In the meantime, both sides had tried ineffectually to shatter civilian morale with long-range missile attacks on each other's capitals. And in April 1988, Washington had the gratification of reaching an agreement with Moscow, enabling the Russians to withdraw from Afghanistan.

In the same month, Saddam opened what was to prove to be the final and decisive offensive. In some of the bitterest fighting of the war, his troops cleared the Fao peninsula by the beginning of July, and drove the Iranians back across the Shatt el Arab. At this psychological moment, the USS *Vincennes*, accidentally shot down the Iranian civilian Air Bus (Flight 655) over the Gulf. This incident seems to have been the trigger, although not the actual cause, of the Tehran religious hierarchy advising the Ayatollah Khomeini that enough was enough. To continue the land war was pointless and would only inflict further enormous losses on their long-suffering people: and at sea, US power in the Gulf was such that a continued tanker war would be counterproductive – Iran needed oil revenues for reconstruction. On 18 July 1988, the Iranian Government accepted the UN Resolution 598 for a cease-fire. The aged Ayatollah, who was to die within a year, described the decision as 'like taking poison'.

* * *

The long Iraq–Iran War was over: the West had enabled the perceived lesser threat to Gulf oil supplies from Saddam's pan-Arab nationalism to triumph over the greater evil of Islamic fundamentalism as propagated by the Ayatollah Khomeini. Saddam had emerged from the struggle with his ambitions enhanced, and with a hardened, battle-experienced army of just under a million men and 5,000 tanks, and an air force with 500 of the latest combat aircraft in hardened bunkers on numerous well dispersed and heavily defended airfields.

On the reverse side of the Iraqi coin, Saddam had received massive loans from other Arab and Moslem states which feared the dire, destabilising influence of the Ayatollah's preaching. Although some of his debts were virtually written off by Kuwait and the Gulf states, other creditors further afield were not so amenable. With the end of the war, the price of oil slumped, making it all the more difficult to go on pursuing his 'guns *and* butter' policy while readying himself for his dream offensive against Israel. Saddam saw overproduction of oil by the Gulf states as ingratitude and deliberate economic warfare designed to weaken Iraq. Had he not protected them from 'rivers of blood' by defeating the Ayatollah?

Casting round for a new source of revenue now that the conquest of the Iranian oilfields was barred to him, he resuscitated Kassim's claim to Kuwait as part of the old Ottoman province of Basra. When Sir Percy Cox had fixed Kuwait's boundaries after the First World War, he is said to have drawn them on a small-scale map after a tiring day of negotiations, giving most of the area of the then undiscovered Rumaylah oilfield and a couple of strategically important islands offshore to Kuwait by mistake. Saddam, in true Hitleresque style, accused Kuwait of stealing $2.4 billion worth of Iraqi oil from the Rumaylah field and encouraging foreign intervention in the Gulf.

Saddam's rhetoric grew in virulence throughout the early months of 1990 as he sought support from other Arab states for his bogus claims on Kuwait. In the third week of July, he started concentrating 100,000 men on its northern border. The general view amongst Middle East analysts was that Saddam would stop short of actual invasion of Kuwait, although there was a possibility that he might seize the Rumaylah oilfield and the islands, which would improve his access to the Gulf. This view was reinforced by assurances that he had given to the US Ambassador in Baghdad, to President Mubarak of Egypt and to King Fahd of Saudi Arabia, and by the announcement of a meeting between the Iraqis and Kuwaitis under Saudi and Egyptian good offices at Jiddah on 1st August. The meeting was turned into farce by the Iraqis walking out. In the early hours of 2 August the Iraqi Army rolled into Kuwait. Resistance was fierce wherever it occurred, but could not be sustained against such numerically adverse odds. The Emir escaped to Saudi Arabia where the Kuwaiti government was set up temporarily at Taif.

★ ★ ★

The international response to the outrageous Iraqi invasion of a neighbouring Arab state was swift. The Security Council met before dawn on 2 August. Fourteen out of the fifteen members (the Yemen abstained) passed UN Resolution 660, condemning Iraqi action; and four days later UN Resolution 661 authorised the imposition of sanctions. Fear also crept through the corridors of power in Washington, London and the Lake Success building in New York that the fall of Kuwait might be only the first phase of operations planned by Saddam to seize all the Gulf oil wells, starting with the Saudi fields just south of Kuwait. He had the military power available, and might have succeeded if he had actually had the intention and the plan, and if he moved quickly enough. The overwhelming defeat inflicted upon him has obscured in many people's minds the full extent of the logistic effort which the assembly and subsequent maintenance of the Coalition forces involved. By his failure to follow through, Saddam enabled the Allies to build up by sea and air over a period of nearly six months. Without that gift of time and the extensive host nation support provided by the Saudi Arabians, the story might have had a very different ending.

★ ★ ★

Saddam made a fatal error of halting in Kuwait and digging in. It was President Bush, encouraged by Margaret Thatcher, who reacted with the greater speed and determination. Naval reinforcements and fighter aircraft were speedily deployed by both countries to the Gulf and the 82nd US Airborne Division was despatched from the States to Saudi Arabia within a week of the crisis breaking. James Baker, George Bush's Secretary of State, began his never-ending round of diplomatic trips, seeking political, military and financial support to back up the Security Council resolutions. Many Moslem countries as well as the former Middle Eastern powers, Britain and France, pledged whole-hearted support and sent contingents for the defence of Saudi Arabia – the Afghan Mujahideen, Bahrain, Bangladesh, Egypt, Morocco, Nigeria, Oman, Pakistan, Qatar, Senegal, Syria, and the United Arab Emirates – all of which came under Saudi Prince Khalid bin Sultan as Commander-in-Chief of the Coalition Forces with the American General Norman Schwarzkopf as operational commander.

Amongst the non-Moslem states, Britain committed Brigadier Patrick Cordingly's 7th Armoured Brigade from Germany in addition to her reinforcement of the Armilla Patrol and the dispatch of 69 Tornado and Jaguar aircraft to the Gulf. All British units – naval, army and air – were placed under command of Lieutenant General Sir Peter de la Billière, who quickly established a close personal and military relationship with Schwarzkopf. France sent the Daguet 6th Light Armoured Division (smaller than a British Brigade Group) to act independently of the Americans in addition to a force of 42 Mirage, Tornado and Jaguar aircraft.

As the Gulf War is too recent to acquire historical perspective, only an outline need be given of this coming together of American and British forces in the closest of military co-operation since the Korean War. It fell into three broad phases. The first was defensive, during which the aim was to secure Saudi Arabia from Iraqi attack while sanctions were steadily tightened and diplomatic efforts were multiplied to persuade Saddam that it was in his own best interests to withdraw from Kuwait. The second was the build-up for offensive action, and the third was the five and a half week all-out air war, followed by the short decisive 100-hour land campaign, which recovered Kuwait, but did not topple Saddam.

In the first defensive phase – *Desert Shield* – which lasted until mid-November, the Americans built up their forces at a rate of over 1,000 men per day to around 350,000, bringing security to Saudi Arabia but failing to force withdrawal on Saddam, who had every confidence that the unnatural Christian/Moslem coalition would break up quite quickly. President Bush had indicated that he was prepared for a long haul, rotating his troops on the Kuwait/Saudi border until sanctions forced Saddam to comply. However, he came under increasing pressure to root out Saddam before the delicately balanced coalition did, indeed, break up. He ushered in the second, build-up, phase with his decision to commit another 150,000 men to make it clear to Saddam that, if he went on prevaricating, he would be ejected from Kuwait by force. The new British government of John Major backed him by sending Major General Rupert Smith's 1st British Armoured Division from Germany with Brigadier Hammerbeck's 4th Armoured Brigade to join 7th Armoured Brigade, bringing the British land force contribution up to 35,000 troops (23 per cent of the British Army) with 200 tanks. The Coalition air strength rose to 1,820 fixed wing combat aircraft of which 1,376 were American. The total air strength was 2,790 aircraft of all types.

Bush's threat of offensive action was given United Nations' backing on 29 November by Resolution 278, authorising Saddam's expulsion by force if he had not withdrawn from Kuwait by 15 January. Planning, training and deployment for the third offensive phase – *Desert Storm* – went on steadily until the UN deadline was passed. The following night, 16–17 January, the air war began, aimed at suppressing the Iraqi air defences, obliterating strategic targets, interdicting supply routes, isolating the battlefield and finally supporting the soldiers on the ground when the land battle started. So successful were the airmen in handling their new high technology weapons, and the sailors in launching their cruise missiles from the US battleships in the Gulf that doubts were soon being expressed about the need for a land battle at all. Airmen have always claimed that they could win wars single-handed, but their accuracy had never been quite good enough. On this occasion, they came nearer to making good their claim than in any previous war through the effective use of their precision guided weapons.

Flying an average of 2,500 sorties per day with an aircraft taking off every 33 seconds, the Coalition airmen overwhelmed the powerful Iraqi air force, driving many of its pilots to seek refuge in Iran and destroying the rest of their aircraft on their airfields or in their hardened bunkers. The precision bombing of strategic targets, such as command posts, was equally successful; and in the interdiction of the main supply routes southwards from Baghdad, in the Tigris and Euphrates valleys, 27 out of the 31 major bridges were cut. With the skies clear of Iraqi aircraft, the Iraqi army around Kuwait was then mercilessly attacked to lower its morale before the land battle started. The only serious Iraqi counter-attacks during the air phase of operations came from their Scud missiles. Eighty-one Scuds were launched: 38 against Israel, 41 against Saudi Arabia and two towards Bahrain and Qatar. The first attacks were launched against Israel on 17 January with the clear intention of involving Israel in the war, thus upsetting the more rabid anti-Israeli states opposing Saddam, and unravelling the Coalition. Few would have predicted the political restraint with which the Israeli Government met this challenge. Patriot missile batteries were rushed from the United States, Germany and Holland to help to defend Israeli cities, and the Israeli Government held back. It did not enter the war, despite Saddam's provocation. The only serious casualties inflicted by the inaccurate Scuds occurred on 27 February when one landed on a warehouse near Dhahran, occupied by American troops as a barracks. Nevertheless, a significant air effort had to be diverted to seeking out and destroying the Scud launchers, which was not very successful. The British SAS deep penetration patrols and later American Green Berets helped the airmen to attack the Scud launchers by marking those that they found with laser target illuminators.

Less serious Iraqi counter-attacks came in the form of creating a massive oil slick in the Gulf, which did more damage to Gulf wildlife than impeding Coalition military operations; and of a spoiling attack in the coastal sector by two Iraqi Mechanised brigades on the deserted border town of Khafji. Arab forces, supported by the US Marines, were able to build up their confidence by repelling the attack and driving the Iraqi force back and out of Saudi territory.

On the waters of the Gulf, there were over a hundred Coalition warships imposing the United Nations sanctions blockade on Iraq. The United States fleet had two battleships (USS *Wisconsin* and USS *Missouri*), five carrier battle groups and an amphibious force of some 33 landing ships of various types with 17,000 marines embarked in addition to their two divisions already ashore. The Armilla Patrol had been increased to four frigates with five mine counter-measure vessels and the helicopter support ship *Argus*. After the initial cruise missile bombardment by the US battleships, the destruction of the small Iraqi Navy was begun. Sixty of its patrol boats were destroyed (15 by the Royal Navy). Sweeping safe channels for the battleships to reach their shore bombardment positions was then put in hand with the RN mine counter-measure vessels co-operating closely with the American mine-hunting helicopters.

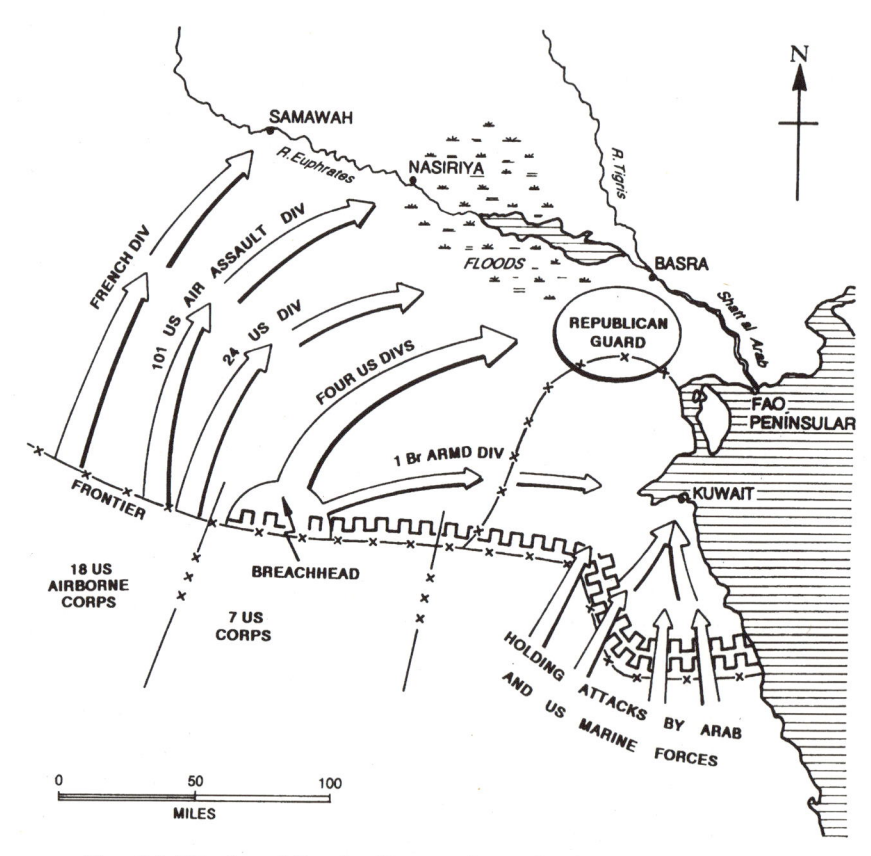

Map 24: The Land Battle: 'Desert Sword', 24–28 February 1991

The problem faced by General Norman Schwarzkopf, the Coalition commander in the field, resembled that of Rommel before the Battle of Gazala in the Western Desert in the spring of 1942. The Iraqi defences on the coast and along Kuwait's southern frontier were immensely strong but faded away into the desert beyond. The obvious answer was to sweep round the desert flank, but there were equally obvious logistic difficulties and operational risks in trying to do so. Supplying the gas-guzzling American Abrahams tanks in a wide left hook would be far from easy, and there was a danger that Saddam's experienced and well-equipped Republican Guard Divisions, which he was holding in reserve just north of Kuwait, would cut off the outflanking force. As Schwarzkopf's directive tasked him to retake Kuwait with minimum Coalition casualties, attacking the strongest sections of its defences was not an option open to him, but pretending to do so would form the basis of his deception plan.

The supply of his left hook was to be solved in the usual American way by throwing logistic resources at it, principally massive truck and fuel tanker columns, supported by a large helicopter lift. The Republican Guard divisions were to be pinned down and demoralised by heavy bombing in the later phases of the air war. If they tried to move during the land battle, they would be harried mercilessly from the air. The large American naval and amphibious forces afloat in the Gulf would be the main vehicle for the strategic deception of Saddam. Several well publicised amphibious landing exercises in the Gulf, and the gradual advance, as mine-free lanes were cleared for them, of the US battleships with their powerful 16 inch guns, ready for shore bombardment, created a level of threat to Kuwait from the sea that Saddam could not, and did not, ignore. He put an enormous, but wasted, effort into strengthening his seaward defences. His shore defences were heavily bombarded, but the Marines did not land.

Schwarzkopf's plan was to pin the Iraqis in Kuwait's main defences, while his main striking force carried out two concentric encircling movements through the desert well to the west. The holding attacks would be launched by the Coalition's Arab contingents, supported by the 1st and 2nd US Marine Divisions, which had been holding the coastal sector for some months and to which 7th Armoured Brigade had been originally attached when it first arrived in October. His inner encircling force was to be the 7th US Corps, containing five divisions, including 1st British Armoured Division. It would attack the western end of the Iraqi defences some 40 miles from the junction of the Iraq/Kuwait/Saudi borders, and then wheel right to surprise the Republican Guard divisions and defenders of Kuwait by attacking them from the west. His outer encircling force was to be the 18th US Airborne Corps with two US airborne divisions, one US infantry division and the French division. It was to cross the frontier well to the west of 7th Corps, using helicopter-borne units supported by armoured infantry formations, and aiming to protect 7th Corps' flank and to cut off any attempt by the Iraqis to withdraw from Kuwait by establishing blocks in the Euphrates valley near Samawah and Nasiriya. All land operations would be given the closest helicopter and fixed-wing air support.

By mid-February, Army planning was complete; all the extra troops had arrived in the theatre and were deployed; and probing attacks, mostly by artillery, attack-helicopters and special forces, were being stepped up all along the front. It was difficult to assess how much damage the airmen were inflicting on the equipment and morale of the Iraqi Army divisions. Subsequent debriefing of Iraqi commanders has, however, suggested that the number of casualties caused subsequently by army indirect fire weapons was far higher than those inflicted by bombing.

Coalition hopes of avoiding a bloody land battle rose on 15 February when Saddam's Revolutionary Command Council announced that Iraq would withdraw from Kuwait. As the terms attached to the withdrawal proposals were totally unacceptable, President Bush issued a final ultimatum to Saddam, on behalf of the Coalition, on the 22nd with a 24 hour deadline. There was no response: the land offensive started at 3am on 24 February – G-Day.

Desert Sword, the land offensive within *Desert Storm*, was one of those operations in which careful preparation paid off with startling results, despite it being fought in the foulest of desert weather with rain and sand storms incongruously intermingled, making target acquisition extraordinarily difficult. At times, the use of night sights was the only way of seeing ahead even in daylight. The 18th Corps' outer encirclement got off to a good start. Forward operating bases had been established half way to the Euphrates by the end of G Day, and preparations to push on to Samawah and Nasiriya were being made. Its thrust, led by combat helicopters and heliborne troops, had gone so well that General Schwarzkopf brought forward 7th Corps' initial breaching of the frontier defences by 15 hours.

The Iraqi obstacle line of anti-tank bunds, mines and wire and their defenders on 7th Corps' front proved far less formidable than expected – many officers in the Iraqi divisions holding the sector had deserted their conscript and reservist units. By early afternoon of G-Day, the 1st US Mechanised Infantry Division had cleared 16 lanes through the defences and had secured the breachhead against faltering resistance. The 1st and 3rd US Armoured Divisions started their advance northwards through the breach, seeking out the six Republican Guard divisions, while 1st British Armoured Division came up on their right and wheeled outwards to protect their right flank and to deal with three Iraqi tank divisions thought to be in tactical reserve close behind the front.

Meanwhile, near the coast, the Marines and Arab formations were pinning down the Iraqi defenders of Kuwait's main defences with highly successful breaching operations of their own. Here again the Iraqi defences were far less formidable than expected, and the weight of US preparatory fire had demoralised their defenders. By the evening of G-Day, the Marines were 20 miles over the frontier, and were ushering their Arab colleagues forward so that they could have the honour of retaking the city. And offshore the two battleships and their escorts were pinning the strong garrisons of the Iraqi beach defences with heavy and continuous bombardment to prevent them moving to reinforce threatened sectors of the front.

★ ★ ★

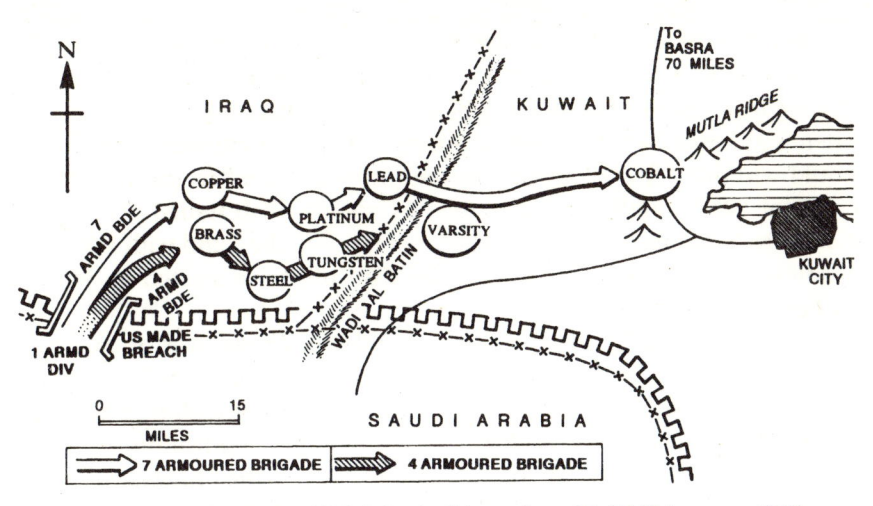

Map 25: 1 Armoured Division's Operation: 25–26 February 1991

In the early hours of the second day, 101st US Air Assault Division was landed by Black Hawk helicopters on the banks of the Euphrates near Nasiriya, cutting the main road from Baghdad to Kuwait, and the rest of 18th Corps followed up to complete the outer ring of the Iraqi encirclement. In 7th Corps, the US armoured divisions thrust on, turning north-eastwards towards the Republican Guard, whose commanders faced the dilemma all too familiar to the German commanders in Normandy in 1944. If they moved out of their prepared positions to counter-attack, they would be destroyed by air and helicopter action; and if they stayed where they were, the Iraqi infantry divisions would collapse under Coalition pressure. Whenever they did attempt to counter-attack, they gave the anti-tank helicopters what their crews called a 'Turkey Shoot', their missiles doing lethal damage to any lumbering tank columns caught in the open.

1st British Armoured Division advanced out of the breachhead during the afternoon and pushed rapidly eastwards across the rear of the Iraqi forward divisions, its immediate objective being the destruction of Iraqi 12th Tank Division. Its probable localities had been identified by air reconnaissance and intelligence sources, and coded with the names of metals (*See Map 25*). 1st Armoured Division advanced eastwards on a two brigade front with 7th Armoured Brigade left and 4th Armoured Brigade slightly echeloned back on the right. Its series of attacks were supported by the division's specially constituted Artillery Group of multiple rocket launchers (MRLS) and heavy 155mm guns, which saturated each objective in turn. Most of the harder fighting occurred during the night of G+1/G+2 while the Iraqis were offering some resistance. By dawn, British troops had overrun objectives Copper, Bronze and Zinc, destroying or capturing over 120 tanks and armoured vehicles and rounding up several thousand prisoners. The speed of their operations was made practicable by their thermal imaging sights and satellite navigation system.

On the coast, the Marines and Arab forces continued to make progress, but were hampered by the black billowing smoke of the burning Kuwaiti oil wells, which had been set on fire on Saddam's instructions.

During the third day (G+2, 26 February), 18th and 7th Corps, closely supported by ground-attack aircraft and combat helicopters, now thrust eastwards into the rapidly disintegrating Iraqi Army. By then, most of Saddam's troops were keener to find safe ways of surrendering than fighting his 'Mother of Battles', which he proclaimed so often and so loudly. 1st British Armoured Division continued eastwards with a rapidly mounted but well supported series of attacks, which brought it up to the Wadi Al Batin, Kuwait's western border, by dusk. Most of the Iraqi positions overrun were facing the wrong way (ie south instead of west), and their men showed a marked reluctance to fight. Taking Iraqis prisoner rather than blasting their positions to pieces became the British commanders' aim.

The reasons for the American and British successes were becoming apparent. In 1st British Armoured Division's operations, the preliminary air bombardments before G-Day were found to have weakened Iraqi morale, but it was the pounding before each attack by the Divisional Artillery Group, which broke the Iraqi infantry. The Challenger tank's long-range 120mm rifled gun with its thermal imaging sights destroyed their tank units. One captured Iraqi artillery brigadier stated that, out of his 100 guns, he lost a mere 13 from air attack, but only 17 survived the British artillery bombardments.

Belatedly, Saddam ordered the evacuation of Kuwait during the third day, but he was too late for his armour to escape, and, in attempting to do so, it created even greater confusion and demoralisation amongst his infantry. The fourth day became one of Iraqi rout. The US armoured divisions set about destroying the Republican Guard; the British ploughed into the backs of the Iraqi defenders of Kuwait itself, cutting the main road to Basra north-west of the city, thus severing their withdrawal route; and the Arab forces entered the city from the south. The cease-fire came at 8am on the fifth day: the carnage being inflicted on the Iraqis by Coalition air and ground forces just had to stop.

In the 66 hours in which 1st British Armoured Division had been in action, it had advanced 180 miles, destroyed the better part of three Iraqi armoured divisions, taken over 7,000 prisoners including two divisional commanders and several brigadiers, and captured over 4,000 major pieces of equipment at a price of 24 British servicemen killed in action. All the American divisions had similar tales to tell. General Schwarzkopf's victory was complete. The political way forward, however, was far from being clear-cut.

Many commentators felt that the Coalition forces should have marched on Baghdad to dictate terms there and rid the world of Saddam. This was deemed unwise for juridical, political and military reasons. Juridically, the Coalition forces were operating under the United Nations' mandate to liberate Kuwait, which did not extend to rooting out the real cause of the conflict: Saddam and his Ba'athist government. Politically, if the American, British and French governments had decided that Baghdad should be occupied to put an end to Saddam's ambitions, the Coalition would have splintered with most of the Arab leaders being strongly opposed to the invasion of another Arab state's territory. When agreeing to allow the vast influx of Western troops into Saudi Arabia, the Arab statesmen always feared that they might not be able to get rid of them when the war was over. They need not have worried: the Americans certainly had no wish to become latter-day imperialists; and both the British and American governments were under political pressure to 'get the boys home'. And militarily, the occupation of Baghdad and the unseating of Saddam would in all probability have led to a long and expensive occupation of most of Iraq while a new and less hostile regime was installed. History might have repeated Britain's so-called temporary occupation of Egypt, which lasted for 70 years after the Battle of Tel el Kebir in 1882.

The United Nations Resolution 687, setting out the terms for the formal cease-fire, was approved on 3 April. The Iraqi Government accepted the terms three days later and they came into effect on 11 April. But against all expectations, Saddam survived as Iraq's leader, and neither of the rogue philosophies in the Gulf – Ba'athist pan-Arabism nor Islamic fundamentalism – had been discredited. It is perhaps worth recalling that the First World War was ended without dictating terms in Berlin, and within two decades the Second World War was upon us. Avoiding marching on Baghdad for the very best of reasons could prove an equally expensive mistake!

* * *

The Gulf War took place almost two centuries after Nelson's lookouts saw the masts of Napoleon's fleet anchored in Aboukir Bay. The Battle of the Nile, which followed, brought British military power into the Middle East for the first time since the Crusades. Thereafter, Britain's strategic interest in the safety of her imperial communications with India, the Far East and Australasia, and her subsequent need for cheap Persian oil, led to her seizing and holding Western paramountcy in the Middle East to fend off the successive challenges of Russia, the Kaiser's Germany, and finally Nazi Germany. The United States played only a limited role in the Middle East until halfway through the Second World War. In the post-war era, superpower status, the Cold War and the birth of Israel drew successive

United States administrations into Middle Eastern affairs, while Britain, withdrawing from empire and avoiding the Israeli entanglement, saw no good reason to spend scarce resources maintaining her position there. The growing disparity of power and interest between the United States and Britain in the Middle East was displayed with regrettable starkness by the Suez débâcle. Since then there has been a steady re-establishment of the Special Relationship in Middle Eastern affairs, which has been consolidated by unity of purpose and victory in the Gulf. The words of an American (not British) academic, Bruce W Watson, in his conclusion in the *Military Lessons of the Gulf War* seem an appropriate tailpiece:

> ... the war re-affirmed the existence of the Anglo-American relationship and its benefit to the world. The latter offers the power and a firm commitment to freedom, the former centuries of experience and possibly a firmer grasp on the world's pulse.[2]

Indeed, for the world's sake, the Anglo-American partnership in the Middle East is of crucial importance. Iraq and Iran are still set on paths of future aggrandisement, which will lead to trouble again before long. The nature of the next Middle East conflict, however, may be very different. Yitzhak Rabin, Israel's Prime Minister and Minister of Defence speaking at the Royal United Services Institute for Defence Studies in Whitehall in December 1992, encapsulated the probable change when he said:

> When I witnessed dogfights between Mirages and MIG 21s during the Six Day War, the ratio of planes lost was 30:1 in our favour. In the Yom Kippur War it was 50:1. In 1982, during clashes in the Lebanon ... the results were 90:1. In fact the Arabs came to the conclusion even before 1981 that if they wanted to reach targets in Israel, they could not rely on their air forces ... The search is on, therefore, for ground-to-ground missiles, the operation of which is not dependent on the capability of the human being at the spearhead.[3]

The Gulf War was certainly a 'high tech' contest. Its successor could be even more so if the Arabs were to try to destroy Israel at long range with weapons of mass destruction. The need for Western nuclear deterrence is as important as ever.

BIBLIOGRAPHY

Anderson, MS, *The Eastern Question* (Macmillan, New York, 1966).
Billière, Sir Peter de la, *Storm Command* (Harper-Collins, London, 1992).
Bowden, Dr Tom, 'The Politics of the Arab Rebellion in Palestine 1936–39', *British Army Review*, 1973.
Boyle, A, *Trenchard* (Collins, London, 1962).
Braeman, John, *Wilson* (Prentice Hall, New Jersey, 1922).
Bulloch, John & Morris, Harvey, *Saddam's War* (Faber & Faber, London, 1991).
Churchill, Winston, *A History of the English Speaking Peoples* (Cassell, London, 1958).
Churchill, Winston, *The Second World War*, 6 Vols (Cassell, London, 1948–1954).
Ciano, Count, *Diary, 1939–43* (Heinemann, London, 1946).
Connell, John, *Auchinleck* (Cassell, London, 1959).
Connell, John, *Wavell* (Cassell, London, 1964).
Dupuy, TN & GP Hayes, *The Campaigns on the Turkish Fronts* (Franklin Watts, New York, 1967).
Eden, Sir Anthony, *Full Circle* (Cassell, London, 1960).
Eisenhower, President Dwight, *Waging Peace* (Heinemann, London, 1965).
Fregosi, Paul, *Dreams of Empire* (Hutchinson, London, 1989).
Gilbert, Martin, *Winston Churchill*; Vol IV (1917–22) (Heinemann, London, 1975).
Glubb, Sir John, *The Changing Scenes of Life* (Quartet Books, London, 1983).
Goldschmidt, Arthur, Jr, *A Concise History of the Middle East*, 3rd Edn (Westview Press, Boulder, USA).
Haldane, Lt-General Sir Aylmer, *The Insurrection in Mesopotamia, 1920* (William Blackwood, London 1922).
Hamilton, Nigel, *Monty*, 3 Vols (Hamish Hamilton, London, 1981–6).
Herzog, Major General Chaim, *The War of Atonement* (Weidenfeld & Nicholson, London, 1975).
Jackson, General Sir William, *The North African Campaign* (Batsford, London, 1975).
Ibid, The Pomp of Yesterday: The Defence of India and the Suez Canal 1798–1918 (Brassey's, London, 1995).

Ibid, Withdrawal from Empire, 1940–43 (Batsford, London, 1986).
Ibid, Britain's Defence Dilemma (Batsford, London, 1990).
Kearsey, A, *A Study of the Strategy and Tactics of the Mesopotamian Campaign* (Gale & Polden, Aldershot, 1934).
Kippenberger, HK, *Infantry Brigadier* (Oxford University Press, Oxford, 1949).
Lawrence, TE, *Seven Pillars of Wisdom* (Jonathan Cape, London, 1935).
Liman von Sanders, *Five Years in Turkey* (Williams & Wilkins, Baltimore, USA, 1928).
Macmillan, Harold, *Autobiography*; Vol IV (Macmillan, 1973).
Montgomery, Field Marshal, Viscount, *Memoirs* (Collins, 1958).
Moorehead, Alan, *African Trilogy* (Hamish Hamilton, 1944).
Roberts, Major General GPB, *From the Desert to the Baltic* (William Kimber, London, 1987).
Rommel, Erwin, Field Marshal, *Rommel Papers* [Edited by Liddell Hart] (Collins, London, 1953).
RUSI Journal, February 1993 Issue (London, 1993).
Sachar, Howard M, *The Emergence of the Middle East: 1914–1924* (Allen Lane, The Penguin Press, London, 1969).
Salmond, Air Marshal Sir John, 'The Air Force in Iraq', *RUSI*, 25 March 1925.
Scoville, Elmer B, 'The RAF and the Desert Frontiers of Iraq', *Aerospace Historian*, Milwaukee, No 2, 1975.
Searight, Sarah, *The British in the Middle East* (Weidenfeld & Nicolson, London, 1969).
Spiegel, Steven L, *The Other Arab–Israeli Conflict* (University of Chicago, USA, 1985).
Stewart, Desmond, *The Middle East; Temple of Janus* (Hamish Hamilton, London, 1972).
Stewart, Desmond, *The Middle East; Temple of Janus* (Hamish Hamilton, London, 1972).
Yapp, ME, *The Making of the Middle East, 1792–1923* (Longman, London, 1987).
Volodarsky, Mikhail, 'Persia and the Great Powers', *Middle Eastern Studies*; (Ministry of Defence Library; 1983).
Watson, Bruce W et al, *Lessons of the Gulf War* (Greenhill Books, London, 1991).
Wilmot, Chester, *Tobruk 1941* (Angus & Robertson, London).

British Official Histories:
Second World War:
Grand Strategy Vol I.
Mediterranean & Middle East Vols I, II, III, IV.

REFERENCES

Chapter 1: Mandates, not Empires

1. Braeman, *Wilson*, pp 69–70.
2. Sacher, *The Emergence of the Middle East; 1914–24*, p 341.
3. Gilbert, *Wilson Churchill*, Vol IV, p 473.
4. Wavell, *Allenby*, p 270.
5. Sacher, p 289.
6. Haldane, *The Insurrection in Mesopotamia, 1920*, p 26.
7. Boyle, *Trenchard*, p 383.
8. Hamilton, *Monty*, p 301.
9. Bowden, *The Palestine Rebellion*, p 13.

Chapter 2: Mussolini's Hollow Challenge

1. Churchill, *The Second World War*, Vol II, pp 369–70.
2. *Ibid, Grand Strategy*, Vol I, p 311.
3. Churchill, *Vol II*, p 376.
4. John Connell, *Wavell*, p 275.
5. Churchill, *Vol II*, p 480.
6. John Connell, p 283.
7. *Ibid*, p 288.
8. *Ibid*, p 289.
9. *Ibid*, p 289.
10. Moorehead, *African Trilogy*, p 67.
11. Ciano, *Diaries*, p 317.
12. Churchill, *Vol III*, p 13.
13. John Connell, p 310.
14. Churchill, *Vol III*, p 16.
15. Jackson, *The North African Campaigns*, p 69.
16. Rommel, *Rommel Papers*, p 95.

Chapter 3: Defeating Hitler's Challenge

1. British Official History, *Mediterranean & Middle East*, Vol I, p xxvi.
2. John Connell, *Wavell*, p 461.
3. Churchill, *The Second World War*, Vol III, p 310.
4. *Ibid*, p 356.

5. John Connell, *Auchinleck*, p 365.
6. Liddell Hart, *The Tanks*, Vol II, p 158.
7. Chester Wilmot, *Tobruk*, p 300.
8. Rommel, *Papers*, p 207.
9. John Connell, p 532.
10. *Ibid*, p 546.
11. Kippenberger, *Infantry Brigadier*, p 126.
12. John Connell, p 628.
13. South African Official History, p 314.
14. Montgomery, *Memoirs*, pp 126–7.

Chapter 4: The Uneasy Anglo-American Partnership

1. Alan Bullock, *Ernest Bevin*, p 242.
2. Churchill, *The Second World War*, Vol VI, p 654.
3. Anthony Eden, *Full Circle*, p 426.
4. *Ibid*, p 440.
5. General Sir Garnet Wolseley, victor of the Battle of Tel el Kebir in 1882, which led to the British occupation of Egypt. See Jackson, *The Pomp of Yesterday* (Brassey's, London, 1995).

Chapter 5: America Takes Over

1. Spiegel, *The Other Arab–Israeli Conflict*, pp 14–15.
2. Eisenhower, *Waging Peace*, pp 182–3.
3. Macmillan, *Autobiography*, Vol IV, p 511.
4. Spiegel, p 246.

Chapter 6: Partnership in the Gulf

1. de la Billière, *Storm Command*, pp 303–4.
2. Watson, *Military Lessons of the Gulf War*, p 214.
3. Yitzhak Rabin, *RUSI Journal, Feb 1993*, p 2.

INDEX

Abdullah 25, 66
Aden 138–9, 141, 143–7, 155
Afghanistan, Soviet invasion of 160–1
Akehurst, Brigadier John 156
Alam Halfa, Battle of 101–4
Alexander, General Harold 100
Allenby, Viscount 10–11, 13–14, 22
Anglo-American relations and the Middle East 109–35
  Special Relationship 109–10, 118
Aosta, Duke of 35, 37, 44, 55–6, 58, 65
Arab League 119, 121, 123
Arafat, Yasser 148, 151, 163
Attlee, Clement 110, 113, 115–16, 119
Auchinleck, General Sir Claude 66, 70, 74–9, 81–2, 84–5, 87, 89–93, 95, 97–8, 99
  failures of British higher command at Battle of Gazala 90–7
  takeover of 8th Army 98–9
Australian forces 96

Ba'ath Party and pan-Arabism 147–8, 175
Bach, Major 72
Baghdad Pact 140
Bahrain 145
Baker, James 167
Begin, Menachem 115, 157–8
Bell, Gertrude 17, 21–3, 25
Ben-Gurion, David 111, 113, 115, 134
Beresford-Peirse, Major General 39, 69, 71, 73–4, 82
Bergonzoli, Lieutenant General 48–9, 53
Berti, General 40–1, 46, 48
Bevin, Ernest 109–10, 114–16, 119
Blacker, Brigadier (later General Sir) Cecil 144–5
Brezhnev, Leonid 153
Brink, Major General 41, 57–8, 77, 79, 81–2
Brooke, General Sir Alan 87, 99
Bulganin, Nikolai 134
Bush, George 167–8

Camp David talks 157–8
Campbell, Brigadier Jock 75, 81
  and 'Jock' columns 75
Campioni, Admiral Angelo 37
Carter, Jimmy 157–8, 160–1
  Carter Doctrine 160
CENTO (formerly Baghdad Pact) 140
China, PR of 109, 118, 124
  and communism 109

Christians in Moslem countries 4–9, 140, 158
  Armenians in Turkey 5, 7–9
  Greeks in Turkey 6–9
  Maronites in Lebanon 4, 7, 140, 158
  in Syria 7
Churchill, Winston 9, 15, 18, 21–2, 24–6, 35, 38–41, 55, 66–72, 74, 77, 83, 87, 95, 97–8, 99–100, 106, 112, 116, 121
  Anglo-Italian war 35, 38–41, 44–5, 49, 51–2, 55
  desert war with Germany 66, 68–72, 77, 83,–4 87, 94, 96–108
  and Iraq 18, 21–2, 24–6, 66
  and Palestine 112, 116
  and Tobruk 77, 84, 94–96
  and Wavell 66–71, 74
Ciano, Count 48
Clemenceau, Georges 6
Commonwealth, development of 110–11
Communism, international 109, 118–19, 124, 139–40
  and Islamic world 139–40
Congreve, General Sir Walter 22
Cordingly, Brigadier Patrick 167
Cornwallis, Sir Kinahan 66–7
Cox, Sir Percy 15–17, 21–4, 26, 166
Creagh, Major General O'Moore 39, 52, 72–4, 77
Crete 69–70
Cripps, Sir Stafford 87
Cruwell, General 78–9, 81–2, 84, 89
Cunningham, General (Sir) Alan 41, 55, 57–8, 77, 79, 81–4, 114, 116
Cunningham, Admiral (Sir) Andrew 35, 37, 49–50, 77, 85

Dalton, Hugh 119
de Gaulle, (later General) Charles 70–1
de la Billière, (later Lieutenant General Sir) Peter 141, 159, 167
de Simone, General 55, 57
Deane-Drummond, Lieutenant Colonel Tony 141
Desert warfare 34–108, 167–76
  Anglo-Italian war 34–58
  war with Germany 49–51, 53–4, 58–108
  Gulf War 167–76
Dill, Field Marshal Sir John 30–1, 50, 87
Dulles, John Foster 124–5, 128, 132–3, 136–7, 140

Eden, Anthony 44–5, 49–50, 55, 120, 123–5, 127, 131–4, 136
Egypt 4, 11–14, 34, 59, 75, 92, 86, 88–9, 97–9, 102, 108, 110, 119–44, 146–55, 157–9, 176
and Aden 142–4
Anglo-Egyptian treaties 121–3
Aswan dam project 123–4, 139
1888 Constantinople Convention 122–3, 125, 128
and Eastern bloc 121–4, 128–9, 134, 140, 152
end of Protectorate 13
and Israel 121, 123, 130–2, 140, 146–50, 152–5, 157–8, 176
Six Day War 146, 149–50, 152, 176
Suez Canal 4, 13–14, 59, 86, 88–9, 96–8, 102, 108, 110, 119–36, 138–9, 150–2, 155, 159, 176
and the US 152, 157–8
Yom Kippur War 152–4, 176
Egyptian-Israeli peace treaty, 1979 157–8
Eisenhower, Dwight D 124–5, 131–4, 136–7, 140, 147
Eisenhower Doctrine 139–40
El Alamein/Line 96–108
Erskine, General Sir George 120

Fahd of Saudi Arabia, King 166
Farouk, King of Egypt 119–20
Farrar-Hockley, Lieutenant Colonel (later General Sir) Anthony 144
Feisal of Iraq 21, 25, 27
Feisal of Saudi Arabia 152
Ford, Gerald 155
France 4, 7–9, 14–15, 27, 34–5, 65, 70–1, 76, 88–9, 90, 94, 125–35, 163–4, 167–8, 171–2
Free French 70–1, 88–9, 91, 93
and Gulf War 167–8, 171–2
and Lebanon 14–15
and Suez crisis 125–35
and Syria 7, 14–15, 27, 65, 70–1
Vichy French 65, 70–1, 76
Freyberg's New Zealanders 61, 65, 77, 81–5, 102, 107
Frusci, General 55–6, 58

Gaddafi, Moamer al 152
Gaitskell, Hugh 125, 129
Gambara, General 78, 82
Gambier-Parry, Major General 51–2, 61–4
Gariboldi, General 60, 62–3, 84
Gazala Line 68, 85–8
Battle of Gazala 90–4, 101
Gazzera, General 58
Germany – the desert war 49–51, 53–4, 58–108
Godwin-Austen, General 38, 57, 77, 79, 81–3, 85, 87
Gott, Brigadier 'Strafer' 40, 65, 69, 72, 77, 79, 81–2, 87–9, 90–6, 97, 98
Grand Mufti of Jerusalem 29, 32–3, 70

Graziani, Marshal 40, 44–5, S2, 54, 60
Greece/Greeks 6–9
in 2nd World War 44, 49–50, 54, 62, 84
Gulf War 166–76
Desert Shield 168
Desert Storm 141, 168–72
Desert Sword 170, 172–5

Haile Selassie, Emperor 41, 57–8
Haining, General Sir Robert 31–2
Haldane, General Sir Aylmer 18–24
Halder, General 68, 83
Hammarskjöld, Dag 131
Hargroves, Brigadier Louis 144
Healey, Denis 145, 150
Heath, Major General 41
Hezbollah (Party of God) 163, 165
Hitler, Adolf 49, 53, 58, 62, 67, 86
and *Barbarossa* 75–6
and 'final solution'
Horrocks, General Brian 101, 104, 105
Horsford, Brigadier Derek 141–2
Hussein, Saddam 148, 160–72, 174–5

Iran 76–7, 107, 110–11, 119–20, 138, 150, 158–66, 175
build-up of defence industrial base 150
Iran-Iraq War 161–2, 164–5
Islamic fundamentalism 159–60, 162, 166, 175
oil supplies to Britain 110–11, 119–20, 138
Shah 158–60, 162
and US hostages 160, 162
Iran-Iraq War 161–2, 164–5
Iraq 3, 15–28, 65–8, 76, 100, 108, 110–11, 119, 122, 138, 140, 148, 160–2, 164–76
Anglo-Iraqi treaties 26, 28, 66
Gulf War 166–76
independence, granting of 28
Iran-Iraq War 160–2, 164–5
oil supplies to Britain 110–11, 119, 138
revolt of 1920 16–21
Islamic fundamentalism 159–60, 162, 166, 175
Israel 113, 116, 121–3, 130–59, 161–3, 169, 176
air attack on Iraqi nuclear weapons plant 162
and Egypt 121, 123, 130–2, 140, 146–50, 152–5, 157–8, 176
and Iraq (Saddam Hussein) 161–2, 169
and Palestinians/PLO 148, 151, 158, 163
Six Day War 146, 149–50, 152, 176
and Suez crisis 130–5
Yom Kippur War 152–4, 176
see also Palestine under Mandate
Italy 6, 9, 14, 29, 34–58, 62, 65, 72, 90, 92
Anglo-Italian war in Africa 34–58
invasion of Abyssinia 29, 34–5

'Jock' columns 75, 78, 83, 100
Johnson, Lyndon B 148–50
Jordan 140–1, 148

Index

Kassim, Brigadier 140–2, 148
Kemal Atatürk
  see Mustapha Kemal 7–10, 27
Kennedy, John F 147
Kesselring, Field Marshal Albert 85–6, 96–7, 98
Khalid bin Sultan, Prince 1–67
Khomeini, Ayatollah 158, 160, 162, 165–6
King, Admiral Ernest 99–100
Kissinger, Henry 151–2, 154–5, 157
Klopper, Major General 88, 96
Koenig's Free French Brigade 88, 93
Korean War 118
Kurdish peoples/Kurdistan 22, 26–8
  Sheikh Mahmound of Sulimania 27
Kuwait 141–2, 147, 164, 166–76
  Anglo-Kuwaiti Defence Agreement 141
  Gulf War 166–76

Laverack's 7th Australian Division 61, 70
Lawrence, TE 17, 21–3
Lebanon 4, 7, 14–15, 140–1, 158, 163, 176
  civil war 158
  Palestinians in 158, 163
  US marines in Beirut 140
Leese, Oliver 101, 103, 105, 107
Levant 139
Lloyd, Selwyn 124–5, 132
Lloyd George, David 4, 6, 10, 13, 15, 21, 24
Longmore, Air Chief Marshal Sir Arthur 37–8, 43–4, 70, 77
Luftwaffe 85–6, 93, 95, 97
Lumsden, Major General Herbert 85, 89, 90, 93–4, 101, 104, 105, 107
Lunt, Brigadier James 144

Mackay, Major General 45, 48–51, 53, 61
Macmillan, Harold 133, 136–8, 140–1
Maitland Wilson, Lieutenant General 'Jumbo' 40, 55, 61, 70–1, 76, 82–3
Major, John 168
Malta 96–8
Marshall, General George 99
McLeod, Iain 138–9
Menzies, Sir Robert 128, 131
Messervy, Major General Frank 71–4, 77, 90, 94
Middle East Department, formation of 21–2
Military operations/Battle plans
  Barbarossa 49, 65, 67, 72, 75–6
  Battleaxe 69–75, 77
  Brevity 69
  Compass 41–8
  Crusader 77–84, 95
  Exporter 70–1
  Limerick 92
  Marita 49, 51, 54, 58, 65
  Midsummer Night's Dream 78
  Musketeer 126–35, 138
  Supercharge 106
  Torch 99
  Totensonntag 80

Mitchell, Lieutenant Colonel Colin 146
Mollet, Guy 131–4
Montgomery, Major General (later Field-Marshal) Bernard 30–1, 46, 97, 100–108
  and battles of Alam Halfa and El Alamein 101–108
  takeover of 8th Army 100–102
Morgan, Lieutenant Colonel Dai 147
Morshead, General 61–4, 68, 95, 106
Mossadeq, Muhammad 120
Mubarak, Hosni 166
Mussolini, Benito 29, 34–5, 37, 44, 49, 51–2, 97
Mustapha Kemal 7–10, 27

Nasser, Gamal Abdel 12, 119–25, 127–32, 134–7, 139–44, 146–52
  and Arab nationalism 140–4, 146
  and Eastern bloc 124, 128–9, 134, 139–42, 151–2
  and Israel 121, 123, 130–2, 140, 146–50
  mutual defence pact with Syria, Iraq and Jordan 149
NATO 121, 140, 144
Naval losses in the Mediterranean 99–100
Neame, Lieutenant General Philip 61–5
Neguib, General 120
Nehring, General 90, 92, 106
Nehru, Jawaharlal 124, 128
Neumann-Silkow, Major General 72–4
Nixon, Richard 151, 153, 155
Non-aligned group of newly independent states 124, 128
Norrie's 30th Corps 77, 79, 82–3, 85, 88–9, 92–5, 97–8

O'Connor, Major General Sir Richard 31–2, 39–41, 43–8, 50, 52–4, 61, 63–4, 84
Oil supplies from Middle East 110–11, 119–20, 135, 137–8, 154–5, 162, 164, 166
  as a blackmailing weapon 152
Oman 141, 155–7
OPEC 152

Palestine under Mandate 4, 11, 14, 22, 25, 28–33, 109–18
  Arab revolt 29–32, 111
  Jewish Agency 111–15
  Jewish defence and terrorist organisations 31, 112–17
  Jewish immigration quotas 111, 113–17
    1939 White Paper on 32, 111, 113
  Jewish settlement/National Home 22, 28–33
  Mandate, ending of 117–18
  terrorist activities 112–17
  see also Israel
Palestinians/PLO 148, 151, 158, 163
Platt, Major General William 41, 45, 55–6

Rabin, Yitzhak 176
Raeder, Grand Admiral Erich 86

RAF 23–8, 44, 46, 57, 78–9, 87, 98, 103
  and *Battleaxe* 72, 74
  and *Crusader* 78–9, 83
  and imperial policing 23–8
Rashid Ali 66, 68
Reagan, Ronald 162
Ritchie, Major General Neil 83–5, 87–95, 97
  failure of Battle of Gazala 90–5
Roberts, Colonel (later General Sir) Ouvry 66–7
Roberts, Colonel (later Major General) Pip 90, 102–4
Rommel, Lieutenant General Erwin 53–4, 60–5, 67–70, 72–4, 76, 78–87, 89–108
  Alam Halfa and El Alamein, battles of 96–108
  Gazala, Battle of 90–4, 101
  and Tobruk 63–5, 68–9, 78–84, 89–90, 94–7
Roosevelt, Franklin D 96, 103, 111–12
Russia
  see Soviet Union

Sadat, Anwar 152–5, 157–8
  plans for destruction of Israel 152
Salmond, Air Marshal Sir John 26–8
Samuel, Herbert 14, 22
Sandys, Dunaan Saudi Arabia and Gulf War 138, 141, 145
Saudi Arabia 122, 145, 150– 154–5, 163–4, 166–76
  and Gulf War 166–76
Schwarzkopf, General Norman 167, 170–2, 174–5
Shearer, Brigadier John 60–1
Six Day War 146, 149–50, 152, 176
Smart, Air Vice-Marshal 66–7
Smith, Major General Rupert 168
Smuts, Field Marshal Jan 4, 55
Sneh, Moshe 115
Soviet Union/Eastern bloc 49, 65, 67, 72, 75–6, 85, 99, 108, 109, 119, 121–4, 128–31, 133–4, 139–40, 151–5, 159–60
  and Afghanistan invasion 159–60
  and Arab world 119, 121–4, 128–9, 134, 139–40, 151–5
  Barbarossa 49, 65, 67, 72, 75–6, 85, 99
  Battle of Stalingrad 108
  and communism 109, 119
  and Suez 128–31, 133–4
Stockwell, General Sir Hugh 134
Stumme, General Georg 106
Sudan 13, 119, 121
Suez Canal 4, 13–14, 59, 86, 88–9, 97–9, 102, 108, 110, 119–36, 138–9, 150–2, 155, 159, 176
  current importance of 159
  nationalisation of 124
  Rommel's/Axis's designs on 88–9, 96–9, 101

Suez crisis 124–35, 138, 176
  Musketeer plan 126–35, 138
Summermann, Major General 78
Syria 7, 14–15, 27, 65, 70–1, 76, 83, 140, 142, 148, 150, 153–4, 158
  Vichy French in 65, 70–1, 76

Tedder, Air Marshal Sir Arthur 70, 77, 87, 98
Thatcher, Margaret 160, 162, 167
Tobruk 63–5, 68–9, 72, 75–85, 88–90, 94–7
Trans-Jordan 22–5, 122
Trenchard, Air Marshal Sir Hugh 22–4, 26
Trevaskis, Sir Kennedy 143
Truman, Harry 113–15, 137
Turkey 3–10, 26–8, 35
  peace settlement 1919–23 5–10
Turner, Colonel Victor 105

U Thant 148
United Arab Republic 140, 142
USA 109–58, 163–76
  Anglo-American relations and the Middle East 109–35
  and the Arab-Israeli tightrope 136–58
  and Gulf War 166–76
  and Iran 159–60, 162, 165
  and Lebanon 163–4

Vance, Cyrus 157
Vincent, Colonel 26–7
von Blomberg, Major Axel 67
von Brauchitsch, General 62, 68
von Kressenstein, Kress 59, 131
von Paulus, General Friedrich 68–9, 72, 74
von Prittwitz, General 60, 68
von Ravenstein, Major General 72–4, 78, 84

Waite, Terry 164
Wavell, General Sir Archibald 31, 35, 37–41, 44–6, 48–55, 58, 60–3, 65–71, 74–6, 84
  Anglo-Italian war 31, 35, 37–41, 44–6, 48–55, 58, 97
  and Churchill 66–71, 74
  desert war with Germany 60–3, 65–8, 70, 74–6, 84
Weizmann, Chaim 14, 113
Wetherall's 11th African Division 57–8
Wilson, Lieutenant Colonel Arnold 17, 19, 24, 44–5
Wilson, Harold 145, 149–50
Wilson, Sir Henry 23
Wilson, Woodrow 4, 11
Wingate, Colonel Orde 31, 41, 55, 57–8

Yemen 142–6, 148
Yom Kippur war 152–4, 176

Zaghlul Pasha 11–13